Canisbay
St. Drostan

Ben Hope

Kildonnan

Navidale
St. Ninian

Dornoch
St. Finbar

Moray Firth

Kilmaluag

Rosemarkie
St. Moluag

Rothiemay
St. Drostan

Deer
St. Drostan

Inverness

Daviot
St. Colm, Bishop in
the Orkneys

Kinnoir
St. Mungo

Methlick
St. Ninian

Temple
St. Ninian

Loch Ness

ALBA
OF THE
PICTS

Lumphanan
St. Finan

Banchory
St. Ternan

CANNA
Kilcolumcille

Inverochty
St. Nidan

Dunottar
St. Ninian

EIGG
Kildonnan

D R U M   A L B A N

G R A M P I A N S

TIREE
Kilmaluag

LISMORE
St. Moluag

MULL

Ben Lomond

Nectansmere

STRATHMORE

Arbirlot
St. Ninian

Iona
St. Columba

St. Andrews
St. Kenneth

COLONSAY

Dunadd

Drymen
St. Columba

St. Ninian's

Culross
St. Serf

Dysart
St. Serf

Firth of Clyde

Bass Rock

Dunbarton

Carnoch

ISLAY

Kilcolumcille

Kilcolumcille

Glasgow
St. Mungo

Antonine's Wall

Dunedin

Traprain Law
or Dunpelder

Kilmoluag

BUTE

R. Clyde

Lanark
St. Mungo

Peebles

Kilcolumcille

ARRAN

Kilcolumcille

S T R A T H C L Y D E

Melrose
St. Cuthbert

St. Mungo's
Hoddam
St. Mungo

Hadrian's
Wall

Kirkmadrine
St. Ninian

Arderyd

Carlisle

Glasserton

Candida Casa
Whithorn
St. Ninian

Maville
St. Finbar

Bangor
Comgall

Maryport

They Built
on Rock

ST. ANTHONY, THE FATHER OF MONASTICISM

They Built on Rock

Stories of the Celtic Saints

DIANA LEATHAM

Hodder & Stoughton

To my Godchild
Diana Wynne

Copyright © 1948 Diana Leatham

First published in Great Britain 1948
This edition 1999

The right of Diana Leatham to be identified as the Author of
the Work has been asserted by the publisher in accordance with
the Copyright, Designs and Patents Act 1988.

10 9 8 7 6 5 4 3 2 1

British Library Cataloguing in Publication Data
A record for this book is available from the British Library

ISBN 0 340 74541 X

Printed and bound in Great Britain by
Clays Ltd, St Ives plc

Hodder and Stoughton Ltd
A Division of Hodder Headline PLC
338 Euston Road
London NW1 3BH

CONTENTS

ILLUSTRATIONS

Maps drawn from designs by Elizabeth D. Jackson.

TAIL-PIECES

ACKNOWLEDGMENTS

THIS book is almost entirely derivative. I therefore owe an immense debt to three groups of people without whom it could not have been written: firstly, to those who wrote the numerous books from which I have borrowed; secondly, to those who made it possible for me to read those books (for the most part out of print) by lending them to me; and lastly to those who have encouraged and helped me to write it.

The works of the first group I have listed at the end of each chapter. The assistants in the National and Public Libraries of Edinburgh lead the second group for no praise can be too high for the quality of their service; then come the generous librarians of Aberdeen University, of the Cathedral Church of St. Mary, Edinburgh, and of the Convent of the Sacred Heart, Craiglockhart; last but not least comes Mrs. Concannon who bravely sent across the Irish Channel almost the only copy still in existence of her excellent *Life of St. Columban*. It would be impossible to mention by name all those in the last group. But only so experienced a hagiographer as Miss Margaret T. Monro could have persuaded me to start the book and, with her helpful criticisms, urge me on with a task which soon began to seem too great for an amateur. Dr. W. Douglas Simpson, too, gave invaluable help by patiently answering lists of what must have seemed to his scholarly mind questions almost too elementary to need asking. All those, named and nameless, I thank for their courtesy and kindness, not forgetting, however, that without the enthusiastic planning of Mr. John Morrison, the publisher of the book, it would probably have had to be content with drab utility clothing.

Lastly I wish to thank the editors of the *New Alliance* and the *National Review* for permission to reprint material I had already used in articles they published on various Celtic saints.

D. M. L.

Chapter I

THE MEN BEHIND ST. NINIAN

THE story of the Celtic Church, with which this book is concerned, is one of the great spiritual dramas. Like all dramas it was played on a stage; and it was acted in a setting already traditional. Without some understanding of that setting we cannot appreciate the dramatic quality of the story. For the setting at once lands us in the unexpected: the Celtic Church drew its ideals and inspiration with singular directness from the first phase of Christian monasticism, worked out in the very different conditions of the Nile Valley.

The sixth century British historian Gildas cheerfully describes his country as " paralysed with icy cold and in a far corner of the world remote from the sun." Yet the lives of those British and Irish monks he so admired, in contrast with the deplorably worldly secular bishops of his time, were faithful copies of those led by the Egyptian monks in a part of the world so close to the sun that a sheepskin coat was a penitential garment, and the monks had sometimes to be allowed to sleep on their roofs. It is indeed startling that austerities heroic enough in a hot climate should have proved an equally beneficial spiritual discipline in a cold damp one, producing there too a glow of the most attractive holiness. The fresh element introduced by the Celtic monks was their evangelistic zeal; all the more astonishing when we consider that their austerities were of a kind to cool the ardour of all but the most devoted followers of Christ. Among the most active and constructive of teachers and missionaries, it was supremely they who carried the light of the Gospel through the blackest of the Dark Ages.

9

All great achievement draws on a great inheritance. Our appreciation of the Celtic achievement will be all the keener if we take a quick glance at the inheritance from which the Celtic saints drew so much of their strength. The story goes back a long way.

It is known that there were Christians in Roman Britain before the third century. Some of them may well have been refugees from the south of Roman Gaul where, at that time, there was a colony of Christians at Lyons under their bishop Pothinus. In 177, during the reign of the Emperor Marcus Aurelius, the colony was attacked, its bishop imprisoned and its members scattered. If these, then, were among the first to preach to their Celtic cousins in Britain it is worth noting how closely linked they were to Christ's life on earth. Before ministering to the Christians at Lyons, their presbyter Irenaeus had studied in Asia Minor under Polycarp, Bishop of Smyrna, who, in his youth had been a pupil of the apostle St. John himself.

By 314 the British Church, always in close contact with the Church in Gaul, had become sufficiently organised to send from the Roman cities of London, York and perhaps Lincoln, three bishops to attend the Council of Arles. This was the first council to be held since the Emperor Constantine had adopted Christianity. Though one historian reckons the number of Christians in the Empire to be as low as one-fifth of the population yet the Church stood out so solidly against the fluid pagan society that Constantine saw her as a force to be exterminated or accepted. As a wise statesman he accepted her realising that her uncompromising attitude towards other creeds would bring new life and unity to the Empire. His decision changed the course of history and made the fourth century a time of expansion and development for the Church.

For the time being the heretics were her worst enemies. The rapidly increasing number of Arians who denied the divinity of Christ made it essential to define that doctrine and the doctrine of the Holy Trinity. In 325 this was duly done under the auspices of the Emperor at the Council of Nicaea, which also banished Arius from Alexandria. The resulting

Nicene Creed is an enlarged and explanatory version of the Apostles' Creed.[1] The Arians therefore found it even less to their taste and as they were increasing in power and numbers so as to rival the Catholics they refused to accept defeat. For a time it looked as though they would triumph permanently. Indeed had it not been for the magnificent stand made against them by the Catholic bishop Athanasius they might well have done so. He fought with them perpetually to win at last, though five times they banished him from his See at Alexandria.

The first time they did this, in 339, he went to Rome, and after six years in Italy moved on to Gaul. Wherever he went, and when he was not engaged in pointing out the insidious danger of the Arian heresy, he enthralled his listeners with stories of his two staunch Catholic friends, Anthony and Pachomius, laymen who had dedicated their lives to God and lived strangely and marvellously with their groups of disciples in the deserts of Egypt.

Ascetics were from the first highly esteemed by the Church. They were revered as practising those virtues of fasting, voluntary poverty and perpetual virginity recommended in the gospels and in the epistles of St. Paul to those Christians in training for the spiritual contest whose prize is eternal life. But it was not till the beginning of the fourth century that at Pispir in Upper Egypt, on the east bank of the Nile, St. Anthony, longing above all for the hermit's life he had led so long, was yet forced to organise the throng of would-be disciples into an orderly group and thus to found the first colony of monks or monastic[2] gathering. His monks, laymen like himself, lived in separate cells reading, praying, singing psalms, and working with their hands. They drew together at regular intervals to hear their master preach and to join the priest in church for the celebration of the Eucharist.[3]

[1] It must be remembered that neither creed was then in its present form; and also that the Apostles' Creed has never been used by the Eastern Church.

[2] The words monasticism, monachism, monk, all derive from the Greek words *monakhos—monos*, meaning solitary. A monk was one who retired from the world to live a religious life.

[3] From the Greek words *eu*, grateful, and *charis*, thanks. Sacrament of the Lord's Supper.

Pachomius had been forced to fight for Constantine. When still a soldier he had been converted by the kindness of Christians and was not only a great lover of God but an extremely practical man. In Upper Egypt he designed monasteries resembling walled cities for his monks and so well did they work in them and on the surrounding land that soon they were sending their surplus goods down to Alexandria in their own two boats. These monks were not semi-eremitical[1] like St. Anthony's but were banded together forty to a house and all obeying the same rule.

How then did the monastic ideal reach the British Isles ? Principally through St. Martin, another of Constantine's reluctant soldiers. He was inspired by Athanasius' *Life of St. Anthony* to build like monasteries in Gaul. What was novel was that in doing so he became the Apostle of Gaul. On his way home from Rome to Britain St. Ninian stayed with him at Marmoutier to study this new way of life. So impressed was he that in 397 his own foundation at Candida Casa in Wigtownshire resembled wherever possible its parent house in Gaul. Moreover St. Patrick and many other fifth century British clerics studied (and one ruled) at Lérins, another important monastery directly following Egyptian models and founded in 410 on an island off the south of France. It too copied St. Anthony in giving its monks separate cells; but much of its system was borrowed from Pachomius.

From the fifth century onwards this originally Egyptian pattern of the monastic life was in active practice all along the Atlantic seaboard.

Let us therefore take a closer look at the original monks of Egypt and learn a little of what so inspired their fellow Christians in far-off Gaul, Britain and Ireland.

At first it was to escape the ties, taxes and persecutions of the Empire that Christians sought refuge in the deserts of Syria, Palestine and Egypt. By the time the pagan persecutions ceased some, at least, of the exiles had discovered they would rather remain alone with God and their fellow worshippers than return to worldly distractions. And by the end of the

[1]Also from the Greek *eremos*, a desert. It now means solitary, like a hermit.

fourth century every available desert was astonishingly alive with monks. There were nuns too, dependent on neighbouring monasteries for hard manual labour and for the ministrations of a priest. If the monastery of the monks was on one side of the river then the dwelling-place of the nuns would be found discreetly situated on the opposite bank.

St. Basil, St. Anthony's pupil, founded in Asia Minor a new kind of monastery where the chief austerity practised was a selfless love of the needy. He emphasised the good of the communal life, taught his monks to run schools for boys, and his nuns to nurse the sick in his hospitals. None the less he ardently admired the contemplative life. He made an extensive tour of the monasteries of Egypt, Palestine, Syria and Mesopotamia, and wrote in one of his letters of their monks as follows : " I admired their continence in living and their endurance in toil; I wondered at their persistence in prayer and their triumph over sleep; subdued by no natural necessity; ever keeping their soul's purpose high and free, in hunger, in thirst, in cold, in nakedness, they never yielded to the body; always as though living in a flesh that was not theirs, they showed in very deed what it is to sojourn in this life for a while and what it is to have one's citizenship and home in heaven."

Copts, Greeks, Latins, indeed all sorts and conditions of men were engaged in like spiritual combat. Palladius spent six years in the midst of the Nile monasteries at the beginning of the fifth century. He wrote their history and tells of an ill-famed robber convert, Moses by name and " an Ethiopian by race, and black." Long and manfully he struggled against the temptations that continued to beset him in the Egyptian desert. They were worst at night; so to occupy himself he would visit the cells of the older brothers and fill their water jugs while they slept. Once four robbers attacked him in his cell. At last he could use his physical strength. " He tied them all together, and putting them on his back like a truss of straw, brought them to the church of the brethren saying : ' Since I am not allowed to hurt anyone, what on earth am I to do so with these ?' "

Sulpicius Severus, a contemporary of Palladius, vies with him in his admiration of the communal monastic life led by Moses and the majority of his fellow monks. He already had a wide public thanks to his much loved *Life of St. Martin*, and to this public he now turned with new material collected on the banks of the Nile. "The monks," he says, "live together generally in separate groups of about a hundred each. Their chief rule consists in being under the authority of an abbot and in undertaking no single act on their own initiative, in obeying in every smallest detail their head on whom they depend. Those among them who aim at a life of greater perfection, repair to the desert there to lead a hermit's life. But this they only do with the full permission of their abbot."

Some of these hermits frankly disliked visitors; for, as one of them explained to his puzzled friends, "if one received men it was impossible also to receive angels." But few men can live by angels alone. Animals were often a welcome addition to the company. Sulpicius Severus describes many such desert friendships, two of which will help to show the close kinship between Egyptian and Celtic hermits. The stories were told to him by his friend Postumianus newly back in Gaul after three years travel in North Africa.

"Well, I was on the borders of the desert, about twelve miles from the Nile; one of the brethren, who was well acquainted with the district, was with me as a guide. We reached the habitation of an old monk who lived at the foot of a mountain, and—a very unusual thing in those parts—there was a well. The monk was the owner of an ox and this beast did nothing but turn a wheel which drew up the water, for the well was immensely deep, over a thousand feet it was said. A garden produced vegetables in abundance, a most unusual occurrence in the desert where the soil, dried up everywhere and scorched by the burning sun, can never afford nourishment to the meanest plants. . . . Well, to continue, when we arrived at our destination in the company of our agreeable host we found a lion in possession, and my companion and I began to tremble and shake. But the holy man, without one moment's hesitation approached the beast;

we followed apprehensively. The lion, as though obeying some heaven-sent command, backed a little, very cautiously and politely. We looked on motionless while the hermit took hold of the lower branches of the palm tree and plucked the fruit. Then, seeing a handful of dates held out to him, the lion bounded forward and ate up the fruit as peacefully as though he had been a tame, domestic pet. And when he had finished he went quietly.

"I made the acquaintance of another equally extra-ordinary hermit who dwelt in a tiny hut just big enough to hold one person. It was said that a wolf was in the habit of sharing his meal. The beast hardly ever failed to appear punctually at the dinner hour. She waited at the door until the hermit handed out any bread that was left over after he had finished his repast, upon which the wolf would lick his hand and having thus expressed her gratitude would quietly take her leave. But one day the holy man was visited by a brother hermit and accompanied his friend on the latter's homeward journey; he was a long time absent and only returned at nightfall. Meanwhile the wolf appeared at the usual dinner hour. She soon perceived that her well-known and kindly host was not at home so she ventured inside. A palm-leaf basket containing five loaves chanced to be hanging near the door. The wolf nibbled at one of the loaves and finally gobbled it up. Then, feeling very guilty, she went away. As soon as the hermit returned he saw that the basket had been meddled with and that one of his loaves was missing, and he felt pretty sure of the identity of the thief. For some days after this the wolf did not appear as usual; she was doubtless repenting her impudent theft and was fearful of approaching her friend. However the hermit missed the little variety which the beast's daily visit afforded and he prayed that she might come back again. And at last, at the end of a week, the wolf appeared as of old, at the usual dinner hour. But her shame and remorse were very apparent. She did not dare to come near her friend. Her head hung down. She seemed cowed and unhappy and was plainly humbly begging to be forgiven. The hermit was very sorry for her. He called her to him and tenderly caressed her drooping head. And then he presented her with a double portion of bread by way of consolation. The wolf saw that she was forgiven and became her own cheerful self, and afterwards appeared punctually every day as usual."

Three hundred years later St. Cuthbert, the last of our great saints to live in the true Celtic tradition, soothed the speechless distress of a pair of repentant ravens who had vowed to steal no more while they shared his island solitude. Perhaps he is a little firmer with them than is his Egyptian forerunner, and perhaps they are grown even more Christian than the wolf for they bring him a placating gift. Otherwise they are the last of a long, lively chain of lions, wolves, deer, cows, hares, horses, bees, monsters, whales, bears, foxes, squirrels, otters, cocks, mice, and even flies—all converted, like Pachomius, by the kindness of Christians. For beasts and birds clearly felt that to befriend and serve these holy men was to live very close to the kingdom of heaven.

And this is scarcely surprising when we remember that the aim of hermits, semi-eremitical monks and coenobitical[1] monks alike was nothing less than to live in a state of perpetual awareness of God. To this end they all studied and prayed; but what was much more remarkable in a world where manual labour was considered only fit for slaves, they all worked daily at their various crafts as a valuable part of spiritual discipline. Not only did the superiors agree with St. Paul that " if a man will not work neither let him eat," but they found it to be true that " a monk who works is tempted by one devil only; the lazy monk by a thousand devils."

So for the good of their souls and for the benefit of the community St. Anthony's monks sat in their separate cells weaving linen or making mats or baskets from Nile rushes. And while they worked they prayed or meditated. In some monasteries the making of mats went on even in church during the communal midnight singing of psalms.

[1]From two Greek words *koenos*, common and *bios*, life—meaning living together in a religious community.

From Pachomius' Life and from his own Rule translated from the Greek by St. Jerome in 404 we learn that the main occupation of his monks too was the weaving of rush mats; but that from dawn his workshops (all his walled cities contained libraries and bakeries; blacksmiths', carpenters' and cobblers' shops) his kitchens, refectories, infirmaries, fields and gardens were alive with silent and well-organised monks the fruit of whose surplus labours went to relieve the famine-stricken and the poor. At noon and in the evening, according to the kind of work they did, these men ate various quantities of bread, cheese, herbs and fruit, and every three days they were given sweets to take back to their cells. They attended daily services in their churches at dawn, sunset and midnight; and on Saturday and Sunday the Eucharist was celebrated and Pachomius spoke to them on such subjects as prayer, hard passages of Holy Writ, and the Incarnation, Passion and Resurrection of Christ. Attendance at these sermons was compulsory, and the monks were bound also to listen to the instruction given them by their House Superiors on Wednesdays and Fridays when they had no mid-day meal.

Just as work was considered necessary for the good of all classes, so all classes had to learn to read; though slaves could only be admitted to a community with their master's permission. Reading, writing and study of the scriptures (for the most part in Greek) went on every day and huge portions were learnt by heart.

Public confession and public repentance of sins against the rule took place on Sundays. Thieves and perverters of souls were whipped; and incurables were expelled. In one of the most severe of the Egyptian monasteries the abbot wrote to the Superior of his neighbouring nuns commanding her to beat twelve of her erring daughters with rods. They may well have deserved it; none the less the letter, still extant, has an unpleasantly harsh flavour unknown in the writings relating to the communities of St. Anthony and St. Pachomius (who had the greatest respect for each other) where the men or women living together in poverty, chastity and complete obedience to their superiors, were undoubtedly charitably treated by them and really did attain amongst themselves to a loving spirit of mutual helpfulness.

Equally happy relations existed from the first between priests and monks. St. Athanasius' pastoral letters were read in all the monasteries of Egypt; his views on Arians were known and heartily shared. He first visited Pachomius and his new walled monasteries in 330 and was received as befitted a hero of the Catholic Church. And again, over twenty year later, when he had told the world how he had seen these men working in the desert barefooted in linen tunics, hooded capes and sheepskin cloaks, looking, when they journeyed, like Old Testament prophets with their staffs in their hands—again it was to the monasteries of Pachomius that he went in search of refuge from a further outbreak of Arian persecution.

As for his relations with St. Anthony, it would be hard to say which of the two men admired the other more. It was St. Anthony's greatest joy to love God alone in his secluded cave—and this despite the fact that because he so excelled in it the devil often used physical force in an effort to stop him. The devil never succeeded. But St. Anthony so loved Athanasius and all he stood for that he gladly deserted his cave at the age of eighty-seven and walked off to Alexandria to stand by his friend the year before the Arians banished him to Europe. Being a monk he had almost no possessions; but when he died he left Athanasius the sheepskin cloak on which he had slept on the ground.[1]

Sometimes a priest joined the candidates who waited so patiently for admittance outside the walls of Pachomian monasteries. Several days would pass before a new batch of penitents was permitted to join the brothers at prayer; and then began a further time of trial and testing at the end of which it was decided whether they should go or stay. Here the trained priest would have the advantage over an ignorant lay brother, but though respected for his special office, he was always completely subject, as they all were, to the rule of the abbot. It is worth while noting the exactly similar position

[1]By the end of his life Athanasius had achieved such fame that in 363 even bishops from the remote British Isles took pleasure in affirming to him their loyal adherence to the Nicene Creed.

held by the clergy in Celtic monasteries. And it is perhaps worth recording that at one Egyptian monastery the long-suffering candidates had to endure ten days of tauntings outside the sacred walls—an exact replica of what was to take place outside St. David's Welsh monastery.

Christ taught that the whole law of life hangs on the following two commandments: "Thou shalt love the Lord thy God with all thy heart, and with all thy soul, and with all thy mind, and with all thy strength . . . and thy neighbour as thyself." By now these words are grown almost too familiar to yield their full meaning. But to thousands of despondent citizens of the still splendid but already corrupt and dying Roman Empire they literally opened the door to a new life. The fourth century was an ominous age; it called for strong spiritual remedies. So dire was the state of the people within, and the pressure of the barbarians without the Empire that men foresaw the end of the world. In 410 Rome fell, and that calamity, lamented by St. Jerome in his far-off monastery near Bethlehem, proved indeed the beginning of the end. Yet St. Augustine cried amidst the anguish that the city of God is eternal; and the men who sought literally to obey the two life-giving commandments were in the forefront of the army of Christians who proved him right. In their frail cells they translated and copied the scriptures, preserved the Catholic faith and upheld the value of the life of sanctity; without them the work of the pioneers would never have been preserved for posterity, that is to say, for us.

When Rome fell Palladius was living in the Thebiad. He estimated that there were then seven thousand monks in that region of the Nile alone. And by then monasticism had emerged from the deserts; had spread from the eastern fringes of the Mediterranean; and taken root in Italy, Africa and Gaul. Five leading bishops of the Catholic Church fostered this lay movement in the West. St. Athanasius explained what monasticism meant; St. Hilary studied it in Asia Minor perceiving its potential force as a weapon against Arianism[1];

[1] In 358 he congratulated the British Church on being almost alone in her freedom from the "detestable heresy."

St. Martin made it the basis of his missionary work in Gaul; St. Ambrose founded an admirable monastery outside Milan; and St. Augustine ruled a purely clerical one for the training of his priests at Hippo. Indeed so swift and wide was the sweep of the movement that while Palladius still marvelled at the monks of the Thebiad, St. Ninian had already set out from Candida Casa to convert the Picts of Eastern Scotland.

Sources:
De Excidio Britanniae. Gildas. Ed. Williams.
Ecclesiastical History of England. Bede. Ed. J. A. Giles.
Irish Monasticism. Ryan. Containing quotations from:
    Life of St. Anthony. Athanasius.
    Church of the Fathers. Newman.
The Lausiac History. Palladius. Ed. W. K. L. Clark.
Life of St. Martin. Sulpicius Severus. Ed. M. C. Watt.
Dialogues. Sulpicius Severus. Ed. M. C. Watt.
The Celtic Church and the See of Peter. MacNaught.
A History of Europe. Fisher.

Chapter II.

ST. MARTIN

T. MARTIN'S life spans the fourth century like a rainbow. It rises faintly from a still sunny pagan landscape; the colours grow clearer as the arch crosses a darkening sky; and as it dips in front of the lowering thunder clouds that are to destroy the Western Empire the rainbow gleams solid against the chaos. The Empire is doomed; but the Church has become an organised and dynamic body prepared to guard the heritage of pagan learning and to tame and convert the barbarous invaders.

That she was equipped for this huge task in Gaul was almost entirely owing to St. Martin. Until he realised his conception of the Church as an active missionary body existing to bring something of heaven to the country districts of Gaul, his fellow bishops had remained inside the cities; and only in the south could the land be said to be in any real sense Christian.

Naturally many of these urban bishops proved hostile to the vigorous, ascetic breed of clergy trained by St. Martin at Marmoutier. They were bound to disapprove, resembling as they did that newly-made bishop described with so sharp a pen by Sulpicius Severus.

"Formerly he travelled on foot or astride an ass; but now he is a personage and he is whirled along by foaming steeds. In the days of old he was content to dwell in a small, poor cell; but now his abode is beneath high-panelled roofs. He makes good use of his well-beloved widows and of the holy virgins who are his friends; some will weave for him a warm, soft birrus, and others will furnish a beautiful floating mantle."

St. Martin, in contrast, he tells us, refused even to sit on his bishop's throne. It was the fact that he lived the gospel and did not merely expound it that so influenced Gallo-Romans of the standing of Sulpicius Severus and of his friend the courtly Paulinus, who, he writes, " had cast off a load of immense riches to follow Christ, and who was in our time almost the only one to follow the law of the Gospel completely."

Both men delighted too in St. Martin's battles for the oppressed against the State. He feared the Emperors Valentinian and Maximus no more than St. Ambrose feared the great Theodosius; and in thus upholding the rights of Apostolic authority he helped to win for the Church the supreme position she was to hold in the future. The two friends were quite intelligent enough to realise the magnitude of his achievements. They revered him; they admired him; but above all they loved him. He combined a perpetual awareness of the presence of God (conversing daily with angels) with so powerful and practical a love for his fellow men that often it flowered into miracles. It was an irresistible combination; and when at last he died in his rural parish of Candes two thousand of his monks followed him to his grave in the Cathedral at Tours. Sulpicius Severus relates that the choirs of nuns among the company " modestly refrained from loud weeping." He himself was stricken. " I am sure," he writes, " that I have now a powerful advocate in heaven; but I have lost the great Consoler of my life here below."

Even before losing his Consoler Sulpicius Severus had finished writing his *Life*. It is an invigorating story; and one well known to St. Ninian who must often have discussed it with the author when they stayed together at Marmoutier.

It starts in Central Europe where St. Martin was born of pagan parents. The family was constantly on the move as his father was a veteran soldier in the Imperial Army. Educated at Pavia in Lombardy, the child there came under Christian influence. At ten he asked to become a catechumen[1], and by twelve he was " dreaming of the desert."

[1]A convert under instruction before baptism.

In the less popular trades of the Roman Empire, however, it had become compulsory to follow the father's profession. So it was as an officer in Constantine's Imperial Cavalry that St. Martin first went to Gaul. Artists all down the ages have felt inspired to paint him at Amiens, leaning from his horse to give his cloak to a shivering beggar. The action reveals the Christian; though when this incident occurred St. Martin was not yet baptised. In this he merely followed the custom of the fourth century when this sacrament was commonly deferred until maturity. For it was argued that as all sins were washed away by baptism and that sins committed after receiving the grace of the Holy Spirit were the more grievous, therefore the longer it was deferred the better. Many only received the sacrament on their deathbeds. Soon after the episode of the cloak, however, St. Martin felt the time had come and " flew to be baptised." Thus fortified he joined the long line of his mounted comrades at Worms. The Legions were drawn up in readiness to attack the approaching barbarians. Swords and spears were in the hands of his companions; but rather than kill his enemies St. Martin faced them unarmed. Fortunately for Christendom the battle was never fought. But as it had become all too plain to his superiors that this young man would never make a satisfactory soldier it was not long before they gave him his freedom.

This brings us to the middle of the century. From then on, till he goes to Tours twenty years later, the would-be hermit prepares all unconsciously for the Apostleship of Gaul guided at first by St. Hilary of Poitiers. When St. Martin first met him St. Hilary had only recently been converted. But he was so fervent a Catholic that a few years after their meeting, in 356, the Arians banished him for four years to Asia Minor. This period of exile greatly profited both master and disciple. Indeed the Arians could not have chosen a wiser way to further the Catholic cause.

Both men were already familiar with the monastic ideals of St. Anthony whose monks strove towards the goal of a hermit's life. But of what his pupil St. Basil had accomplished in Asia Minor they knew little till St. Hilary found it out at first hand. As has already been stated St. Basil had directed the emphasis from the contemplative and ascetic to the active and social. Instead of nightly vigils and daily fasts his monks and nuns practised a selfless devotion to the sick, the needy and the helpless under their care. St. Basil widened the scriptural meaning of the word neighbour; for those he taught, nursed and fed were from outside the monastery walls. Fired by the stories told by St. Hilary on his return, St. Martin was to stretch the meaning of the word still further.

He had left Poitiers before St. Hilary's enforced departure, driven by a dream to return to his birthplace and convert his parents. He went as an exorcist,[1] having, despite his theological studies, refused to accept more than this humble rank in the Church. None the less so marked was his Catholic zeal that he had only succeeded in converting his mother when the Arians, all powerful in Central Europe, drove him, like his master, into exile. Having learnt of St. Hilary's similar plight he did not return to Poitiers but settled for a time in a hermit's cell at Milan. From this cell he conducted so fierce a war with the Arian bishop that he was once more expelled. This time a longing for peace took him to an island off the coast of Liguria. And it was probably there that he achieved the nearest approach to the solitary life he had longed for ever since his first dreams of the desert.

But it was merely a time of preparation. As soon as he heard of his master's return he followed him back to Poitiers.

He now became a priest. But he begged and obtained permission to continue to live as a solitary monk. St. Hilary, no doubt aware that his remarkable disciple was destined to attract others, gave him some farm land nearby at Ligugé, on which to build his White Hut[2]. The fame of his miracles and of his great sanctity soon drew to him a host of visitors. These visitors persuaded him to turn his hut into the first of the monastic White Houses so common afterwards throughout Gaul and in the settlements of the Celtic saints in Pictland

[1]Orders in the fourth century Church were as follows:—Doorkeepers, Funeral undertakers, Readers, Exorcists (spiritual healers), Sub-Deacons, Deacons, Presbyters (officiating priests), Bishops, Metropolitans and Patriarchs.

[2]From the Celtic *Logo-Tigiac* translated by St. Ninian into the Latin Candida Casa.

ST. MARTIN SPANS THE FOURTH CENTURY LIKE A RAINBOW

and Britain. Then the disciples became (in the Celtic language) his *muinntir* or family and he their *pápa*[1] or father having over them the same authority as the chief of a Celtic clan. He was still at Ligugé in 371 perfecting that combination of the contemplative with the active and social life which was to prove the strength of the Celtic Church, when he was called away to Tours to heal a case of dangerous illness. Long before the end of the journey he had learnt that the sickness was a mere blind. His admirers had determined to make him the new Bishop of Tours.

They had their way. But though his authoritive position in the Church enlarged the field of his activities from the boundaries of the farm at Ligugé to the whole of Gaul, he continued to live as a monk. Nor would he consent to dwell inside the city walls like his fellow bishops, but found for himself another spot outside Tours secluded enough to ensure some approach to desert conditions. So many disciples flocked to him that the place became known as Big Family (the meaning of the Celtic *Mar-moutier* or *muinntir*).

For the last few years of St. Martin's life, during which period St. Ninian stayed with him, Sulpicius Severus too was constantly at Marmoutier. "The bishop," he relates, "occupied a cell of wood. Many of the brethren lived in similar cells, but the greater number dug out caves in the overhanging rock in which to instal themselves. There were here about eighty disciples all following the example of their blessed master. No one possessed personal property, everything was in common. To buy or to sell as do many monks, was strictly forbidden. No arts were practised save the art of transcribing and even this work was reserved for the young monks, the older ones being entirely given up to prayer. The monks rarely left their cells except to meet together in the spot appointed for public prayer. They all ate together after the great fast; wine they never tasted, unless compelled by sickness to do so. The greater number were clothed in camelor, for in this place it was a sin to wear dainty clothing. These austerities were the more to be

[1]The word was borrowed from Greek-speaking monks and taken to Scotland by St. Ninian.

admired in that many of the monks were of noble birth. Several of them we have beheld in after years as bishops.''

Though St. Anthony's monks were not nobles and seldom entered the priesthood the way of life described here is clearly his. And like him St. Martin slept on the bare ground with sackcloth for his sole covering, a custom followed faithfully by his Celtic successors in their yet damper lands. The main difference between Egyptian and Gallic monks lay in the latter's use of the monastic life as a background and school for widespread missionary work.

These mission bases became ever more numerous. From time to time twelve disciples under an acknowledged leader would break off from the parent cell at Marmoutier and, with the blessing of St. Martin, would depart to make the core of a new *muinntir* following the rule of the mother house. Two of the earliest of these *muinntirs* became Landonart and Landevenech[1] in what we now call Brittany. Thus, very much after the fashion of the primitive Church, did monasticism spread in an ever widening orbit from the centre at Tours. The city bishops, living at ease among their secular populations, might dislike these purely religious communities springing up throughout the countryside and producing priests and laymen intent on the conversion of the peasants; but they were, for several generations, powerless to interfere. St. Martin, within his rights as bishop, himself consecrated men famous for their sanctity to be the bishops necessary to make his new *muinntirs* independent. It was an important step towards the reformation of the Church in Gaul and one which decided the position of bishops in the Celtic Church. Sometimes (as were St. Martin and St. Ninian) the rulers of monasteries were themselves bishops. But far more often the monastic bishop lived, as did all the members of the *muinntir*, under the supreme authority of the *pápa*.

It is sad that we know so little at first hand of how the monks were trained. To Sulpicius Severus the spirit of St. Martin's experiments mattered far more than their form.

[1]The Celtic word *lan* or *llan* originally meant an enclosed place but came to mean a church and was always followed by the name of the founder.

As in Egypt the scriptures formed the principal study. There were Latin versions of the psalms and the New Testament for daily use in church and these would be largely learnt by heart. Probably the Old Testament was also studied. By the time St. Ninian arrived at Marmoutier from Rome St. Jerome's new translations of the psalms and the New Testament were available. No doubt so keen a student brought copies with him and though these innovations may not have been welcome to monks already familiar with other translations it was certainly an early version of the *Vulgate*[1] that St. Ninian carried to Scotland. At that time professional copyists had made the works of Greek and Latin authors reasonably cheap in Rome. Surely they also formed part of his luggage. Fresh from his studies there he probably helped to introduce them to the monks of Marmoutier. After all he had been given the same Roman education as had Sulpicius Severus to whom Homer, Plato, Socrates, Terence and Statius are so familiar that he obviously takes his pagan heritage for granted. St. Martin was no scholar; but if he had not encouraged secular learning besides the study of the scriptures it seems most improbable that Candida Casa should so soon have won fame among the Irish as the leading school among the earliest monasteries. They mention with relish the library of which they made such good use.

Because of her geographical position Ireland escaped both Roman and early Anglo-Saxon invasions. When, in the ninth century, the Vikings[2] reached her the damage they did was appalling but they had already vented their worst fury on England and Scotland. It is therefore from her written sources, alone preserved, that we learn not only of the proud position of Candida Casa but of the early forms of Celtic liturgy originally brought by St. Ninian from Gaul and therefore used by St. Martin. The form of worship used in Gaul seems at first to have closely resembled desert liturgies. Psalms

[1]The name given to St. Jerome's superb translation of the Bible into simple Latin begun in Rome by order of Pope Damasus (d. 384) and finished in St. Jerome's own monastery in Bethlehem. It was in use throughout the churches of Christendom until the Reformation.

[2]The word means literally " creekers." They were Norsemen and included Danes.

were chanted or intoned by the hour, but to what kind of music we have, alas, no idea. St. Ambrose, whose services were also much influenced by eastern customs, wrote for his congregation at Milan hymns to melodies so piercingly sweet that they made St. Augustine weep. Celtic saints sang on the slightest provocation so it is safe to assume that there were musicians too among the noble Celtic and Latin priests and laymen gathered together at Marmoutier.

For the missionaries produced by the *muinntirs* in Gaul were by no means all priests. Many of the monks were masons, blacksmiths, farmers, cooks or gardeners. Through their efforts the whole face of rural Gaul was changed. Down crashed the idols, the temples, the consecrated trees. In their place there rose little parish churches—each one in charge of a priest—to be the centres of the new Christian settlements where the peasants were provided with seed and taught to farm and to build more intelligently. Such settlements were planted in the regions of Paris, Trêves, Chartres, Viennes and Luxembourg; in the Rhône Valley; and all over the south of Gaul. To each congregation the great event of the year was the bishop's visit. St. Martin never failed to arrive, escorted by a troop of monks and travelling sometimes on foot, sometimes on a donkey and sometimes sailing at ease down the broad rivers of Gaul. His dynamic presence revived jaded priests to attack afresh the frequent signs of reviving idolatry. His converts rejoiced to show him what had been accomplished since his last visit. The following graphic account from Sulpicius Severus' *Life*, of the conversion of a district is too pertinent to condense.

" In a certain town, after destroying a very ancient temple, Martin desired also to fell a pine tree which stood close to the site of the pagan sanctuary. But the priest of the place and all the heathen population obstinately set themselves to oppose him. These men, who, by the grace of God, had silently allowed the destruction of their temple, were now determined that the tree should not be felled.

" All in vain did Martin forcibly represent to them that there was nothing worthy of veneration in a mere tree, that they should not worship it, but rather the great God whose minister he was, and that this tree which had been dedicated to a devil ought to be cast down.

" At length one of the assembled heathen, bolder than the rest, exclaimed: ' If thou hast conquered in the name and by the power of this God whom thou pretendest to adore, we, ourselves, will fell this tree, but only on condition that thou place thyself beneath it, so that in its fall it will crush thee. If thy God is ever with thee as thou declarest, thou wilt run no risk.'

" Bold and confident in the Lord, Martin at once agreed to this proposal.

" This strange bargain caused a vast concourse of pagans to assemble. They were resigned to the loss of their sacred tree if only in its fall it might cause the destruction of the enemy of their faith.

" The great pine tree had grown to one side and it seemed certain that in falling it would crash in the direction towards which it leant. Martin, therefore, was bound and placed in a certain spot indicated by the peasants and where they were convinced the tree must fall. And then the pagans began themselves to fell the tree—joyfully, eagerly, did they go to work in full view of a crowd of persons who, all amazed, watched from afar.

" Soon the pine tree shook and trembled and it seemed that the Saint must surely be crushed to death.

" The monks, standing afar off, grew pale, terrified at the imminent peril. They had lost all hope, all courage, and were convinced that Martin must die.

" He, however, strong in the Lord waits fearless, undisturbed, and as the crashing noise made by the falling tree reverberates through the air, he calmly raises his hand and makes towards it the Sign of the Cross. The tree seems to be caught backwards by some unseen power and it falls in quite the opposite direction to which it had inclined, so that the peasants, who were gathered in what had appeared to be so safe a place, have a narrow escape from being crushed to death.

31

" At once, a great shout rises up to Heaven—the pagans are amazed and confounded by the miracle and all the monks weep for joy. All acclaim the name of Christ and indeed on that day salvation was vouchsafed to the whole district, for in all that great crowd of heathen there was hardly one who did not implore the laying on of hands in order to believe in the Lord Jesus and abandon the errors of paganism.

" And truly before Martin's day, very few, hardly any indeed, in these regions had professed Christ, but now the Holy Name became so well known, thanks to the miracles and the examples of Martin, that the whole district is full of churches and monasteries, Martin's practice being, wherever he destroyed heathen sanctuaries to replace them immediately with churches and monasteries."

As a missionary in training St. Ninian surely accompanied St. Martin on some of the journeys he made towards the end of his life. And Sulpicius Severus in his capacity of biographer undoubtedly took care to witness many of the events he describes. But in the south of Gaul even the stones give evidence of St. Martin's presence. Many tombstones have been found adorned by his masons with the Chi-Rho monogram.[1] Constantine carried this Christian symbol on his Imperial banner and in those days it was as much in evidence as was the swastika in the heyday of Nazi power. What is remarkable about the carvings found in Southern Gaul is that the Rho is open as it can be seen in the photographs of the early stones found at St. Ninian's Kirkmadrine. Now to write the Rho thus was an eastern habit. In the west it was commonly closed. The use of the open Rho in Southern Gaul (and its subsequent introduction to Pictland where, combined with the Chi and encircled with a ring of glory, the monogram developed into the Celtic wheel cross) is a concrete example of how deeply St. Martin was influenced by St. Hilary's sojourn in Greek-speaking lands, and through him, of course, by St. Basil and the Desert Fathers.

Like those hermits St. Martin was often subtly tempted

[1] Made by combining the first two Greek letters of Christ's name χ(CH) and ρ(R).

while he meditated in solitude. Here is one such experience given in the words of Sulpicius Severus.

"But one should not omit to relate, it seems to me, with what skill the Devil, about this period, tempted Martin. One day he appeared to the Saint preceded and illumined by a blinding light, thus producing an effect of borrowed splendour. Robed in a kingly mantle, crowned with a golden crown set with jewels, shod with gilded sandals, with serene aspect and joyous mien, he did not in the least degree resemble the Devil. And thus he stood erect, near the Bishop, who was praying in his cell. Martin, when he first caught sight of his visitor, seemed almost stupified. And for some time the two were absolutely silent. Then the Devil made the first advance. 'Martin,' he said, 'behold me, here before thee; I am the Christ, and, having come down to earth, I have desired to reveal myself to thee before all others.'

"Martin remained silent and answered nothing. The Devil dared not reiterate his impudent assertion: 'Well, Martin, why hesitate to believe, now that thou beholdest with thine eyes ? I am the Christ.'

"Then the Bishop, enlightened by the Holy Ghost, knew that it was the Devil and not the Lord. 'The Lord Jesus,' he said, 'has not said that He would come robed in purple with a glittering diadem. For me, I will not believe in the advent of Christ unless He bear the aspect and look the same as on the day of His Passion, unless He show me the wounds of His Cross.'

"At these words, the other immediately vanished like smoke, and the cell was filled with a vile stench—indisputable proof that it was indeed the Devil.

"This tale, just as I have told it, I had from Martin's own lips. So do not imagine that it is a mere fable."

But on the whole Sulpicius Severus is inclined to contrast the simplicity of the solitary warfare undertaken by those Desert Fathers with the complex and exhausting battles continually fought by the Bishop of Tours. "Martin lived in the midst of men, in the world amongst the people; he was surrounded by a hostile clergy and by angry bishops, scandals were of almost daily occurrence and he was perpetually assailed from all quarters; and amidst all this his piety remained unshaken and his miracles are greater than those worked by famous hermits who live or have lived in the desert." Hermits might fight the devil more or less in person; but they did not feel obliged to fight the Emperor for the life of a heretic nor to attempt to wrest from the State the power to judge ecclesiastical offences. It is small wonder that towards the end of his twenty-six years episcopate St. Martin had grown so bruised with these battles that he would no longer attend a synod. It was more important to win rural Gaul for Christ before it should be too late. The heedless bishops sorely distressed him. Nor was he comforted when on one occasion he had particularly impressed a snake. "The serpents hear me," he said sadly, "but men hear me not." It was much easier to rescue a terrified hare from the chase or give sanity to a poor mad cow than to wean proud men from the devil. Even at Marmoutier he had need of all his courage and patience. When asked how he could tolerate in his monastery the presence of a certain protégé of his, relapsed, after entering the priesthood, into a scandalously godless state, he replied: "If Christ could tolerate Judas, surely I can put up with Brictio."

We owe it to the lively pen of Sulpicius Severus that we can still catch such glimpses of the great mystic evangelist who moulded St. Ninian and who spent twenty-six years preparing rural Gaul to meet the heathen invaders. The author was from the first happily aware that through his book a worthy place had been ensured for his beloved Martin in the hearts of all Christians. The self-righteous bishops of Gaul might consider the saint uncultured; but the Celtic saints always thought him to be the spiritual equal of those earlier apostles St. Peter, St. Paul and St. John. Armed with his powerful blessing St. Ninian worked tirelessly in Scotland and Ireland. He made it so clear that his methods were those of his master and that his church at Whithorn[1] was the daughter church of Marmoutier, that the Irish were wont to call Candida Casa

[1] Simply the Anglo-Saxon version of White House.

Martin's House. And indeed it was : having been called after the first White House at Ligugé.

Later, despite the fact that in 405 Gaul fell before the Teutonic invaders leaving the British Isles more or less isolated from the continent, St. Patrick, St. Columba and St. Columban each made his way to Tours to pray at St. Martin's tomb.[1] The collapse of the empire failed to stem the world-wide flow of pilgrims drawn as by a magnet to that sacred spot. Right through the Dark Ages Sulpicius Severus' proud boast remained true : '' The Ethiopian knows of his fame ; the Indian too has heard of it as have also the dwellers in Persia and Parthia. Armenia has not been left in ignorance, nor has the region beyond the Bosphorus ; and surely, if there be dwellers in the Fortunate Isles and the Arctic regions, they, too, must have heard of the fame of Martin.''

To-day we still remember his name. Martinmas, St. Martin's Summer, St. Martin-in-the-Field all vouch for that. But in this enlightened age too few of us have heard of the fame of the father of our Celtic Church.

[1]Though Dr. W. Douglas Simpson thinks it '' chronologically impossible '' that St. Columba should have brought back *St. Martin's Gospel*, there seems no good reason to doubt his visit to Tours.

Sources :
Life of St. Martin and Dialogues. Sulpicius Severus. Ed. M. C. Watt.
St. Ambrose, His Life and Times. F. Homes Dudden.
The Celtic Church in Scotland. W. Douglas Simpson.
The Pictish People and its Church. Archibald B. Scott.

CHAPTER III.

ST. NINIAN

AS St. Ninian what we call a well-educated man ? In what kind of surroundings did he grow up ? And what kind of people were the Picts to whom he was sent as a missionary by Rome in a final effort to bring them into the Empire ? The true answers to these questions are not, at first, easy to find. There must have been contemporary records of St. Ninian's life ; but they were all lost in Anglo-Saxon and Viking raids. The Latin authors certainly mention the Picts, but inevitably they see them as naked savages. For the Picts stripped for battle, and were only known to Roman historians in their capacity of unconquerable warriors.

However, modern historians and archaeologists have done much to reveal Pictish culture. Moreover by patient research they have succeeded in piecing together an historical portrait of St. Ninian, enabling him at last to take his rightful place in the story of the Celtic Church. But to accomplish this they had first to study the two earliest authorities to mention the saint's existence.

It has been observed with some truth by modern critics that those hagiographers conveniently separated from their subjects by several centuries incline to dilate on the miraculous in far greater detail than do contemporary writers. There are, however, interesting exceptions : among whom are Aelred, St. Ninian's twelfth century biographer, and our friend Sulpicius Severus writer of St. Martin's life. To believers in spiritual power it is delightful to find a fourth century Gallo-Roman scholar of so wide a repute veritably encrusting the life of his still living friend and master with miracles. An attitude so far from classical might well have ruined his literary career. But as we know the book became a best-seller throughout the whole Latin-reading world. A copy of the famous *Life* surely followed St. Ninian to Candida Casa.

36

It was the very book to inspire his *muinntir* when they set out unarmed to follow the route used long before by the departed Roman garrisons. For they were about to plant in Alba, the mountainous country of the Picts, a chain of the same type of fertile Christian communities as those already introduced by St. Martin with such startling success into Gaul.

And by written evidence alone we know that they too prospered in their enterprise. The historian Bede, seated at his eighth century desk, has something to say on the subject. Glancing at Ptolemy's map of the British Isles, in which Scotland juts eastward into the North Sea, and discoursing the while on St. Columba's activities among the Northern Picts (who, on our maps would have lived in the West), he writes as follows: " For the Southern Picts themselves [really the Eastern Picts] . . . had long before abandoned idolatry and embraced the faith of the truth, by the preaching of the Word by Bishop Ninian, a most reverend and holy man, of the nation of the Britons, who had at Rome been regularly instructed in the faith and mysteries of the truth; the seat of whose episcopate, dedicated to St. Martin, and a remarkable church (where he resteth in the body along with many saints) even now belongeth to the nation of the Angles. That place, in the province of Bernicii, is commonly called ' The White House,' because there he built a church of stone in a way unusual among the Britons."[1]

Our next authority is Aelred. A prolific writer of his day, he quotes these words from Bede's *Ecclesiastical History of England* at the beginning of the *Life of St. Ninian* he was commissioned to write about the middle of the twelfth century by Christianus, Bishop of Whithorn. Like all devout Christians up to the time of the Reformation Aelred was given to " straying from Cross to Cross " and had been on pilgrimage to Candida Casa from his own monastery at Rievaulx, Yorkshire. But he was seven centuries away from his subject. Far from loosing a stream of colourful miracles from his pen, the fact that he himself knows nothing at first

[1] It has been proved conclusively that the Romanised Picts and Britons were quite familiar with stone buildings. The White House was called after St. Martin's hut at Ligugé, the word " white " being used, apparently, as synonymous to holy:

hand of St. Ninian's life so curbs him that except for sundry pious ejaculations and several alarming distortions and additions to the truth he does little more than translate from the Anglic into an elegant Latin that " book of his Life and Miracles written in a barbarous style " (probably in the eighth century from yet older manuscripts) in which longer account he obviously trusts as firmly as he does in Bede's brief paragraph.

As far as it goes, then, Aelred's *Life* inspires a cautious confidence, though due allowance has constantly to be made for the different complexion of the Roman Church for which he wrote his richly embroidered book. He it is who tells us that St. Ninian stayed with St. Martin on his way home from Rome. He rescues too from the Anglic Life the invaluable fact that it was while Candida Casa was being built that St. Martin died. His death is known to have occurred in 397 which thus becomes the first date in the history of Christianity in Scotland. But how the two saints (both mystics but both so practical) would have laughed at his description of their time together! " The pillars in the tabernacle of God are joined one with the other; sometimes borne up on the wings of virtue they soar to God, sometimes standing and folding their wings they become edifying to each other." Exalted the writing may be; but it is a most inadequate account of St. Ninian's training, especially when Aelred admits to have studied Sulpicius Severus' *Life of St. Martin*. Nor is it in the least likely (as Aelred would have us believe) that when St. Ninian left Gaul he asked St. Martin for masons, desiring even in buildings " to imitate the Roman Church." St. Ninian was a true Catholic; but he studied under the greatest religious pioneer of his age. It was not masons that he needed (this idea seems derived from Bede's unfortunate remark on the unusual appearance of Candida Casa[1]) but a *muinntir* of brave and practical Christians to help him gather his new congregation.

Aelred's readers would doubtless have been shocked to

[1]Celtic religious buildings were always small and simple. Romanised British masons used to constructing roads, baths, villas and temples could easily build them.

learn that the great St. Martin wandered all over his country in the same untidy way as did his followers the Celtic saints who so annoyed their orderly contemporaries from Rome; so though again he must have known this fact from his reading of Sulpicius Severus, he merely observes somewhat misleadingly that after St. Ninian's departure St. Martin remained " in his own See."

Now and then, however, Aelred does acknowledge Celtic customs. After telling of the conversion of the so-called Southern Picts and the miracles that confirmed the word preached by St. Ninian, he continues : " The holy Bishop began to ordain presbyters, *consecrate bishops*, distribute the other dignitaries of the ecclesiastical ranks and divide the whole land into distinct parishes." In Aelred's church it was unheard of that one bishop alone should consecrate another; it required at least three. But for obvious reasons the precedent created by St. Martin was generally followed in the Celtic Church.

The histories of the Celtic saints constantly mention their *bachalls* or staffs and their little hand-bells. So carefully were these preserved that at least one Pictish staff and several Pictish bells have survived fifteen hundred stormy years. Among other interesting information the reverence in which St. Ninian's *bachall* was held is made very plain in the following story.

" Meanwhile many, both nobles and men of the middle rank, intrusted their sons to the blessed Pontiff to be trained in sacred learning. He indoctrinated these by his knowledge, he formed them by his example, curbing by a salutary discipline the vices to which their age was prone, and persuasively inculcating the virtues whereby they might live soberly, righteously and piously. Once upon a time one of these young men committed a fault which could not escape the saint, and because it was not right that discipline should be withheld from the offender, the rods, the severest torments of boys, were made ready. The lad in terror fled, but not being ignorant of the power of the holy man, was careful to carry away with him the staff on which he used to lean, thinking that he had procured the best comfort for the journey, if he took with him anything that belonged to the saint. . . . It is the custom in that neighbourhood to frame out of twigs a certain vessel in the form of a cup, of such a size that it can contain three men sitting close together. By stretching an ox-hide over it, they render it not only buoyant but actually impenetrable by the water.[1] Possibly at that time vessels of immense size were built in the same way. The young man stumbled on one of these lying at the shore, but not covered with leather, into which, when he had incautiously entered, by Divine providence, I know not whether by its natural lightness (for on a slight touch these float far out into the waves) straightway the ship was carried out to sea. As the water poured in . . . the unhappy boy, repenting his flight, beheld with pale countenance the waves ready to avenge the injury done to the father. At length, coming to himself, and thinking that St. Ninian was present in his staff, he confessed his fault, as if in his presence, and in a lamentable voice besought pardon and prayed that by his most holy merits the divine aid might be vouchsafed him. Then trusting in the known kindness as well as power of the bishop, he stuck the staff in one of the holes, that posterity might not be ignorant of what Ninian could do even on the sea. At once, at the touch of the staff, the element trembled, and, as if kept back by a divine influence, ventured not to enter further by the open holes. . . . The staff, acting for sail, caught the wind; the staff as helm directed the vessel; the staff as anchor stayed it.'' And so, to the amazement of the onlookers, the boy floated rejoicing back to the shore.

That is one of the six miracles from the Anglic Life related by Aelred as occurring during the saint's lifetime. Another concerns the brethren's garden where he once produced miraculous leeks of so rare a quality that they left the guests partaking of them '' much better refreshed in mind than in body.''

The following miracle underlines the saint's known kindness to man and beast. '' It sometimes pleased the most holy

---

[1] An excellent description of a Celtic coracle. Amazingly long voyages were made in these lively little vessels.

ST. NINIAN BLESSES HIS FLOCKS ON SUNDAY.

Ninian to visit his flocks and the huts of his shepherds, wishing that the flocks, which he had gathered together for the use of the brethren, the poor, and the pilgrims, should be partakers of the episcopal blessing." For this purpose he had the beasts gathered together and having duly commended them to the Divine protection he enclosed them for the night in a holy circle drawn on the ground with his staff. He was far from home and had to spend the night nearby " in the house of a certain honourable matron." After finishing the solemn service of prayer he went out into the darkness to find that thieves had broken into the circle deceived by the apparently unprotected state of the cattle. The leader lay dead, gored by the bull; while the rest, wild with terror, attempted in vain to escape from their invisible prison. The sight was more than St. Ninian could bear. He begged God to restore the dead thief. " Nor did he cease from tears and entreaties till the same power which had slain him restored him not merely to life, but made him safe and sound." The rest implored pardon. " And he, benignantly chiding them and impressing upon them the fear of God and the judgment prepared for the rapacious, giving them his benediction, granted them permission to depart."

Comparing St. Ninian's way of life with the less admirable habits of his own contemporaries Aelred points out that the missionary saint was profitably employed even during his frequent and arduous travels. " For whithersoever he went forth, he raised his soul to heavenly things either by prayer or by contemplation. But so often as turning aside from his journey he indulged in rest either for himself or for the beast on which he rode, bringing out a book which he carried with him for the very purpose, he delighted in reading or singing something. Whence the Divine power bestowed such grace upon him, that even when resting in the open air, when reading in the heaviest rain, no moisture ever touched the book on which he was intent." Except, that is, on one occasion when, with a travelling companion, he was seated on the ground chanting from his psalter. It was, as usual, raining. Because of widespread forests St. Ninian's Scotland was even wetter than ours. " But during the singing the most blessed Ninian turned off his eyes from the book, affected a little by an unlawful thought, even with some desire he was tickled by some suggestion of the devil. Whereupon at once the shower, invading him and his book, betrayed what was hidden. Then the brother, who was sitting by him, knowing what had taken place, with gentle reproof reminded him of his order and age, and showed him how unbecoming such things were in such as he. Straightway the man of God, coming to himself, blushed that he had been overtaken by a vain thought, and in the same moment of time drove away the thought and stayed the shower."

After dwelling with real eloquence on the beauty of the saint's death Aelred relates that from the first his tomb was frequented with the greatest devotion.[1] This reverence pleased the Divine Power which (in his charming words) " gave evidence by frequent miracles that he whom the common lot had removed from earth was living in heaven." He then sets forth the four miracles mentioned in the Anglic life as having taken place at the tomb: the healing of a poor man afflicted with a scab; of a blind girl; of two lepers; and of a vividly described cripple. This last sufferer was left by his sorrowing parents to spend the night by the sacred relics. " And behold in the silence of the midnight hour the poor wretch saw a man come to him shining with celestial light and *glittering in the ornaments of the episcopate*, who touching his head told him to rise and be whole, and give thanks to God his Saviour. And when he had departed the wretched being, as if awakening from a deep sleep, by an easy motion, twisted each member into its natural place, and having recovered the power of them all, returned to his home safe and sound."

It is a pity that Aelred did not add to the eighth century Anglic life an account of at least one of the miracles he mentions as still occurring at Whithorn in his own day. For if he had heard the story of the cripple from a contemporary witness he could scarcely have added to the celestial light that

[1] Dr. Scott holds that there was no veneration of relics in the Celtic Church till after Candida Casa had conformed to Rome in 730. But the tombs of the Celtic saints, St. Ninian's among them, soon became places of pilgrimage, as did St. Martin's.

44

surrounded the vision of St. Ninian such unsuitable additions of his own as glittering ornaments. Medieval bishops glittered, no doubt, but St. Ninian and his monks wore long hooded garments of native undyed wool with sandals on their feet. Far from being studded with gems St. Ninian's staff was of plain wood. It was valued, as was his little iron bell, purely because he used it. If Aelred knew these facts he thought them better ignored. Because of this attitude his little book is for the most part merely tantalising to the modern reader athirst for accurate information. But it exactly met the requirements of the medieval public for whom it was written. Like the author his public was far more interested in true stories of miracles than in a true historical background.

With the later Celtic saints of the Dark Ages that background is so chaotic that it can be almost ignored. But St. Ninian is not a solitary light shining amidst confusion. He is one of a number of great Christian figures building for the future within the framework of the dying Roman Empire. To understand him rightly it is necessary first to place him within that historical framework.

When he was born in what we now call Cumberland, the country north of Hadrian's Wall had been lost to the Romans for nearly two hundred years. He was a Briton living near the Imperial Frontier and familiar with the Romanised towns of Carlisle and Maryport where the houses were centrally heated, had glass windows and were timbered or built of stone. Looking west across the Solway, easily reached by coracle, he could see the low-lying Brito-Pictish peninsular on which he was to found Candida Casa. Though on the wrong side of the Wall the peninsula was on the verge of the Empire and shared with St. Ninian's part of the country a large measure of Roman culture imbibed through centuries of commercial intercourse.

In fourth century Cumberland and fourth century Galloway alike most men were bilingual; they could write Latin; and their Celtic names were Latinised. Christianity had been the official religion of the Empire since the beginning of the century. Among the still flourishing Roman temples the British Church was already active as far north as the Wall.

In his Brito-Roman home (probably far more comfortable than Aelred's) St. Ninian learnt not only the elements of a Latin education but the rudiments of the Christian faith. "His soul was hot within him with zeal for perfection in all things of holy religion, and, discerning that matters were not conducted according to the Word, he longed for that instruction which would enable him to become a worthy minister of Jesus Christ." In short, he left Northern Britain and went to Rome.

In 383 the Spanish general Maximus (who twenty years before had helped to repel a strong Pictish attack on Hadrian's Wall) was in charge of Britain's northern frontier. He himself has it that his British army, already famous for its turbulence, persuaded him to march against Gratian, the unpopular young Emperor of the West. At any rate, posing as the champion of Christian orthodoxy, Maximus proceeded that year to raise so large an army for continental warfare that the Wall was almost denuded of defenders. He was, according to Sulpicius Severus, a man endowed "with many excellent qualities." It is tempting to imagine that the young Ninian may have heard him harangue his devoted soldiers. Carried away like them by thoughts of adventure, and perhaps by the usurper's Catholic propaganda, he may have decided then and there to take advantage of the free educational facilities offered at that time by Rome to all students within the Empire who could produce certificates from their local magistrates. The dates certainly fit perfectly. It is quite probable that Ninian started his journey along the straight Roman roads in the train of the rebel army. If he did he fared better than the British soldiers. They are remembered to this day in Wales as the "Lost Army." Gratian met the expedition in Gaul but his army deserted him and he fled only to be captured and executed at Lyons. Maximus took his place at Trêves and from that noble city he proceeded to plan the conquest of Italy and after that the capture of the whole vast Empire with the overthrow of the man who instead destroyed him—Theodosius, Emperor of the East.

Rome, when Ninian arrived there, was no longer the seat of emperors. Maximus ruled at Trêves; Gratian's young brother Valentinian had his court at Milan and was a mere puppet emperor torn between his Arian mother and the mighty St. Ambrose; while Constantinople was the base from which Theodosius dealt so ably with the west-moving tide of Goths, Vandals and other barbarians.

But Rome was still the mighty capital of the world. Another ambitious young man drawn to her in 383 was St. Augustine. He came from Carthage, a brilliant professor of rhetoric as yet unconverted to Christianity and very eager to try his eloquence on the students gathered in this greatest of cities. Writing of why he chose to go there he says : " My chief and almost only reason was that I heard that young men studied there more peacefully and were kept quiet under a restraint of more regular discipline." But he left for Milan in less than a year because the well-governed students failed to pay his fees. It is quite possible that Ninian heard him speak then or in 387 when St. Augustine returned to Rome for a year, after his conversion and baptism in Milan. For in the heart of Christendom it was still the custom for students to learn the rhetoric that made such fine preachers of some of the Christians. They explored too the beauty and humour of pagan literature in the works of Virgil, Cicero, Horace and Terence. Only when he had completed this secular course would St. Ninian concentrate on " the disciplines of faith and the sound meaning of Scripture," which subjects are alone mentioned by Aelred. Then, " with the greatest eagerness, with enlarged mouth receiving the word of God, like a bee he formed for himself the honeycombs of wisdom by arguments from the different opinions of doctors, as of various kinds of flowers."

There were, however, weeds among the flowers and if he expected Rome to be a fount of purity the young Briton must have been startled at their rank growth. Within the Church herself there appears to have been at that time a shocking amount of worldly intrigue, ambition and disunity. St. Jerome never tired of railing against the lives and vices of the fashionable clergy.

Only in the eventful year of 383 did St. Ambrose at last

persuade Gratian to disestablish the pagan worship still con-
tinuing in the stately temples of Christian Rome. These
buildings and the contemporary Christian basilicas of St. Paul,
St. Mary and St. Costanza still overpower us though we live
in a world of towering concrete. How much more must they
have astonished St. Ninian. He would, however, be more
familiar than we are with the style and standard of the Roman
tiles, mosaics, sculptures and paintings that decorated these
vast-domed, hollow groves of pillars. In Britain he had seen
baths; but none so huge as those used as clubs by Roman
gentlemen. St. Jerome, following the custom of the time,
often visited the catacombs on Sundays. He thought them
" so dark that it almost seems as if the psalmists words were
fulfilled: ' Let them go down alive into Hell.' " St. Ninian
was probably equally awestruck by underground cities of
Christian dead.

And giants moved among these marvels of architecture.
St. Ambrose, Bishop of Milan, and virtual ruler of the Church
in the West, battled with emperor after emperor for the
supreme authority of the Church in matters of faith and
spiritual discipline. Eventually, in 390, by sheer moral force,
he drove Theodosius to his knees in public repentance for a
political massacre. And that great emperor, by then the ruler
of the whole Empire, cried out: " I know of no one except
Ambrose who deserves the name of bishop."

Ambrose deserved the name in many ways. In an Empire
tottering under the weight of barbarian invasions and full of
discontented soldiers, ill-treated slaves, corrupt officials, idle
rich and groaning taxpayers he stood fearlessly for the kingdom
of God on earth. And among the often tempting religions
constantly introduced by travellers from the East, and the
heresies continually springing up within the Christian fold, he
stood firm for the Catholic faith. Perhaps St. Ninian visited
his Cathedral where the whole congregation sang his
courageous hymns and where even the girls joined sweetly in
the singing of the psalms. He would be less shocked than we
would be by the talking and laughing so often heard during the
reading of the lessons. St. Ambrose lamented it; and (following

the universal practice of the Church since the second century) he saw to it that only those of the faithful who were baptised and therefore spiritually mature were permitted to attend the solemn mysteries of the Mass which followed the sermon. As in the Eastern Rite the celebrant was hidden from the congregation by screens; and the people, who provided the bread and wine themselves, received communion standing. During his stay in Rome St. Ninian himself was probably baptised. He would prepare for it during Lent and make his first communion on Easter Sunday.

Another giant was St. Jerome, the renowned scholar and slashing critic of the age who had recently described Ambrose's treatise on the Holy Spirit as " flaccid and spiritless, sleek and pretty, and decorated with purple patches." He was merciless to friend and foe alike; but all respected his mighty intellect. When St. Ninian arrived in Rome St. Jerome was secretary to Pope Damasus and because of his knowledge of Greek and Hebrew had been newly commissioned to retranslate the Bible into a more correct and simpler Latin. This was the translation that came to be called the *Vulgate*; an early version of which the Celtic saints were to copy so carefully and lovingly beyond the far-off fringes of the fallen Roman Empire. They were to carry it back from their remote islands to a continent ravaged by Teutonic invasions.

At Rome, then, in the midst of great men and great buildings Aelred tells us that St. Ninian spent many profitable years. Finally Damasus' successor Siricius, " the Roman Pontiff, hearing that some in the western parts of Britain had not yet received the faith of our Saviour, and that some had heard the word of the gospel, either from heretics or from men ill instructed in the law of God, moved by the spirit of God, consecrated the said man of God to the episcopate with his own hands, and, after giving him his benediction, sent him forth as an apostle to those people."

It took St. Ambrose exactly a week to change from a layman into a bishop.[1] But the Celtic saints spent a large part

[1]The circumstances leading to his rapid promotion were, however, exceptional. The Roman branch of the Catholic Church also took to heart the admonition: " Lay hands on no man suddenly."

of their lives preparing for their ministries. Even after some ten years in Rome St. Ninian did not consider himself ready for the Pictish mission field. Consecrated by the Church and apparently backed by the Roman State still interested in the taming of the recalcitrant Picts, he went to study the novel methods of St. Martin; the greatest missionary of his age.

How much the Celtic Church owed to St. Ninian's sojourn at Marmoutier has already been explained. It remains now to give some account of the Picts; and to show how far-reaching and long-lived were the effects of St. Ninian's Christian penetration of their country.

Only two branches of the Celtic race were so placed geographically that they escaped being moulded into the Roman pattern. These were the Scotic or Gaidhaelic branch living in Ireland, and the Pictish branch living beyond Hadrian's Wall in what we now call Scotland. In this latter country there is much archaeological evidence of trade with the Empire. But it failed to affect the purely Celtic culture which reached its highest artistic development from the fifth to the ninth centuries. Here is a description by Dr. W. Douglas Simpson of the activities of the men St. Ninian introduced to Christianity.

" We must imagine our Pictish predecessors in those early ages as an energetic and intelligent agricultural population tilling the soil and tending herds of oxen and swine and flocks of sheep. They were possessed of a high degree of practical and artistic knowledge. Their metallurgic skill is evidenced in the beautiful brooches, rings, pins, massive embossed armlets, and harness mountings all wrought in bronze, some-times finely enamelled in various colours; and in the heavy double-linked silver chains which are a peculiar characteristic of this period. A similar degree of skill is exhibited in their iron tools of ordinary domestic use, and by their beads of variegated glass and their implements and ornaments in stone, bone and wood, sometimes beautifully carved. They wove cloth in bright colours and varied patterns. Their construc-tional skill, no less than their power of combined effort and capacity for organisation are revealed in the immense stone hill-forts . . . and on a smaller scale in the earth-houses which they constructed as subterranean adjuncts to their hut dwellings."[1] Ships abounded—Candida Casa possessed its own fleet—and well-to-do Picts drove their own two-wheeled carts.

Over in Ireland the Scots and their cousins the Irish Picts[2] enjoyed a fairly similar culture though there the Roman menace had not driven the tribes to combine when need arose, as the Picts did, under one democratically elected overlord. By the fifth century the latter were already a nation, the Picts of Alba. One strange example of this national unity can be traced from St. Ninian's time till the coming of the Vikings. During that period the Picts carved on stone slabs a series of unique and highly artistic symbols. The same abstract designs are found all over Pictland; but nothing remotely like them has ever been found anywhere else in the world.[3] What these incised symbols express remains a mystery. But because they are so often found on stones near the sites of early Celtic churches; and because on the same stone the symbols and the primitive equal-armed cross are often carved close together, it is thought that they had a Christian significance.

One thing is clear to anyone pondering over this curiously mature symbolism (it is as highly developed on the earliest as on the latest stone) and that is that the Picts were no savages. Fierce they might be in warfare, but in peace they were a pastoral people showing all the pleasing characteristics of shepherds down the ages. When a Pict wished to express affection he turned to the names of his three most precious possessions: his dog, his flocks and his pastures. St. Kentigern's pet name, Mungo, means literally " my dog."

By the time St. Ninian returned to his country the Picts had over-run Hadrian's Wall. Their inroads were such that in 396 the Romans had reorganised the frontier as a chain of

[1] *The Celtic Church in Scotland*—page 37.

[2] Till fifth century they occupied the whole east coast of Ireland when the Scots drove a wedge through them in Meath.

[3] Not one example of this art is to be found west of Drumalban because that part of Scotland was colonised by the Scots from the end of the fifth century onwards.

forts running roughly from Carlisle to the Humber. A glance at the map makes it seem most likely that St. Ninian crossed over from the Cumberland coast by boat to his first mission station among those remarkable people. No doubt some of his British friends helped to swell the number of the *muinntir* and to build Candida Casa on the small promontory still known as the Isle of Whithorn. Of his church, his kitchens, his refectory, his barns, his school buildings, not a trace remains. But his cave is unchanged. As befits the retreat of a busy *pppa* it is a mile or so away, hollowed out of the rocks that back the Glasserton shore. Here, alone with God, he achieved the spiritual strength to heal and convert the local chieftain Tuduvallus who, at first, threatened to wreck his plans. It was by no means the habit of the Celtic Church to start by winning kings. But without the support of Tuduvallus the position of so young an offshoot from Gaul clinging to the Pictish coast would indeed have been precarious. One glad Easter the chief was baptised and from then on the *muinntir* throve. Pupils poured into the school—boys and girls alike: some to be trained for work in the Church and some to lead valuable Christian lives in their own homes. Apparently the parents of these children gave land to the good monks. Before his death St. Ninian's property stretched so far that, as we have seen, he had to spend the night away from home when visiting his more distant flocks.

Most of the monks in the *muinntir* were what would now be called lay brothers, each one the master of some craft essential to the spiritual, mental or physical welfare of the community. As the numbers grew, more and more Pictish scribes, teachers, smiths, gardeners, masons, farmers, cooks, shepherds, fishermen and carpenters were to be seen among the original founders. It was on these new monks that the future life of the Church depended. They were trained as apostles prepared to carry the gospel they had learnt to the very ends of the earth. That does not mean they were prepared to preach to the benighted Picts. It means rather that they were prepared to live in their small Christian colonies in a state of purity, holiness and constant self-denial, surrounded by a pagan people too often violent, immoral, selfish and unjust. Only when the astonishing qualities of those within the *muinntir* had won the respect of their neighbours, and when deeds of mercy and charity had transformed respect into love —only then did the priest of the *muinntir* explain why they had come. Unlike the parson who is reported to have begged his parishioners not to do what he did but to do what he said, the Celtic Church relied above all on the force of example.

As soon as sufficient men were ready one of the priests ordained by St. Ninian was elected by his own twelve disciples as their leader in the same way that the Pictish clans were accustomed to elect their overlord. The thirteen missionaries would then depart to found a new *muinntir* on a suitable site. Perhaps the first offshoot was at Kirkmadrine, near enough to be visited by St. Ninian. When this proved a successful venture, then the whole monastery must have concentrated on the preparations for their *pápa's* momentous journey into the heart of Pictland.

There was no elaborate packing of stores and luggage. Like the apostles of old St. Ninian and his monks took nothing with them save a little bread in their wallets, and, hanging from their shoulders, their gospels carefully encased in leather satchels. The craftsmen must have carried their tools, and the agriculturists probably took seed as did the monks of St. Martin. Priests, carefully chosen, were in charge of the sacred vessels and psalters that were to be the treasures of the future churches.

No doubt a good deal of extra copying had to be done before the expedition considered itself properly equipped. There was, however, even for the Britons, no new language to learn. British and Pictish dialects were very similar, and like the Britons the Galloway Picts were well acquainted with the Latin they read and sang. It must be remembered too, that the Eastern Picts to whom they were going, might be expected to have at least a smattering of Latin.

For the most part, then, the preparations would consist in a mighty effort to become spiritually fit for the task ahead. Prayer and fasting played a large part in this discipline.

On St. Ninian would fall the burden of choosing from the mass of eager applicants, the body of monks to man the chain of *muinntirs* he had already planned.

For there is no doubt that he knew exactly where he was going. Indeed it almost looks as though, with a well-informed Roman staff-officer beside him, he had plotted his course on a map showing the route of penetration so often followed by the unsuccessful legions.

When they were ready to leave Candida Casa, the party set off due north towards the remains of Antonine's Wall which once guarded the plain between the Clyde and the Forth. South of the Wall, at Glasgow, they planted a Christian colony. In his life of St. Kentigern, Joceline mentions that the saint chose to build his new church there, on the site of a cemetery consecrated long before by St. Ninian.

Turning east and crossing the plain to the Forth, they next established what was known in the thirteenth century as *Eaglais-Ninian*[1] and is now known simply as St. Ninian's. The site is south of Stirling and close to a Roman camp. From there the Roman route runs north-east up Strathmore, keeping the Grampians on its left, and making for the easiest pass into east Aberdeenshire. St. Ninian followed it obediently, only once making a slight diversion to the east to found a *muinntir* at Arbirlot, near Arbroath, on the Forfarshire coast. Here there is documentary proof that a monastery associated with St. Ninian's name survived till the beginning of the thirteenth century; and on a stone in the manse garden, are incised (among some odd Pictish symbols) two equal-armed crosses of the type which developed early at Candida Casa out of the Chi-Rho symbol.

Following the coast north from Arbirlot, the dwindling party rejoined the Roman route just south of the pass. Here, at Dunottar, on a magnificently rocky promontory, they founded another church. In the thirteenth century the parish church still stood in this inconvenient position proudly bearing the name of St. Ninian. The site and the name combined are

[1]*Eaglais* from the Greek *ekklesia*, Assembly or Church. When it occurs in association with ancient Pictish foundations it is always attached to the founder's name.

almost sufficient proof of the saint's presence there; but to make it certain there are nearby St. Ninian's Den and St. Ninian's Well.

Then, crossing the pass he founded the last of his churches to bear what was almost certainly the imprint of an Imperial political plan. It was at Methlick in Aberdeenshire, a little to the east of the north-running line of Roman camps and almost at the limit of Imperial penetration. The site is called Andet or Annat which, in the ancient language of the Celtic Church always meant the Mother Church of the district; and on this site it is recorded that St. Ninian's chapel stood. As for the surrounding district it is called Formartine or Martin's land— surely a fascinating link with St. Ninian and Gaul.

If St. Ninian was working with and for the Empire what must have been his dismay when he heard first of the Teutonic invasion of Gaul, next of the Roman retreat from Britain, and lastly of the fall of Rome herself? These gigantic disasters left him marooned on an island at the mercy of the first invaders. Yet he never wavered. It was plain that Alba could never become part of the Western Empire—not through any fault of his, but because there was no longer an Empire; but it was also plain that like St. Martin's Gaul she must be made ready to play her part in keeping the faith alive. He completed his chain of *muinntirs* each with its bishop and its dependent group of churches. Making for the heart of Pictland he planted a church at Temple[1] on the west bank of Loch Ness strategically close to Inverness, the chief fortress of the Pictish kings. On a slab there another primitive cross is incised, and the church has always borne the name of Ninian.

The Celtic saints could never resist water, however cold or rough. The last unmistakably Ninianic site is at Navidale[2] on the east coast of Sutherland on a rocky promontory as exposed as Dunottar to the North Sea gales. The Pictish monks turned this unlikely spot into a sanctuary called by its founder's name. Again, near the churchyard are St. Ninian's

[1] *Temple* or *teampull* was a Celtic word in common use in Christian Pictland denoting a stone church—it originally meant a sacred heathen enclosure.
[2] *Dale* is Norse, but *navi* or *nevay* is a very old Pictish word meaning sanctuary.

Well and St. Ninian's Field. Obviously this most distant of the *muinntirs* from its mother church was to serve the Picts of the far north.

Having thus planted Christian colonies over the whole of Pictland north of the remains of Antonine's Wall and east of Drumalban (the range of mountains running north from Ben Lomond to Ben Hope and cutting Scotland in two) St. Ninian returned to Candida Casa. It would seem that he shared with St. Columba the gift of prophetic vision. For he did not attempt the conversion of the eastern lowlands so soon to be ravaged by the Angles. Instead he made the move that was to ensure the preservation of his far-flung *muinntirs* in the worst times ahead. He retreated west from Candida Casa and crossed the North Channel on a mission to the Picts of Ireland.

The old Irish Life only mentions that he founded a church in Leinster. Here he was commemorated on 16th September as " 'Monenn'[1], the shout of every mouth." But his name was surely shouted in Ulster too, for the Leinster church was almost certainly the southernmost of a chain of *muinntirs* planted along the Pictish coast of Ireland. If St. Ninian landed at Strangford Lough as seems most probable, obviously the first thing he did was to found a *muinntir* there within easy reach of Candida Casa. And that is exactly where the fifth century Pictish foundation of Nendrum was situated. Whether or not St. Ninian was the founder, Nendrum, on Mahee Island, Strangford Lough, was undoubtedly a daughter house of Candida Casa, relying on her for the help and advice brought over regularly by boat, and sending her more advanced pupils to be finished in the already famous school across the water. At the beginning of the sixth century one of these pupils was Finbar, who sailed to Alba in a boat belonging to the Candida Casa fleet. Returning later to Strangford Lough full of learning, he founded his own *muinntir* not far from Nendrum and became the famous St. Finbar of Moville.[2] Before long that

[1]*Nen* or *Nan* are the British forms of his name—*Mo* is a prefix meaning " my " and implying respectful affection.

[2]This British form of his name is used to avoid confusion with a famous contemporary —in Ireland he was called Finnian.

corner of Ireland, first introduced to Christianity by St. Ninian, was sending forth missionaries not only to the stricken country of her first teacher but to Gaul, to Italy and to Switzerland.

St. Patrick landed at Strangford Lough in 432 ; and in the same year St. Ninian died at Candida Casa, his task accomplished. It was hard to part from his sorrowing people, " yet to be longer separate from Christ was intolerable." " Wherefor blessed Ninian, perfect in life and full of years, passed from this world in happiness, and was carried into heaven accompanied by the angelic spirits to receive an eternal reward."

From then on, until the Act of 1581 prohibiting " pilgrimages to Chapelles, Welles, Croces and sik other monuments of Idolatrie," Whithorn was a famous place of pilgrimage. Thither went Kenneth II in 970 to give thanks to the great St. Ninian after he had expelled the Vikings from Galloway. Robert the Bruce also knelt before the holy tomb. No less than eight pilgrimages were made by James IV and his wife, the last one being undertaken on the year before the king was killed at Flodden. When Mary, Queen of Scots visited the monastery the end was very near. The prior had confessed to celebrating Mass and had been carried off to prison in Dumbarton. But the founder of Candida Casa was still there, ready to hear the prayers of one who, like him, had left sunny Gaul to make history in Scotland.

Sources :
Ecclesiastical History of England. Bede. Ed. J. A. Giles.
Life of St. Ninian. Aelred. Ed. Bishop Forbes of Brechin.
Celtic Scotland. Vol. II. W. F. Skene.
The Pictish Nation. Archibald B. Scott.
St. Ambrose, His Life and Times. F. Homes Dudden.
St. Ninian and the Origins of Christianity. W. D. Simpson.
The Celtic Church in Scotland. W. D. Simpson.
St. Ninian. Booklet by Sir Herbert Maxwell.

CHAPTER IV.

ST. PATRICK

T is fascinating to discover how the lives of the Celtic saints are linked one to another. At first glance it would seem that St. Patrick is the exception that proves this rule. But this is not so. There appears to have been a living link between St. Patrick and St. Ninian in the person of the Briton Caranoc. Trained at Candida Casa in its earliest days, this ardent missionary is known to have succeeded St. Ninian in 432. Though he had many years of travel ahead of him and was only abbot of Candida Casa till a suitable successor could be found, Caranoc was at the time of his appointment, already a middle-aged man who had laboured long among the Picts of Alba, among his fellow Britons, and among both the Picts and Scots of Ireland. He appears to have shared with his master the prophetic knowledge that because of her geographical position in a world invaded from the east, Ireland was to prove the most vital of St. Ninian's mission fields. It was there that he spent the last years of his life, planting *muinntirs* among Picts and Scots alike in a brave effort to form a Christian federal union out of tribes too often hostile. Eventually this pioneer work led to his becoming Ireland's first martyr; but not in vain. He had a glorious reward.

For there are three orders of Celtic saints in Ireland (which being interpreted means that there were three phases in the Irish Celtic Church). The first, founded by St. Patrick, consisted of secular bishops and founders of churches. The second, founded by St. Caranoc (and therefore a direct off-shoot from Candida Casa) was that monastic order of abbots —for the most part presbyters—that proved the crowning glory of the Celtic Church in Ireland. The third order of Irish saints scarcely concerns us here but is of interest because it consisted of hermits who completed the Celtic circle of development by reverting to the purely contemplative habits of their Egyptian ancestors.

Both the Books of Ballymote and of Lecan record that Caranoc baptised Patrick and was his friend. If this be true (and there seems no reason to doubt it) the meeting between the two young Britons must have taken place before 412 on one of Caranoc's first missionary journeys in Ireland and when Patrick was still a slave in Antrim. St. Patrick was, of course, already an ardent Christian, but knowing the custom of the times it is extremely unlikely that he had been baptised in Britain before being kidnapped by the Scots at the age of sixteen. And he would certainly make every effort to go south to meet them if he heard of Christians working from a base on Strangford Lough. Lastly, no one need be surprised that he never mentions meeting Caranoc then, or again after 432 when they are said to have divided Ireland amicably between them, Patrick agreeing to work to the south and Caranoc to the north. After all there is, in the Confession, scarcely a single proper name.

In spite of its extreme vagueness where facts are concerned St. Patrick's Confession brings him astonishingly close to us. An incomplete copy of it and a copy of his letter denouncing Coroticus, are to be found within the covers of the Book of Armagh together with two valuable *Lives* written from older sources by seventh century bishops when Irish learning had reached its highest peak.[1] Any attempt to reconstruct his story must rest primarily on these earliest foundations.

At the beginning of the fifth century the Scots of Ireland troubled Britain even more than did the Picts. With the slackening of Roman defences they could raid the west coasts almost with impunity, and in the year 405 a whole fleet of their ships appeared, nosing their way up either a Welsh or a Cumbrian river. The raid had been organised by the High King of Ireland, Niall of the Seven Hostages; and this time the young Patrick was among the thousands of captives carried back to Ireland. He left behind him a country where the law and order maintained by Roman troops had already become a mere memory, and where the cleanliness and comfort of Roman ways were also rapidly vanishing. Indeed Christianity

[1] *Life of St. Patrick* by Muirchu Maccu Mactheni.
Memoir of St. Patrick by Tirechan.

59

alone seemed strong enough to remain unquenched by the tragedy of Rome's desertion of Britain.

Patrick's father Calpurnius was a Christian deacon who owned a small farm outside a Romanised British town. There seem to be almost equally good reasons for believing this town to have been either on the Welsh or the Cumberland coast. However, the pattern of life in all Romanised British towns was much the same. St. Patrick would learn the Grammar and Rhetoric taught to citizens of the Empire whether he lived outside Maryport or near a town on the coast of Wales. What much more affects the story of his life is the fact that his lessons did not interest him. Nor did he heed, as he afterwards lamented, the constant admonishments of the priests who taught him the psalms. He was as other boys. Then, one day, without any warning, he was rowed in a hide-bound boat to a land Rome never reached. Like Alba, the land of the Picts, Ireland still lay apart following the old tribal ways in a strange and often beautiful Celtic twilight already faintly tinged with Christianity. There, instead of being surrounded by a devoted family, he had to lead the life of a solitary slave. It was a tremendous shock.

"Before I was afflicted," he writes, "I was like a stone which lies in the deep mire. And He that is mighty came and in His mercy lifted me up and set me on the top of the wall, fool that I am, into the midst of those who seem to be wise and skilled in everything. Now after I came to Ireland, daily I pastured flocks. I stayed even in the woods and on the mountains. Before daylight I used to be roused to prayer in snow, in frost, in rain. And I felt no harm, nor was there any slothfulness in me because the spirit in me was then fervent."

It seems probable that he was first taken to the west coast of Ireland and that it was there, by the Wood of Fochlut —"the oldest wood that ever grew in Eire and the gloomiest," as an ancient writer has it—that he was touched in his loneliness by the kindness of those Irish children whose voices haunted him over the years and changed the course of his life. He learnt their Gaidhaelic or Scotic dialect which differed considerably from British and Pictish speech, and soon

ST. PATRICK FINDS PEACE ON HIS MOUNTAIN.

delighted so much in the heroic tales sung at his master's fireside that he feared the listening must be a sin. His eyes too lacked for nothing when they feasted on the rich hangings in the *dun*[1] and on the colourful clothes and gold ornaments of the chiefs.

There were children too in Ulster where he spent six years as Milchu's slave tending his sheep and swine on the slopes of Slemish. Like Scotland, Ireland was then thickly wooded — Slemish yielded few green pastures for sheep. This mountain is near Ballymena in County Antrim and there in the daytime St. Patrick taught his small converts while at night he himself was instructed by angels. They bade him be of good courage as he would see his fatherland again. When his spirits flagged they comforted him coming sometimes in the shape of beautiful birds. But though he already inspired in the young that love that much later made the little Benen cover him with roses while he slept and hang desperately on to his foot as the saint mounted his chariot to leave him behind, yet he led on the slopes of Slemish the lonely life of an exile. The meeting with Caranoc, a Christian and a Briton, would show him how deep was his loneliness. The revelation probably decided him to escape.

At last the time came and St. Patrick heard a voice in the night say: " See, your ship is ready." " And it was not near but was far off about two hundred miles. And I had never been there nor had I knowledge of any person there. And I came in the strength of God Who prospered my ways for good, and I met nothing alarming until I came to the ship." About the ship lying, probably, at the mouth of the Boyne, there certainly was something sinister. She was about to sail for an unknown port with a cargo of those shaggy deer-hounds still bred near Londonderry. If St. Patrick hoped the ship would carry him back to Britain he was disappointed. Deer-hounds were in great demand in the East and undoubtedly the ship behaved furtively in port because the dogs hidden on board were stolen property. All deer-hounds were the monopoly of the chiefs.

[1] The Celtic name for the type of circular fortress built by the chiefs.

Undaunted by the odd habits of the rascally pagan crew Patrick "hoped that some of them would come into the faith of Christ Jesus" and he certainly did all he could for their souls and bodies. He was their slave for the next three months. For they landed in a part of Gaul so ravaged by the Vandals that it took all the power of his prayer to produce a herd of swine in time to save their lives and revive the remaining dogs many of whom, he says, "had fainted and were left half-dead by the way." Perhaps because of this power the crew seem to have kept him with them till they reached Marseilles, the main port for eastern trade. From there St. Patrick travelled to Tours, probably visiting the Christian communities at Arles and Auxerre on his way. What St. Martin foresaw had come to pass. Christian settlements were surrounded, and often engulfed, by a stormy sea of barbarism. It must have been a sad and even a dangerous journey through land wasted and stricken by the Teutonic conquerors.

Writing to God of the first time he heard of how Christians lived and worked in monasteries, St. Augustine of Hippo says: "We were amazed to hear that so lately and almost in our own days, such wonderful things had been wrought by Thee, in the true faith and in the Christian Church." But when confronted for the first time with monasticism at Marmoutier St. Patrick (though always a monk at heart) remains silent. He has, as he owns himself, "a slow tongue." Only the great turning points of his life can rouse his pen. So he tells us nothing of St. Martin's town where the citizens still spoke of the saint as though he were alive; nothing of the monks with whom he is sure to have spoken at Marmoutier. Perhaps he is silent because it was at Tours that he first saw himself as "the most illiterate and inconsiderable of the faithful," and realised how long and steep was the path of knowledge he had to climb if he wished to become a priest of the Church.

"Again a few years later I was in Britain with my kin who welcomed me as a son and in good faith besought me that now at least, after the great tribulations I had endured, I would never again go away from them. . . . And there verily I saw in the night visions, a man whose name was Victoricus, coming as it were from Ireland with countless letters. He gave one of them to me, and I read the beginning of the letter which was entitled ' The Voice of the Irish,' and I heard the voice of those that lived beside the Wood of Fochlut which is beside the western sea. And thus they cried out, as if from one mouth, ' We beg you, holy boy, to come and walk with us again.' And I was deeply broken in heart and could read no further and so I awoke. Thanks be to God that after a great length of time the Lord dealt with them according to their cry."

The experience is perfectly expressed. But of what he did during this great length of time there is not a word in the Confession. It is from the two *Lives* that any information must be gleaned. He himself merely says: " Towards Ireland I did not stir of my own accord until I was almost worn out. But this was all to my good since thus I was amended by the Lord. He fitted me to become something which was once quite beyond my grasp." Yet as he wrote these words as an old man in Ireland St. Patrick must have seen in his mind the beautiful sunny island of Lérins where he spent some nine years equipping himself with a knowledge of Theology, Law and Scripture to make him a fit teacher for so intellectually vigorous a people as the Scots of Ireland. He found it hard work to keep up with the noble and distinguished company of monks gathered from far and near to worship God in this Mediterranean island refuge; but he tells us that later he often yearned to see them again.

It may well be asked why he chose to train for the Irish mission field so very far from home. The answer is simple. Such was the state of the world at that time that, with the exception of Candida Casa, there was really no suitable theological college any nearer. Perhaps Candida Casa was too close to Ireland to appeal to an escaped slave. Britain might have been safer; and it is true that for the time being she had rallied from the onslaughts of the Picts and Scots under the brilliant leadership of Cunedda. But the country was still so unstable that the British Church remained an offshoot of the

Church of Gaul. Gaul herself was flooded with barbarians; so that it was apparently to far off Italy that the would-be monk had to go in search of advice. He seems to have carried an introduction to that good friend of St. Martin and Sulpicius Severus, St. Paulinus of Nola. This man was known throughout cultured Europe to have sacrificed a brilliant career for the monastic life. He now corresponded with St. Augustine and St. Jerome; indeed he was acquainted with everyone worth knowing in the Christian world. It is apparent that in putting his case before so eminent an authority St. Patrick was determined to have the very best advice available. And he got it. Lérins was the place selected for him by Paulinus and we know now that in the fifth century there was not another monastery to touch it for the standard of its spiritual discipline and its learning.

The island lies off the coast of Var near Cannes and is now known as St. Honorat in honour of the man who, about 410, changed it from an evilly disposed desert island into a veritable garden of Eden in which both Eve and the serpent were conspicuous by their absence. St. Patrick did found some monasteries in Ireland, so it is worth while to glance at this their pattern. The monastery at Lérins was designed on the Anthonian model, each monk having his own separate cell; but much of the strict system, in which work and learning played a considerable part in a life whose chief object was prayer, was borrowed by Honoratus from Pachomius. The hermit's life was the goal of the senior monks, and if he did not excel in his studies St. Patrick does seem to have been among these spiritually advanced monks permitted to go into retreat from time to time in caves on the mainland at Cappo Rosso. Even now there is a Cistercian monastery on the island and it must comfort St. Patrick—always so sensitive about his illiteracy—to know that the monks still remember him when so many of the great ones he met there are forgotten.

In 426, to the great sorrow of the community at Lérins, Honoratus left them to become bishop of Arles. Perhaps St. Patrick accompanied him and attended the synod there in

428. If so he would sit absorbed while the assembled bishops discussed his country. At the beginning of the century St. Jerome had remarked that " Britain in common with Rome, Gaul, Africa, Persia, the East and India adores one Christ, observes one rule of faith." But since the pagan Teutons had poured into Gaul and more or less cut her off from the continent Britain was said to have lapsed from orthodoxy and to favour the doctrine of her too clever son Pelagius. Like many alive to-day he held that men are born perfect. There was no original sin. So serious did the Synod of Arles consider the implications of this heresy that the bishops decided to send the great warrior monk Germanus to win the misguided Britons back to the true faith. Two of St. Patrick's early biographers state that when on the continent he learnt most of all from Germanus; while one of them has it that he accompanied Germanus when the latter " put to sea, and was calmly wafted over into Britain." Those are Bede's graphic words. He relates the British adventures with relish showing it to have been a most successful mission. Perhaps St. Patrick's knowledge of the language helped to vanquish the heretics as did St. Germanus' knowledge of war when he won his stirring battle against the Picts.

These cheering events soon reached the ears of Christians in Ireland. It was probably priests from the group of churches fed from the British Church in Wales, and existing in the south or south-east of Ireland who wrote eagerly asking Germanus to send them an able man to reorganise their church. At any rate it was from Auxerre, where Germanus was bishop, that in 431 " Palladius, ordained by Pope Celestine, was sent as their first bishop to the Irish believing in Christ." These facts are recorded in the Annals of Ulster for that year.

It may seem odd that St. Patrick was not chosen; but he says: " It did not seem meet in their eyes on account of my illiteracy." It was the same with St. Martin. The Gallic bishops would never have appointed so uncultured a man to the See of Tours had it not been that the people forced their hands. But Germanus recognised a good man when he saw one and he had chosen St. Patrick to go to Ireland a year later with the second batch of missionaries. Indeed he and his party had just set out when the news reached Auxerre that Palladius was dead.

St. Patrick's hour had come. It is said that while he was consecrated at Auxerre the church rang with the harmonies of three rival choirs. The choristers sang; some passing angels joined in; and high above all could be heard the far-off voices of the children of the Wood of Fochlut.

As the natives of America foresaw the coming of the white man, so did the druids of Ireland prophesy the coming of strange men to their land, " their mantles hole-headed, their staves crook-headed, their tables to the east of their houses. All their people shall answer Amen, Amen." In one small corner of the land the prophesy had already been fulfilled in the arrival of St. Ninian and his monks. But St. Patrick and his followers were to make it come true all over the country.

The first to hear of the fresh batch of strange men was Dichu, a chief living on the south-west shore of Strangford Lough. Warned of the arrival of a foreign ship in the lough he hurried down to meet it. The sight of a dozen men already ashore alarmed him and he set one of his dogs at their leader. This dog was St. Patrick's first convert. His voice and his touch won it instantly. On coming nearer Dichu was so impressed by the stranger's face and by the Gaidhaelic words he spoke that his fears vanished and he bade the whole party welcome to his *dun*. Next day Dichu's barn became St. Patrick's first church in Ireland.

It was an auspicious beginning. No doubt St. Patrick well knew what he was doing when he landed so far south of his Antrim home. One of the *Lives* has it that he had kept in touch with his old master's children and knew that one of them had married and settled in this district; or he may have wished to make contact with Caranoc's Christian settlements on the lough. Whatever the reason, he was no sooner settled than he set off north to visit Milchu and to pay the ransom without which he was not legally free. He knew

Milchu to be hostile; but he never suspected that at the approach of his now powerful Christian slave his old master would shut himself up in his *dun* and burn it to the ground. St. Patrick could only repeat again and again: "I know not; God knoweth." If Milchu was so obstinate a pagan his grandson St. Mochaoi atoned for him. At Nendrum, Candida Casa's daughter house on Strangford Lough, he became the first independent resident abbot.

But to St. Patrick it seemed a bewildering tragedy. He returned sadly to Mag Inis to tell the terrible story to Dichu. The party of missionaries spent the winter in this district with the friendly chief "and there the faith began to grow." By March they were ready to sail down the east coast and up the River Boyne to take a leading part in the great Spring Feast held at the High King's court at Tara. It was vital for the success of their future work among the many tribes or clans of Ireland that they should come to terms with Leary, and at Tara they would meet him and all the sub-kings gathered together for the lighting of the sacred spring fire. The druids lit it annually on the 25th March and that day, until they had struck the new fire, all the hearths of Ireland must remain cold. It was therefore with horror that the waiting crowd saw on the distant slopes of Slane a great glow of fire. Up there in his camp St. Patrick was defiantly celebrating Easter. He had ordained his first native priest and bade him light the Paschal fire "which in Eire shall not be extinguished for ever."

The battle was on. Complete with druids and nine chariots, Leary rushed off to quench the forbidden fire. But he was no match for St. Patrick; and after the saint's terrible voice had blown his chariots all over the plain the king thought it prudent to pretend to acquiesce in the new religion. He politely invited St. Patrick and his nine followers to join him at Tara the next day. Then he dashed off in his chariot to make quite sure they could never arrive.

But they did reach Tara. Nothing could stop St. Patrick. He led his little band through the valley of the shadow of death singing his glorious hymn "I bind unto myself to-day the strong shield of the Trinity '' which we still know as '' The Breastplate of St. Patrick.'' The Irish call it '' The Deers' Cry '' because the waiting murderers could see nothing but a string of eight deer walking down the valley, '' and behind them a fawn with a bundle on its back. That was Patrick with his eight, and Benen behind them with his tablets on his back.'' Benen was among the first of the many little boys who refused to be separated from the saint. Destined to share all his journeys he eventually succeeded him as Archbishop of Armagh.

On they went so girt about with faith that they marched straight through the locked and guarded doors of the great hall of Tara. There they found the king feasting with his guests. After a short interval during which an attempt was made to poison the saint, the chief druid rose nobly to the occasion and suggested that things should be settled once and for all by a contest of Miracles between the two of them. This took place outside before a large audience. The druid showed a doleful resemblance to modern man. He produced great and horrible marvels but had no idea how to control or get rid of them. It was St. Patrick's power to do this that won the people's admiration. Even when he saw that the Christians had without doubt won the day, Leary could not bring himself to forsake his old religion; but having no choice he gave the necessary permission to preach under his protection throughout his whole kingdom.

As we know the country was not entirely pagan. Caranoc was at work in the north where St. Ninian had worked before him : Christians from the south had begged Germanus for help. But it was the preaching of St. Patrick up and down the land that was to turn a small helpless minority into the first secular phase of a Church which, when adjusted by monasticism to fit the tribal system, grew so strong in faith and learning that her ardent missionary saints were, in a miraculously short time, carrying the faith to places as far apart as Spain and Iceland and Russia. This fact alone shows how passionately alive St. Patrick's message must have been; and something of the burning faith born of experience that his listeners caught is communicated to us in fragmentary sentences from his Confession. Had he not felt the Spirit wrestling within him " mightily and with groanings ?" Had he not heard in his sleep a voice—" whether within me or at my side I cannot tell "—saying things far beyond understanding but ending gloriously by telling him: " He who laid down His life for you He it is who speaks in you." Writing of his mission he says: " And He shed on us abundantly the Holy Ghost." This knowledge that God was not only on his side but within him fortified St. Patrick stoutly when men mocked. " Let who will laugh or insult," he says, " I shall not keep silent nor conceal the signs and wonders which were furnished to me by the Lord." When such a man told his people: " Beyond all doubt we shall rise in that day in the glory of Christ Jesus our Redeemer," and added: " And we look for His Coming any day now," his words carried conviction.

One of the most important converts to be baptised shortly after the first memorable Easter at Tara, was Prince Conall, one of Leary's brothers. He built a church for the saint at Donaghpatrick—no mean gift, for in those days a church, whether of wood or stone, cost fully six cows. For the next year it was from this base that St. Patrick spread the faith over those parts of Meath under Conall's rule. One of the churches founded in this district, he gave into the care of three British brothers and their attractively named sister Catnea. Women are frequently mentioned among the missionaries. They cleaned, they cooked, they embroidered; and they taught and cared for the women and children among the converts. The priests under whom they worked were for the most part bishops. St. Patrick seems to have placed one (with an assistant presbyter where necessary) in every church he founded.[1] These numerous bishops welcomed the women's help for " founded on the Rock of Christ they feared not the blast of temptation " as did the second monastic order of saints.

It was probably from Donaghpatrick that St. Patrick set

[1] In this he merely copied continental customs. At that time, in Asia Minor alone, there were over 400 bishops.

out for Mag Slecht, the Plain of Prostration. This centre of heathen worship was in what is now County Cavan. There stood Crom Cruach, "the chief idol of Ireland," a great stone figure covered with gold and round him his twelve sub-gods covered with bronze. The accounts of what happened when the saint joined the worshippers are confused and varied. It seems that, using his episcopal staff and cursing vehemently, he brought out the demon of the place for all to see. "And they feared they would all perish unless Patrick should cast him into Hell." This, with a mighty shout, he did. Afterwards he found he had lost his brooch in the fray. But much was gained. He had shown the people his invisible God could overcome their idols: and (though for the most part he naturally built his churches wherever a chief granted him land) he had won an important site for a church.

Leary was a reluctant spectator on this occasion. By next Easter so great was their following that he found it expedient to allow these extraordinary men to hold their annual ceremonies at Tara. Because Erc, Leary's chief lawyer, was to be baptised by St. Patrick, nobles had come from far and near to watch the mysterious ceremony. Walking among them the saint overheard a local chief ask one of these strangers whence he came. "I am Enda," he answered, "from the western shores and from the Wood of Fochlut." "Now when Patrick heard the name of the Wood of Fochlut," says his biographer, "he rejoiced greatly and said to Enda, 'I will accompany thee back if I am alive because the Lord bade me go.'" When Enda objected that the journey was dangerous as they had to pass through the territory of many hostile tribes, St. Patrick merely warned him that if that were so, then he, Enda, would be far safer with him as "It was on my account that thou didst come hither."

One of the *Lives* tells us: "Thrice did Patrick wend across the Shannon into the land of Connaught. Fifty bells, and fifty chalices and fifty altar-cloths he left in it, each in its own church. Seven years was he a-preaching to the men of Connaught, and he left his blessing with them when he departed."

His heart must have been sore within him when he gave them his final blessing. During all the seven years spent answering so fully the prayer of those who dwelt beside the Wood of Fochlut that he would come and walk with them once more, dark clouds of discontent and jealousy were gathering behind him. In 439, when he turned his back on the western sea, he met the storm.

His colleagues from Gaul had always disliked the mission to Connaught. They did not object openly; but behind his back they said: " Why does this fellow thrust himself into danger among hostile folk who know not God ?" To this he replies in his Confession that he had to obey his Lord's command. Through his labours, he writes proudly, " the gospel has been preached to the places beyond which no man dwells." They then accused him of lack of culture; and of dishonesty in the handling of church funds. He vindicates his honesty with ease. But that he, a bishop, should still have his rudeness thrown at him bites very deep. None the less he points out that grace without learning is of more value than learning without grace.

St. Patrick's Church in Ireland was, of course, under the jurisdiction of the Church in Gaul from whom she constantly received funds and fresh missionaries. Thither a deputation appears to have gone to ask for his deposition. Knowing that they would never succeed on these charges alone they sought others and, he says, " they found as an occasion against me a matter which I had confessed before I became a deacon. In my anxiety, with sorrowing heart, I disclosed to my closest friend what I had done in my youth on one day, no, in one hour, because I had not then triumphed." It had been like a reprieve when his friend—" a man to whom I trusted even my soul "—absolved him, saying that despite a sin committed at sixteen he was still " a man to be raised to the rank of bishop." Now, for his own lamentable purposes, this priest, whose name St. Patrick conceals for very shame, betrayed a secret confided thirty years before.

Incredible though it may seem, on hearing the disclosure the council decided to deprive him of his rank. Secundius, the bishop chosen to succeed him, appears to have followed him to Connaught to break the news. St. Patrick was stunned by so unexpected an onslaught. That night he was only saved from furious despair by the knowledge that God was angry too. He came to tell him so. Through the agony of this disgrace he was thrust back into his Irish childhood. Then, as before, God was his only shield. Naturally he sought once more the solitude in which he had first learnt to trust in the Lord. He turned back to the western sea and spent the Lent of 440 alone on the top of Croagh Patrick.

He did not at first find consolation. Far from it. He had to explore the depths of that Dark Night of the Soul which hardly a saint escapes. " And heavy birds were towards him and he could not see the face of heaven or earth or the sea." At last an angel appeared and wiped away the tears that soaked his chasuble. Then " the whole mountain top was filled with beautiful birds which sang most tuneful strains and the voices of the mountain and the sea were mingled in their melody so that the Reek became for a time as it were the Paradise of God."

Those few who while still on earth journey down to hell and up to heaven make indomitable fighters. Before he left the Reek St. Patrick fought for the souls of the Irish. He might well have lost the battle if the angel with whom he wrestled had not appeared so desperately anxious to be left once more in sole charge of the mountain. He had only to refuse to leave to be granted grudgingly but instantly those indulgences without which he doubted the ability of the people of Ireland to keep on the road to heaven. Having eased their way he then made sure that barbarians should never have dominion over their land. Lastly, having none of our faith in progress, he asked that the sea should cover Ireland seven years before the day of judgment.

Then he fought for himself. How he did this is far from clear. Some think he made a journey to Rome and was there vindicated by the Pope. These pin their faith on the mention in the Confession of " a journey on which I had resolved," and on the entry for 441 in the Annals of Ulster; " Leo is

74

ordained bishop of Rome and Patrick the Bishop was approved in the Catholic faith.'' Others stress the fact that he says himself that once dedicated to Ireland he never left her even to go '' as far as Gaul to visit the brethren. God knows I used to yearn deeply for it.'' They maintain that the Tripartite Life is probably correct in saying: '' When Patrick was on Cruach Aigli [the Reek's name before it became a place of Christian pilgrimage] he sent Munis to Rome with counsel to the Abbot of Rome and relics were given to him.''

It does seem that by his own efforts he was not only reinstated as head of the missionary church from Auxerre: but also that by 444 he had achieved for Ireland a new position as an independent ecclesiastical province directly under the jurisdiction of the Bishop of Rome. He chose to build the new church that was to be his See as Primate of Ireland, on the top of a hill at Armagh. There is a legend that newly acquired relics of Peter, Paul and Stephen were housed in a small church at the foot of the hill during the building of the cathedral: that there they remained: and that every Sunday the congregation of the church above came down in procession to visit the Shrine of the Martyrs. It is too charming a story to neglect: but there can scarcely have been traffic in relics at so early a date.

Armagh soon became a delightful refuge for the ageing saint. Because it was the custom among well-to-do Scots and Picts to send their sons for instruction in the ancient Celtic folk-lore, learning and art, to the druids or other foster-parents equally well-equipped, St. Patrick had no need to stress the importance of education. The school he built at Armagh was rapidly filled by boys entrusted to him by their Christian parents. We know the progress they made in their lessons: for they were destined to become the teachers of some of those who made famous the great Irish monastic schools in which St. Columba was to be so ardent a student. None the less it may well have been one of these young scholars who caused his despairing master to write of '' a youth whose scrawl is so bad that none can tell whether it is caused by a human hand or by a bird's claw.'' If so, St. Patrick would deal lightly with him. Indeed, remembering his own trials, he probably consoled him with one of those titbits so often brought to the school by friendly neighbours with the message: "This is for the little boys."

From this happy home St. Patrick would journey forth to strengthen and confirm his churches in Ulster and Connaught. There were monasteries to visit also for he speaks proudly of his many "monks and virgins in Christ." But most of his time would be spent discussing the work accomplished by the secular bishops and presbyters, who with "Christ as their head and St. Patrick for their leader" achieved a unity of liturgy and tonsure quite absent from the second monastic phase of the Celtic Church in Ireland. By thus binding his little churches together he strove, as did Caranoc before him, to form the constantly warring chiefs into a Christian federation looking to him as its religious chief. But in spite of his great knowledge of and respect for the tribal and cultural customs of the country it cannot be said that the form of Church adapted by St. Patrick from the continental pattern he knew best was to prove typical of the Celtic Church at its greatest in Ireland. Yet his brave pioneer work prepared the people for the next successful monastic phase. Had he and his fellow saints, the bishops, not ploughed the land so tirelessly and patiently the presbyter saints could never have reaped so early and rich a harvest.

St. Ninian appears to have traversed Scotland unmolested by the Picts. In Ireland the perpetual rivalries, feuds and quarrels over tribute and hostages indulged in by the Scotic and Pictish chiefs alike made travel distinctly dangerous. "Daily I expect either slaughter or to be defrauded or to be reduced to slavery or an unfair attack of some kind," says St. Patrick. He therefore took with him on his journeys a formidable bodyguard among whom was his personal champion who not only defended him in danger but who carried him across such common obstacles as rivers. It was considered an honourable position; but at last the once strong man complained that he was too old to continue his work. He begged St. Patrick to give him a church and to make him a bishop like so many of his contemporaries. St. Patrick was loath to lose the company of so stout a friend, so he installed him in a church near enough to Armagh to be "convenient for visiting." Besides his bodyguard he took with him also his personal attendant, his judge (to interpret Gaidhealic laws and customs when necessary), his chaplain, his cook and his brewer.

After 450 Leinster and Munster became in turn the fields of his labours. Though British missionaries had been at work there since the beginning of the third century there were still churches to be built and chiefs to be converted. So, besides the escort already mentioned, St. Patrick took with him his bell-ringer, his smiths, carpenters and masons (for the building and furnishing of the new churches) and three ladies to embroider vestments and altar cloths. Small wonder that the chiefs were, for the most part, respectful when they beheld so impressive a retinue.

It is nowhere stated exactly how these Christian priests were clothed but St. Patrick had associated too long with monks to wish to depart from their simple garments. We know that he and his priests were tonsured from ear to ear—that is, the front of their heads were shaved—while the rest of their hair hung down their backs uncut. Though it is hard to visualise St. Patrick it is easy to see how greatly his people loved him. In one place they remembered, and it was recorded, how one of his teeth fell out ; in another they told the story of how his nose bled. His biographers dwell on such trivial human accidents with as much enthusiasm as they naturally felt for his miracles. He probably owed his success to the very real man he was as much as to the very great saint.

Twenty-two years before the missionary expedition into Leinster and Munster—on the day that St. Patrick had sung his way into the great hall of Tara—the Druids had forbidden King Leary's guests to rise in greeting to the Christian strangers. It may have been the magnificent words of the invocation St. Patrick sang, or perhaps they saw with their inward eye what manner of man he was, but two men had boldly risen in defiance of the order. Their names were Dubhthach and Fiacc and they were both Leinster poets. Indeed Dubhthach was considered the greatest bard in Ireland. His subsequent conversion to Christianity had done much to smooth the paths of the missionaries in that land of bards.

Now at last, St. Patrick came to Leinster to baptise Dubhthach's king. This meant a new bishop in a new church, and the saint chose Fiacc. In spite of his episcopal duties Fiacc continued to write poetry. Even now we may read the famous elegy he composed after the death of his spiritual father.

The kings of Leinster and Munster were related, which meant that when the missionaries left Fiacc and moved on to Munster they were bound to be well received. Indeed the King of Munster listened gladly and very soon embraced the new faith. "While Patrick was baptising Oengus, the spike of the crozier went through Oengus's foot. Said Patrick: 'Why didn't thou not tell this to me?' 'It seemed to me,' quoth Oengus, 'that it was part of the ritual.' 'Thou shalt have thy reward,' said Patrick, 'thy successor shall not die of a wound for ever.'"

The people of Munster grew so fond of the saint that when they heard he was about to leave them they hurried after him determined to say good-bye. When they caught up with him "the men and women of Munster uttered a great cry and a great clamour for gladness at looking upon Patrick." As for St. Patrick he loved them so much that he blessed everything they had, down to their bare flag-stones.

That he was so wholly devoted to these children of his, "begotten in God," was one reason for the startling success of his mission to Ireland. When Coroticus, a British chief, raided the south-east coast of Ireland and carried off to slavery a party of his converts, he wrote him so wild a letter that it is directed as much to these lost sheep (the little "flock of the Lord which verily in Ireland was growing up excellently with the greatest care" only to be "sold and enslaved amongst

78

the wicked, abandoned, and apostate Picts[1] ") and to the priests who were to read it in British churches, as to the perpetrator of the crime himself. So common were these slave raids, made on Christian communities by such " fellow citizens of the devil," that the church in Gaul regularly set aside sums of money to ransom its members. Though he cries out in anguish to think of the fate of his innocent Christian girls, the saint does not ransom them. One of his biographers tells us that when his letter failed to move Coroticus " he prayed that the chief should be banished from this world and the next." " Coroticus then when he was in the midst of his court, took on the form of a little fox—a pitiable object—and departed in the presence of his friends," never to be seen again.

Another engaging story; which perhaps reveals the kind of people St. Patrick met rather than the nature of the saint himself.

About 457 Benen took St. Patrick's place at Armagh; and the old saint, weary with his labours, retired to Mag Inis to make ready for the greatest of all his journeys. There he wrote his Confession. He would feign have died at Armagh ("a dear thorpe, a dear hill, a fortress which my soul haunteth ") and after four years he made an attempt to reach it. But his angelic advisers had never looked with favour on his fondness for places. In the past they had been wont to hurry him on whenever he thought to find an earthly refuge. Now one of them sternly bade him return from whence he came. And so he died close to the first church he founded in Ireland. That night there was no darkness in the sky so great was the company of angels that swept down to the Island Plain. They filled the church where his body lay, keeping vigil there all night and leaving behind them in the morning that " most sweet odour as of honey and a delicious fragrance of wine " so often noted about the graves of saints.

How right it is that Benen, the little boy of the roses— St. Patrick's fawn on the road to Tara—should succeed to his

[1]The apostacy of the Picts can hardly have been widespread considering the number of well-trained missionaries known to have been working among them at that time.

inheritance and become the first Archbishop. It is right too that the saint should end where he began. But then it is no accident that the lives of saints are so exquisitely shaped. The life of a great artist may be a poor, patternless thing, strangely at variance with the satisfying forms he creates. But a great saint makes his masterpiece out of his life. The splendour of St. Patrick's is seen through the mighty shield he holds before it. "None shall ever say it was my ignorance which achieves whatever tiny success was mine or whatever I showed in accordance with God's will. But make your judgment, and let it be most truly believed that it was the Gift of God. And this is my confession before I die."

Sources:

St. Patrick's Confession and Epistle against Coroticus. Ed. Gogarty.
Book of Armagh. Ed. Gwynne. Containing the following works:
    Confession and Letter against Coroticus.
    Memoirs of St. Patrick. Tirechan.
    Life of St. Patrick. Muirchu Maccu Mactheni.
Breviarum of Tirechan.
Tripartite Life.
Dicta Patriccii.
Ecclesiastical History of England. Bede. Ed. J. A. Giles.
St. Patrick, His Life and Mission. Helena Concannon.
Irish Monasticism. Ryan.
Celtic Scotland. Skene.

CHAPTER V.

ST. DAVID

FOR a knowledge of the impressive set of links and clasps that moor St. David so securely to St. Ninian and Candida Casa we have to thank that learned champion of the Celtic Church, Dr. Archibald Scott. Without his brilliant piecing together of important facts distorted almost beyond recognition but none the less rescued for us from the ancient Celtic *Life* by St. David's ignorant eleventh century biographers, that saint would seem to float free on a colourful but mysteriously alien sea. Not that it is an empty sea; far from it.

For if, without the work of Dr. Scott it would be hard to imagine who could have influenced St. David, there is no difficulty in realising how deep was his influence on the saints who constantly crossed the water to visit his Welsh monastery. First and foremost of these was " the Master of the Saints of Ireland," St. Finnian of the famous monastery of Clonard in Meath. This Irish Pict had the greatest respect for the Britons, having been educated among them; and though St. David was his junior in years he came eagerly across to study the stricter form of monasticism practised at Menevia. Indeed, like all great teachers, the bishop Finnian was a born learner. It was through him that the Second Order of presbyter-abbot saints achieved their special Missa or liturgy drawn up by the Britons St. David, St. Gildas and St. Cadoc. Gildas was twenty years younger than St. David. Nevertheless St. Finnian, like Alcuin of York, recognised Gildas to be " the wisest among the Britons " and when he could no longer make the arduous journey to Britain he continued to write for his advice until he died at Clonard in 549.[1]

Among St. Finnian's " twelve apostles of Ireland," destined to become the flower of the Second Order of Irish

---

[1] It is worth noting that St. Finnian had already to ask advice of Gildas on a subject later to become so pressing that by the beginning of the seventh century St. Columban asked St. Gregory's advice on it : What was to be done about the ever more numerous monks desiring to leave the monasteries and become hermits ?

Saints, were the Scot St. Columba who founded Derry in 546 and Iona in 563; the Irish Pict St. Kenneth who first worked in Scotland and then founded Achabo in 578 near the head of the Nore in Queen's County; and the Scot St. Brendan who founded Clonfert in 559 after much useful work among the Picts of Perthshire and the Scots of the Western Isles. Passionately in love with the sea, St. Brendan became one of the most daring navigators of his time, rarely staying long in his monastery. It is therefore not at all surprising to find him calling upon St. Columba at Iona and upon St. David at Menevia. The Briton St. Kentigern too, while exiled from Scotland in Wales about 567, naturally hastened to pay his respects to the famous Bishop of Menevia; to learn from him how best to organise the monastery he had founded at Llanelwy in Glamorganshire, later to be known as St. Asaph's; and to regale his host with news of the north where St. David had lived and worked as a young man before the invasions of the Scots in the west and while the pitiless Angles remained as yet in the south-east lowlands. St. David no doubt rejoiced to hear how the Irish Picts had swelled the ranks of missionaries from Candida Casa still at work along the east coast feeding the old Ninianic centres with fresh faith and learning.

Because of its effect on St. David's life the history of Candida Casa itself is of special interest. When the Briton Caranoc left it for his last mission to Ireland, his place as abbot was taken by Ternan, a Pict. Ternan was a native of the east coast district of Scotland where St. Ninian had founded his *muinntir* at Dunottar. Converted by the mission, Ternan was later baptised by one of the best known of St. Ninian's British helpers, Paul the Aged. After his training he founded the famous school of Banchory[1]—Ternan in Aberdeenshire. Paul the Aged was so-called because even after founding his own White House on the river Davi in Carmarthenshire at the advanced age of seventy, he continued his widespread and indefatigable missionary labours. He was still alive and teaching in his Carmarthenshire monastery (now called Whitland

[1] *Banchory*, or in Britain and Ireland, *Bangor* is a word meaning the kind of monastic establishment with educational facilities attached first founded by St. Martin.

ST. DAVID BLESSES THE BEES BOUND FOR IRELAND

Abbey) when Ternan died and one Ninian took his place as fourth abbot of Candida Casa. Paul and his friends called this man Manchan, which means the Little Monk, to distinguish him from his great predecessor.

According to Dr. Scott, Paul the Aged, St. Ninian's disciple, and Manchan, St. Ninian's successor, both taught St. David in the early years of the sixth century. But it must be remembered that these facts—and much other invaluable information—could never have been revealed without a patient study of the *Lives* of St. David written during the early years of the Norman Conquest, the most valuable of which is the *Life* by Rhygyvarch. If, through ignorance of the past, he produces little or nothing approaching history, Rhygyvarch does rescue a wealth of delicious stories from the ancient Celtic Life. Even the shortest study of St. David would be barren without them and without the best of the stories gleaned from the other contemporary lives.

When William the Conqueror thrust his relentless way through Hastings, the news of his arrival in England appeared to the already harassed bishop of St. David's in Pembrokeshire to be yet another portent of fresh danger from the east. The Metropolitan See of the ancient British Church stood, significantly, on the extreme westernmost tip of Wales. It could be conveniently reached across the sea by those from kindred monastic churches in Ireland, Iona, Devon and Brittany. Spiritually it faced west. For though St. David had founded it five hundred years before the coming of the Normans, the Angles and the Saxons had for long made the east parts of the country into a mighty battlefield. When at last that battle was over the Welsh Church was again and again plundered and destroyed and her priests martyred during the annual summer expeditions of persistent Viking pirates from the Orkneys; and now, in 1066, the independence of the foundation was threatened by more fierce Norsemen coming this time from France.

Bishop Sulien's fears proved to be all too well founded. This successor of St. David had four sons, for he had studied long in Scotland, Ireland and Wales before entering the

Church.[1] These young men grew up full of his infectious love of learning. Ieuan wrote poetry; and Rhygyvarch shared his father's growing anxiety about the fate of the independent Welsh Church. Nine years after William's ominous visit to St. David's in 1081, Rhygyvarch wisely decided to write the life of the first Archbishop of Menevia before it should be too late.

" These few things," he explains, " we have collected together. They have been found scattered in very old writings of the country, especially in the monastery itself, which have survived until now eaten away by the constant devouring of moths and the yearly boring of ages, and written according to the old style of the ancients. I, sucking as it were with the mouth of a bee, have brought them together in one place from a flowering garden of diverse plants. And so for me, Rhygyvarch, who have rashly applied the capacity of my small intellect to these things, let those who read them with devout mind, render aid with their prayers that because the clemency of the Father, like that of spring, has conducted me to a tiny flower of intelligence, it might at length lead me by mature works to the fruit of a good harvest. So that when the reapers shall separate the tares and fill the barns for the heavenly country with most carefully picked bundles, they may place me as a tiny sheaf of the latest harvest within the hall of the heavenly gate to behold God for ever."

At times Rhygyvarch's flowery Latin prose makes the reader long for the " old style of the ancients." But he surely had his reward, for without his bee-like industry we should know almost nothing of St. David.

It is from an Irish catalogue of saints, drawn up about 730, that we learn that with the historian Gildas and his fellow missionary St. Cadoc, St. David gave to the Second Monastic Order of Irish Saints their particular way of celebrating Mass. As this Second Order flourished in the sixth century, this proves that St. David must have been already famous during the first half. The most reliable dates in his

[1]That is one view. But he may well have been a married bishop just as St. Patrick's father was a married deacon. In the history of the Celtic Church married clerics are often mentioned.

life are to be found in Irish records: the British purposely ante-dated his life. From Brittany comes the news that because (as Rhygyvarch puts it) " he led a blessed life in God on bread and water only," he was known as " David the Waterman "; and in an early ninth century martyrology he is called " David of the monastery of Menevia."

This marshy spot is doubtfully said to have been coveted by St. Patrick when on his way back to Ireland from Gaul in 432. Indeed he was apparently about to settle there when, to his extreme chagrin, an angel came to inform him that it was already reserved for another servant of God. " But the Lord loved Patrick much," and the angel was allowed to appease him by miraculously showing him across the water the far greater kingdom of Ireland in store for him.

In due time, at the end of the fifth century, David, the servant of God, was born. His grandfather Ceredig or Coroticus[1] was the famous military leader of that district still known, because of him, as Cardiganshire. He had two sons: the warrior chief Non, David's father, himself the founder of several churches after he turned cleric; and Caradoc who abandoned a military career to follow St. Patrick to Ireland. Even before his birth there were signs that David was to be no ordinary mortal; and when the leprous priest, who held him while the bishop baptised him, afterwards sprinkled himself with the remains of the holy water, he " recovered the sight of his eyes and the full completion of his countenance." As it is most unlikely that St. David was baptised before reaching maturity this story of Rhygyvarch's is told for its charm alone.

As for the child, he " grew up lovely to behold." His father sent him to school nearby in Cardinganshire at Hen Vynyw, which means Old Menevia—so called to distinguish it from David's later foundation. There he first met Guistilianus, the bishop who was to become one of his greatest friends. The monks here taught him to read in the Latin psalter thus completing the elementary part of his education. Naturally his clerical father was acquainted with the most

[1]The same chief against whom St. Patrick wrote his famous letter.

87

revered and venerable of British priests. He next sent his son south to Carmarthenshire where the abbot Paul the Aged still lived a monastic life " most pleasing to God." " And David tarried there many years, reading and fulfilling what he read." Through these studies and through the monastic discipline, he began to acquire " saving knowledge and the power of governing demons." Paul the Aged suffered much from his failing eyes; they ached continually. He therefore begged his disciples to examine them and by their faith to cure them. Not one of them could ease the pain; and when it came to David's turn he refused even to look at them. " These ten years have I laboured at scripture with thee," he said, " and so far I have not glanced at thy face." Paul was so moved that he gave him leave to continue in his modest ways and found to his joy that the boy's touch alone sufficed to give him sight.

It was almost certainly this wise old man who advised Non to send her remarkable son to study at the famous school at Candida Casa. At any rate St. David next sets out for " Rosnant," the name given by Irish sailors to the promontory on which Candida Casa stood. And we find his father advised in a dream to send to the " monastery of Manchan " an offering of honey, fish and the dressed carcase of a stag on behalf of his son studying (as one biographer so aptly puts it) among the monks of the " Isle of Whitelands." One can only hope that Non was also advised to have the fish caught while crossing the Solway; for it is even now a long journey from Wales to Galloway. St. David is also said to have trained at " Glaston," which is surely Glasserton, close to the Isle of Whithorn where St. Ninian's unchanging cave can still be seen. The " Isle of Whitelands " has been thought to be the Isle of Wight, and " Glaston " to be Glastonbury; but even had Glastonbury existed in St. David's day, in neither of these places did Manchan rule.

At Candida Casa, then, St. David completed his education. Among the missionaries he met there was St. Finbar of Moville. It will be recalled that St. Finbar sailed over from the Irish monastery of Nendrum on Mahee Island, Strangford Lough, at the beginning of the sixth century to

complete his studies in the mother house, being ordered to
do so by his abbot St. Mochaoi, grandson of St. Patrick's
pagan master. St. Finbar had become an active missionary and
a keen teacher of the boys and girls studying at Candida Casa.
They knew his passionate love of books so well that we find
Drusticc, daughter of the Pictish Sovereign, bribing him with
" all the books which Mugent has," in a vain effort to get her
own way. When he was not wrestling with his amusing pupils
St. Finbar went off to visit all St. Ninian's Pictish foundations
finally planting a *muinntir* himself at Dornoch in Sutherland.
Only after many years of work among the Picts of Alba did
he return to Ireland to found Moville near the head of Strangford Lough. It is most probable that St. David accompanied
him on his journeys up the east coast of Alba as part of his
education as a future missionary.

It would be hard to find a greater contrast among
influential sixth century Christians than there is between the
contemplative, ascetical David and that unhappy lover of
moderation in all things, the wise counsellor and historian
Gildas, so much admired by St. Finnian of Clonard. Yet both
men were products of Candida Casa, Gildas arriving there
from Dumbarton some twenty years after St. David, during the
rule of the fifth abbot Mugent. It was to the library originally
founded by St. Ninian that Gildas owed his great learning;
while the liturgy that he, St. David and St. Cadoc gave to the
Second Order of Saints in Ireland must have been derived for
the most part from the form of service used at Candida Casa.
St. Cadoc worked with Gildas in the north and in Wales, and
fled from there with him to Brittany when the Saxons burst
through into South-West Britain in 546. " If you wish for
glory march faithfully to death," St. Cadoc said and bravely
returned to his Welsh monastery of Llangarvan in 570 to be
martyred by the Saxons.

When St. David's training was completed he returned to
Wales; so it was from his native land that he eventually set
out to plant a chain of *muinntirs* among the pagan invaders in
the east. The Irish inform us he was made a monastic bishop
in 540, just ninety years after the first Saxon invasion of the

Humber district. Rhygyvarch says his powerful voice was first heard preaching the word of God in Somerset, then in Lincolnshire, Derbyshire, Radnorshire, Herefordshire, Monmouthshire and Glamorganshire. And just as St. Patrick's Irish wanderings can be traced by the churches he built to strengthen, confirm and consolidate his scattered groups of converts, so St. David left behind him in England and Wales a chain of Ninianic monasteries to be oases of Christianity in a more or less pagan desert. Judging by Gildas' strictures on "harmless good" secular British bishops ("Where is your strength; your energy; your daring; your uncompromising zeal for the glory of God's house?") St. David's fresh outlook was badly needed even in Christian Britain.

This important period of his life was apparently rounded off by a return to his first school where the bishop and he "comforted each other with religious talk." There was now in David a great longing to settle in his own country; but he had no sooner selected what he took to be a suitable place in which to serve God, than an angel, intent on the fulfilling of the prophesy made to St. Patrick deterred him by telling him that it so abounded in evil spirits that "scarcely one in a hundred will be able to escape to the kingdom of God." He then led him to Menevia from which pure spot "few shall go to hell." There is, in the valley, an ancient well called after Guistilianus which makes it seem probable that this old friend of St. David's joined the other disciples, among whom were Aeddan and Eiludd, in the building of the new monastery.

At first the neighbours were hostile, and the settlers were much troubled by the attentions of a jealous druid. The man's wife too was determined to get rid of them and continually tempted the brethren with the sight of her slave girls in the little river Alan, nakedly and wantonly at play in full view of the monastery. It was indeed more than the monks could stand. "We cannot dwell here owing to the molestations of these spiteful sluts," they cried. But David refused to go and waited calmly till the Lord should remove his enemies. One by one they were destroyed, each more horribly than the last, till "the malice of enemies having thus been expelled by the good God," the brethren were able to concentrate on their new life.

Far more austere than most of the contemporary Irish rules; and certainly far more strenuous than the discipline of Candida Casa St. David's way of life called forth all his monks' powers of endurance. Everything they needed must be produced by themselves, from the skin garments they mostly wore to the roofs that sheltered their ever hungry bodies. Gildas—usually so admiring of monks in contrast to the licentious secular bishops of his day—writes of St. David's monks as "those who drag ploughs and dig mattocks into the ground with presumption and arrogance." When he heard that they ate nothing but bread, herbs and salt and only assuaged their "ardent thirst with a temperate sort of drink" he remarked that they gave preference to fasting over love. "Better are they," he said, "who preserve a clean heart than those who eat no flesh." But in forbidding the use of cattle St. David sought to avoid that accumulation of wealth which led to the plunder of so many monasteries, his own included, by the Vikings in the ninth and tenth centuries. And in spite of their meagre diet it must be owned that his monks continued to feed and tend the poor; they read, they wrote, they sang, and above all they prayed. No matter how they were employed, at the first stroke of the bell they abandoned all and hurried to the church. If only the top of a letter had been formed, then the bottom half must wait till the next period of writing.[1] Instant and total obedience in all things was the rule. "They open out their thoughts to the father and obtain his permission even for the requirements of nature."

"As long as they prayed in church none dared unrestrainedly to yawn, none to sneeze, none to spit." But so greatly did men desire the spiritual benefits to be obtained through this constant discipline, and through the public and private penances introduced into the monastic system by St. David and his disciple St. Finnian of Clonard, that eager

[1] It should be remembered that the scribes not only wrote but made their own ink, ground their own colours, cut their own quills and pared the vellum pages.

candidates would stand outside the monastery for as long as ten days to be taunted and tested till their broken pride gained them admittance. Once inside they were privileged to see the saint " pouring forth fountains of tears daily and blazing with a double flame of charity, consecrate with pure hands the due oblation of the Lord's body." Bede gives a like description of St. Cuthbert's emotional nature, and it is interesting that the two saints cooled their transports in the same way. For, when matins was over St. David " proceeded alone to angelic discourse. After this excitement he immediately sought cold water in which by lingering a long while wet he subdued every heat of the flesh." New courage would pour into exhausted novices when they passed the place " where the angel was wont to talk to him."

Thus fortified, St. David himself was tireless, and it is plain that his extraordinary character made him a man greatly loved or greatly hated. It is to the credit of Rhygyvarch that he collected the bitter poison of jealousy he occasionally found and placed it beside the sweet honey he gleaned from the love of the saint's friends. These friends had often real cause to fear that he would be treacherously destroyed within the precincts of his own monastery.

Settled nearby on Ramsay Island was a saint from Brittany called Justinan. Since his first visit to Menevia St. David had gladdened his heart by becoming his Soul-Friend; this meant that so perfect was the concord between the two saints that St. David made Justinan his confessor and, after God, the guardian of his life. It was therefore with anguish that Justinan heard from the sailors in a strange boat approaching his island that his Soul-Friend was in mortal danger. He had been meditating on the beach and now he waded straight out to the boat and bade the men row him with all speed to the mainland. It was not till they were half-way across that he was calm enough to observe that the faces of the men rowing " were more than humanly ugly "; that, in fact they were nothing more than demons intent on deluding him.

No doubt the two saints laughed together afterwards over the subtle wiles of the devil, and no doubt St. David heartened

Justinan by telling him the story of that memorable day when he had so upset his monks at Menevia by a mad rush to the nearby wood with only one boot on. He had just stretched out his hand for the second boot when he was smitten by a vision of his beloved young disciple Aeddan collecting wood in the forest and about to be killed by a laybrother's axe. When he reached the edge of the forest the would-be murderer was suddenly unable to move and stood before his victim holding the axe, " his hands raised aloft, dried in the air." And as Aeddan left the dark wood to run to him, St. David had seen " innumerable troops of angels round about the boy as he came."

This young scholar from Ireland dearly loved to read out of doors. But when anyone called to him to run a message, in his eagerness to obey he often abandoned his book. Once, when this happened the precious volume was only preserved from the onslaughts of a deluge of rain by a miracle. Another time we find St. David hurrying to the sea-shore to accuse him of doing it yet again; and the boy, prostrate on the beach, confessing to his fatal absence of mind. This time the saint was so angry that he finally turned and left Aeddan without bidding him to rise. So the child stayed there and the tide crept towards him. It was some time before he was missed at the monastery; and when at last they found him they had to pull him out of the water with a rope; for he still lay prostrate on the incoming tide.

Though there is no word of it inconveniencing him while he worked among the Picts of Alba yet Aeddan's forgetfulness proved incurable. When at length he returned to Southern Ireland to found his own monastery of Ferns in County Wexford he left behind him the thing he valued most. Back came a boat containing one of his boys to ask for the " dear little bell " which had been St. David's parting gift. But St. David, knowing his young friend so well and loath to keep him in suspense, sent the boy back empty-handed while the bell he despatched across the water by a swift-flying angel. Aeddan received it joyfully but he was somewhat distraught as he was about to return to Menevia himself, having quite forgotten to ask St. David for the name of a suitable Irish Soul-Friend. To save him the tiresome crossing the angel kindly recommended St. Molua, Confessor also to the great St. Comgall of Bangor in Ulster.

Sixth century saints, however, were so much at home in the water that the angels were only troubled in grave emergencies; though no doubt they escorted unasked the strange craft so often to be seen in the Irish Channel in those days. One Irish abbot, Barre by name, visited Menevia on his way home to Cork from a pilgrimage to Rome. He waited there for a ship but when none came he was in despair. His mind seethed with visions of his abbotless monastery so alarming that he decided he could not wait. "He searched with anxious mind and found a wondrous path." Having got permission from St. David to borrow his horse and "having received the father's blessing he goes to the harbour, enters the sea, and putting his trust in the blessing of the father and the support of the horse he uses it as a ship, in as much as the horse ploughs through the swelling masses of the waves as through a level field." Proceeding further into the sea he arrived at length to the place where St. Brendan was "leading a wondrous life on a marine animal." As Barre passed him the two saints greeted each other and St. Brendan (considering the miraculous life he was wont to lead himself) was curiously surprised to see a man horse-riding in the sea, and exclaimed "God is wonderful in his saints!" If there had been dissensions in his monastery at Cork they vanished as soon as the abbot appeared triumphant on horseback. All were united in praise of the miracle. And after the death of the horse (which was never allowed to return to St. David) they made a gold-covered image of it. Renowned for its miracles, this image was still visited by pilgrims when Rhygyvarch wrote in the eleventh century.

But there was no image made of the obliging monster who saved St. David's life. It was late one Easter Eve when an angel sped down to Aeddan's monastery at Ferns. He revealed a hideous plot by which the abbot of Menevia would be poisoned the very next day. It did not occur to Aeddan to ask the angel why he had brought so urgent a message to Ireland and not to Wales. But he did remember that on such a festival he could not leave his monastery himself. He therefore chose Scutatus to carry the alarm across the water. There was no boat in the harbour, none the less he ordered his unhappy disciple to set out at once. " The disciple obeys, goes to the shore and enters the water to his knees. Then a monster took him and carried him across to the confines of the monastery." It proved a slow-moving monster for Scutatus only arrived at Menevia next morning at the end of the Easter Mass. But St. David emerged alive from the church and in private the messenger divulged to him what his prior, cellarer and deacon had planned. Then they proceeded to dine and the guilty deacon stepped forward with the poisoned bread. Pleading to be allowed the honour of serving the abbot, Scutatus took it from him and watched him withdraw " conscious of the crime and rigid with astonishment." St. David divided the bread into three pieces. One he gave to a small dog that stood outside by the door. In a twinkling of an eye all its hairs fell off, its skin split all over and it died wretchedly. The second bit he gave to a raven seated in its nest in an ash tree and at once it fell lifeless to the ground. The third bit he blessed; and before the horrified assembly he ate it himself. For three hours they watched him and then, still miraculously unharmed, he told them all. Loud were the lamentations and curses of the faithful brethren and vehemently they declared that the treacherous men " should never have a part in the heavenly kingdom."

When Modomnoc[1] left Menevia for County Dublin he crossed over in a perfectly normal craft. But he had long been in charge of the monastery bees and so great was their affection for him that " the whole multitude of bees followed the ship he had entered and settled with him on the ship's prow." Modomnoc had no wish to deprive the monastery of its one source of sweetness, so he ordered the return of the

---

[1]Celtic saints were so tenderly loved that the words " my " " little," " dear," are constantly attached to their names quite altering their appearance. Thus Aidan is often Maidoc (" my dear Aidan ") and Modomnoc's real name is Dom.

ship and " reappeared in the presence of the holy father attended by the swarm of bees," which, seeing he was safely home, discreetly returned to its own quarters. St. David praised Modomnoc's thoughtfulness and waved him farewell once more. But the wise bees had set a watch and the boat had not gone far before they were all comfortably ensconced once more in the prow. As he returned again Modomnoc must have stifled a wicked glow of pride at their flattering behaviour. And when they followed him a third time St. David had no choice but to reward their perseverance by blessing the whole swarm. " May the land to which you hasten abound with your offspring," he said kindly as they surged and hummed about their dear young master's head. And thus encouraged the party set off in peace; and so (according to Rhygyvarch) did Modomnoc bring to Ireland her first bees.

Sixth century angels not only supervised all journeys to heaven; they often arranged and conducted continental tours. It was they who gave St. David such short notice to set out for Jerusalem with his disciples Eiludd and Padarm. They smoothed the long road for them by temporarily endowing the abbot with the gift of tongues so that he might speak with the foreigners whose lands they traversed. They warned the Patriarch of the approach of " three Catholic men from the limits of the west " and prepared him to consecrate them as bishops. The Patriarch of Jerusalem was an intelligent man. He acted on these suggestions and after spiritual conversation he promoted St. David to archbishop. Then he sent the three of them off as missionaries to the Jews " that they might quieten down, knowing that the Christian faith is spread abroad to the limits of the west." It cannot be said that their mission was permanently successful; but the Patriarch was highly enough impressed by their efforts to give to each a bell, a staff and a tunic woven with gold. Because these presents flew back before them to their respective monasteries—the Patriarch thoughtfully sent them across Europe by angelic transport—the British people took them to be gifts from heaven. For the whole story there is, of course, no historical foundation though British pilgrims of those days are often mentioned as having reached Jerusalem.

But there is historical evidence of the two important synods referred to by Rhygyvarch. The first was at Brevi in Cardiganshire in 560. It was attended by one hundred and eighteen British bishops and a vast concourse of clergy and laity. Rhygyvarch says the cause of this gathering was a new outbreak of the Pelagian heresy so ably quelled a hundred years before by Germanus of Auxerre. But it seems more probable that the acts of two British synods recently discovered in France and readily identified as the proceedings of those attended by St. David, reveal the real reason to be simply the need for a general discussion on the discipline of the clergy and laity of the British Church. Rhygyvarch himself found in his researches that at Brevi " Decrees of Catholic and ecclesiastical rule were confirmed. They are found in part in the oldest writings of the father written in his own sacred hand."

And yet oddly enough St. David was not, at first, one of the one hundred and eighteen bishops who gathered together. By that time he dearly loved the seclusion of his monastery. It was only when the voices of those bishops had failed to reach the ears of more than a fraction of the huge crowd gathered together that one of St. David's friends remembered him. " There is one bishop approved in religion," he said to the worried priests, " who has an angel as comrade—a lovable man. I advise you to invite him." By this time the frantic bishops had promised to promote to metropolitan the man who succeeded in holding and converting the impatient multitude. Reluctantly St. David came. And standing in the midst of the people he " expounded the gospel and the law as from a trumpet. In the presence of all a snow-white pigeon sent from heaven settled on his shoulder and remained as long as he preached." The people heard and were filled and " they gave thanks to God and St. David." So was he elected primate of the Cambrian Church transporting the See at once from Caerleon to Menevia. But Caerleon remained ecclesiastically important and there, in 569, he held the Victory synod at which some useful new rules were made and those adopted at Brevi were renewed and confirmed. " So," says Rhygyvarch thinking with dismay of the impending Primacy of Canterbury, " from these two synods all the churches of our country take their standard, and rule by Roman authority."

There followed a period of great religious activity. " Throughout the whole country brethren built monasteries. Everywhere indications of churches are heard. Everywhere sounds of prayer are raised to the stars." As for St. David, in his old age he was renowned as the supreme religious head of all the British race. He had the rather dubious power to give sanctuary to " every evil person flying from place to place." With his peculiar interest in bees Rhygyvarch has it that the saint " engendered every swarm of monks in the land shining as he did in a blaze of miracles."

According to the Chronicum Scotorum St. David died in 589. He was ready to go, for one day at matins an angel interrupted the service to warn him saying: " Prepare and gird thyself. On the first of March the Lord Jesus Christ accompanied by a great host of angels will come to meet thee." The brethren heard the conversation and were fallen to the ground in terror; but St. David heard the friendly voice joyfully. And while the monastery overflowed with tears and lamentation he continued to rejoice. In one day the angel carried the news throughout the whole of Britain and Ireland. " Then from all sides came assemblies of saints like bees to a hive at the approach of a storm.

" And so on the third day of the week at cock-crow the monastery is filled with angelic choirs and with the sweetest fragrance. At the hour of matins the Lord Jesus Christ deigned to bestow his presence for the consolation of the father as he had promised by the angel. When David saw Him he altogether rejoiced in spirit, saying, ' Take me after Thee.' With these words he gave back his life to God. With Christ as his companion and surrounded by the angelic host he went to the abodes of heaven."

Judging by his extreme austerity and by his love of the contemplative life St. David would seem to have read St. Ninian's copy of Athanasius' *Life of St. Anthony* with even deeper interest than his copy of Sulpicius Severus' *Life of St. Martin*. As far as he was concerned it was useless for the sensible Gildas to rail against the absurdity of men attempting to live in a wind-swept, treeless, Welsh swamp after the manner of the sun-soaked monks of Egypt. Gildas' efforts to steer a middle course between the worldliness of the princes and secular bishops and the fanatical severity of St. David's monks ended in a retreat to Brittany. For all his excellent preaching and his treasured letters to the great ones of his time there is not one ancient Welsh church called by his name. Whereas for the next five hundred years St. David's way of life with its emphasis on penitence, abstinence and humility, appealed irresistibly to the people of Wales; and even after it was swamped by a flood of Norman ideals he continued, and still continues, to be their beloved patron saint.

Sources:
Life by Rhygyfarch. Ed. A. W. Wade-Evans.
Bollandist *Life of St. David* from *Acta Sanctorum*. Vol. VII.
Stories told by Giraldus Cambrensis.
De Excidio Britanniae. Gildas. Ed. Williams.
Anglo-Saxon Chronicle. Ed. J. A. Giles.
Vitae Sanctorum Hiberniae. Ed. Plummer.
Historia Regum Britanniae. Geoffrey of Monmouth.
Irish Monasticism. Ryan.
The Pictish Nation, Its People and its Church. Archibald B. Scott.

saint david

Chapter VI.

ST. BRENDAN

H my God, help me, for my boat is so small and Thy sea is so great." That prayer has been used all down the ages by Breton sailors and was quite possibly taught to them by St. Brendan when he visited the British refugees fled to Brittany in 546 under the religious guidance of St. Gildas and St. Cadoc from the wrath of the pitiless Angles. It is certainly a prayer well-suited to the bravest of sailor saints and one likely to have been very often in his heart.

Perhaps the great breakers of the Atlantic put a spell on him from the first, seeing that he was born about the beginning of the sixth century in what is now County Kerry, where Brandon Hill, Brandon Bay and Brandon Head still tell us of his favourite haunts. He was an outstanding child; so much so that the local bishop, Erc, took a special interest in his welfare. He sent him for his first lessons to Kileedy[1] in Limerick where the great St. Ita, "Foster-Mother of the Saints of Ireland," ruled a monastery in which the nuns not only prayed, fasted and meditated, but ran an already famous school for small boys. "True faith in God with purity of heart; simplicity of life with religion; generosity with charity." Such were the precepts of St. Ita's wise rule. At first glance the following episode from St. Brendan's childhood, taken from the Lismore *Life*, would seem to contradict this rule.

Bishop Erc had driven over to see the abbess. While his guardian was closeted with her in holy talk, the small Brendan, aged ten, had mounted the bishop's chariot and was sitting in state in the driver's seat happily holding the reins when up came a little princess. She thought nothing of his proud position but begged him to come down and play with her. Not once did she ask him, but, despite his constant refusals,

[1]From Kil-Ita, the church of Ita. Originally *kil* held its Latin meaning *cella*, a cell. When used it is always to be found attached to some version of the founder's name.

again and again. At last, feeling in some small measure that " blast of temptation " to which only St. Patrick's clerics were able to boast immunity, the young saint rose from his seat in fury and leaning over he flogged the little girl with the reins till she ran screaming to her parents. Nowadays such unchivalrous behaviour would have called forth another flogging for Brendan. But so common was sexual immorality in a land only just emerged from paganism that the bishop and the abbess both praised him for the strong line he had taken with the designing young female.

It is easy to understand why the boy was so happy in this school that eventually he had to be removed by Bishop Erc. " Go off now," said St. Ita, " and learn the rules of holy men who have practised what they preached; and do not study with virgins lest evil be spoken of you by men."

So, reluctantly, he crossed the country to the monastery of Clonard in Meath, where, because of his excellent grounding, he rapidly excelled in his studies, even among the large and brilliant gathering of students living under the rule of St. Finnian. At last, with his friends St. Columba and St. Kenneth, he became a presbyter and won the coveted title of one of St. Finnian's " Twelve Apostles of Ireland." St. Brendan, St. Columba and St. Kenneth all won their title through missionary work undertaken, not in Ireland herself, but in what we now call Scotland. Great changes had taken place in the population of that country since the days of St. Ninian. Scots from the north of Ireland had colonised Argyllshire and the Western Isles. They called their new kingdom Dalriada after the Irish district they had left. The Picts did not welcome their strange-tongued and semi-Christian cousins; but on the whole the penetration seems to have taken place peacefully.

Spreading northwards and westwards along the Firth of Forth were the pagan Angles. South of the Forth they had already occupied the rich coastal area as far as the Pentlands.

Farther south in what is now called England these same Angles, and their friends the Saxons, spreading across the country from their original base at the Humber, had succeeded in driving a wedge between the South Britons of Wales and the Britons in Cumberland who had, in consequence of the invasion, fled north of the Solway. These refugees formed the new British kingdom of Strathclyde with its capital at Dumbarton on the Clyde.

North of the Tay and east of Drumalban (the huge range of mountains running north from Ben Lomond to Ben Hope and cutting Scotland in half except for the deep cleft of the Caledonian Canal) the Picts still lived unmolested under their pagan king Brude mac Maelchon.

St. Kenneth was an Irish Pict. On one occasion he accompanied St. Columba as interpreter when that Scotic saint went to interview King Brude at Inverness on the subject of his kinsmen the Dalriadic Scots. But though St. Kenneth was a good enough Christian to help his Scottish friend it was to his own kinsmen the Picts that he naturally preached. Before founding the monastery of Achabo at the head of the Nore, Queen's County, he went to work in Fife and founded a monastery where the town of St. Andrews now stands.

Like St. Columba St. Brendan naturally occupied himself while in Scotland with his fellow Scots in the west. He started to explore the Dalriadic islands about 545, some twenty years before St. Columba landed in Iona. In Tiree, in Bute, and on three other islands he left Christian settlements that bore his name. So tireless were his voyages among the islands that even on the remote island of St. Kilda, far out to the west from the Outer Hebrides, it is recorded that there was once a chapel called after St. Brendan.

It must have been during this period of voyaging through the magic of the western seas that St. Brendan first became obsessed with the idea that somewhere in the fallen world the Garden of Eden must still exist in all its primeval innocence. Like his friend St. Columba, he was gifted with a marvellous voice and was often, like him, transformed to shining ecstasy by visions of the divine. Where he differed from his fellow saint was in thinking that it was not enough to strive to make in his monasteries small patches of heaven upon the earth; he determined to spend as much time as possible hunting for

ST. BRENDAN PREACHES ON THE GREAT WHALE'S BACK

the place itself in his coracle. It was quite useless for his friends to reason with so inspired a fanatic. No sooner had he returned to Ireland to found his monastery of Clonfert in 555 in a sheltered meadow by the Shannon where that great river now forms the easternmost corner of County Galway, than he set out on his first voyage. It was unsuccessful; but he returned from it with a fund of stories so wonderful that such sceptical friends as St. David, St. Columba and St. Cadoc were enthralled. Even that mournful realist St. Gildas could hardly fail to be carried away by the lure of those Blessed Isles men had always thought to be secreted in the vast Atlantic.

It seems that St. Brendan did not confide in St. Ita, though she had always remained his good friend and councillor. He judged (and rightly) that she would disapprove of so unusual a way of breaking through to heaven. Sure enough, when she learnt how eccentric her pupil had become she sent for him and said: " My dear son, why didst thou go on a voyage without consulting me ? The land that thou seekest from God thou wilt never find under these dead-stained skies." But perceiving that it was impossible to deter him, and loving him as she did, she added: " Howbeit, let wooden ships be built and maybe thou wilt find the land later."

According to a hundred or more versions of his next tremendous voyage St. Ita's soothing words actually came true. The story grew world-famous in the tenth century through the publication of St. Brendan's *Navigatio* or Log Book by a gifted, anonymous Irish writer. It is told here as much as possible in the words of an early sixteenth century connoisseur of the tale. There is something irresistible about the beautiful Celtic legend when told by a serious believer a thousand years later in the inimitable language of Tudor England.

It appears that the man who did first find this blessed land, one Meruoke, was not looking for it. He happened on heaven while searching, as did so many contemporary monks, for a lonely island on which to lead the life of a hermit. His father (weeping annoyingly and inexplicably the while) had just arrived at Clonfert and was engaged, somewhat incoherently, in breaking the glad news to St. Brendan, when, with the aptness of a dream, Meruoke and his crew walked into the monastery their clothes still smelling of the " sweet and joyful place." It was an island, they said, where was " ever day never night." They had been astounded when the stern young guardian of this " paradise terrestre " had bade them leave. " Ye have been here half a year without meat or drink or sleep," he said, and they, bewildered, thought it was but half an hour, " so merry and joyful they were there."

Thus were St. Brendan's theories gloriously vindicated. At once a ship was built and victualled. This time he gave it a triple layer of skins, collecting much butter to keep them supple. For forty days his monks prayed and fasted. Meruoke appears to have given no directions to the crew. They left all that to God.

When all was ready two extra monks rushed down the Shannon shore begging to be taken. St. Brendan had only to look at them to know that one of them was bound for hell and would never return to Ireland. Thinking to be rid of them he told them this. But each naturally supposing it to be the other, they climbed eagerly in. " And then St. Brendan bade the ship-men to wind up the sail and forth they sailed in God's name."

After sailing " plain east " through curiously empty seas, cliffs at last loomed ahead. It took them three days to find a little haven among their gauntness. They landed; and at once a fair hound came bounding over the sand. Going up to St. Brendan " he made him good cheer in his manner." They followed this hound to a hollow hall where a meal and beds were prepared; though with never a sign of a human being. Tired and trusting " they said graces, ate and drank; and rested after their long labour."

After this comfortable adventure they sailed on till they reached the Island of Sheep. The guardian here was an old man who explained the exceeding greatness and whiteness of the sheep by telling them " here is never cold weather." The herbage was green and deliciously scented. The mariners rejoiced in it till their host set them off on their search once more, advising them, strangely to keep on " right east."

This time land was soon sighted—it was only a small island but a convenient place on which to stretch legs and cook a meal. " When the fire was right hot and the meat nigh sodden, then this island began to move." Indeed it sank rapidly from sight and the monks abandoned it only just in time. St. Brendan, who had remained in the boat, explained calmly that it was a great fish who tried always to get his tail in his mouth " but for greatness he may not."

Here is another explanation given by Philippe de Thaun. He wrote it in Latin for the enlightenment of the many medieval readers of these adventures. " Cetus is a very great beast which lives always in the sea. It takes the sand of the sea, spreads it on its back, raises itself up in the sea and remains motionless. The seafarer thinks it is an island and lands there to prepare his meals. The whale feels the fire and the ship and the people. He will plunge and drown them if he can."

Such a beast was far from Christian. But St. Brendan's whale was soon converted. Indeed it might almost be said to have been consecrated. During the seven years of journeyings back and forth the saint made a habit of using the patient monster as a church on which to celebrate Easter. The monks were always glad to see it and recognised it by their cauldron which it kept thoughtfully on its back. The last time they landed there they were exhausted after battling with a " full great tempest." The huge whale felt this, and waited devoutly till they had finished singing Mass. " Then he began to move and swam forth fast into the sea whereof the monks were sore aghast that stood upon him . . . but by the will of our Lord God this fish set all the monks a-land in the Paradise of Birds all whole and sound."

During his seven years search St. Brendan annually visited this last island. When they first came there they were awed and amazed at one of the trees. This was white, not with blossom, but with birds and " they sang so merrily that it was an heavenly noise to hear." St. Brendan knelt on the shore, weeping, and thanked God for so much loveliness.

He then begged to be told why birds lived there in such profusion. " One bird then and with flickering of his wings made a full merry noise like a fiddle." After this delicious prelude he left his fellows and came to the group of ecstatic monks. He told them that all these birds were really angels, followers of their one-time master Lucifer, and fallen with him out of heaven. Lucifer for his monstrous pride had naturally fallen far lower than they for their smaller offences. All over the world, he said, were fallen angels thus disguised, and placed by God " after the quality of their trespass. . . . Because our trespass is but small we are allowed to serve Him on this tree in the best manner that we can; and every Sunday we are made white as snow for to praise Our Lord in the best noise we may."

This island, an enchanted patch of fallen heaven, stirred the searchers to new endeavours and the angelic bird's small trespass must have been swiftly expiated by its helpful behaviour to them. It prophesied only a short stay in paradise when they should reach it and many perils and troubles before then. To ease these it often flew with them and protected them. Once it pierced the sullen eyes of a great grype that assailed St. Brendan's boat. And so, though it proved true that those who strive to come close to God are the more besieged by their adversary the devil, this frail craft survived; but the monks were often " right weary for lack of land " and " set little price on their lives."

St. Brendan himself never lost hope or courage. Once when his tired monks begged him to refrain from singing lest he wake a mass of sleeping fishes below them in the clear water, he not only went on singing mightily; but looking down he gave a great laugh to think that men who had tamed a whale could still fear these. The fishes awoke and they crowded so thick that they hid the water; but when the song was finished they melted decorously away.

Blown northwards through that clear water they reached an island " full dark and full of stench and smoke." Here they heard " great blowing and blasting of bellows but they might see nothing." Sore afraid they " blessed them oft " and hurried away—but horrible fiends followed fast. All the sea was " on a fire " with them. This was too much for one of the company. Throwing the blame for his behaviour on to his parents and cursing the day he was born, he leapt into the blazing sea. It was the doomed monk bound for hell.

St. Brendan declared afterwards that this island was undoubtedly an outlying part of that dominion; though many now incline to place it in the nearer region of Iceland. Truly he moved, like God, in a mysterious way; for where, then, should we place the other islands in this loose-lying archipelago ? What of that ghastly rock (fit subject for El Greco's brush) on which the mariners found the wasted, tortured form of Judas. Even in this comparatively late edition of the voyage, published by Wynkyn de Worde in 1527 at the Sign of the Sun in Fleet Street, it is presented with a horrid realism. Though constantly beaten by ill-gotten canvas that flapped wetly above him, and lashed by the waves that surged below, this rock was to Judas a sort of holiday resort where, on Sundays, he was allowed respite from hell. St. Brendan was appalled at the tale he told and banished for one extra night those fiends that came to fetch him back. " Off they went roaring and crying towards their master the great devil." But back they came the next morning. " And they take then Judas trembling for fear with them to pain."

This small outpost of hell, though startling, is as vivid as the rest of the islands they discovered, but the heaven they reached at last had the uncomfortable vastness and vagueness of an unmapped continent. They recognised it as God's own country, of course (was it really America ?), but though it resembled Meruoke's description in many pleasant ways they undoubtedly felt lost there and were perturbed by the great river they durst not cross. Almost they were relieved (after forty days and nights of undiluted sunlight) to be sent safely back to Ireland deservedly enriched with the fruits and precious stones of paradise.

For in truth St. Paule's island (where they found the aged hermit attended by an upright otter dutifully wearing a necklace of fresh fish) was much more the sort of place where a Celtic saint could feel at home with God and dream peacefully of heaven. Short cuts are notoriously misleading, even for saints. But so powerful is the urge to try them that for the next twelve hundred years after St. Brendan had eventually reached heaven by the usual long and lonely road men had only to read of his voyage to be fired to find his land. As late as 1721, with the Age of Reason already born, yet another ship set out to sea to seek it. These sailors placed it (as did Columbus' cartographer in 1472), somewhere west of the Canaries. Their ship was large and fast. They even had telescopes. But they achieved no more than an occasional momentary glimpse. They lacked St. Brendan's vision. And if they were not troubled with grypes, neither were they guided by angelic birds. They were incapable of converting a whale or changing an otter's life.

Indeed they suffered a double handicap. They searched in the wrong direction and the eyes they used were not the eyes of a saint. It must be owned that even St. Brendan's trained sense of direction was a little warped; but if he too looked in the wrong places, heaven was always his goal; and so great was the driving force behind this motive that many now believe it carried his coracle to Iceland, the West Indies, Mexico and America.

It may well be asked why the monastery of so dauntless a sailor monk was not placed upon an island. Even if he felt that to live within sight and sound of the sea would prove too strong a temptation why did he not elect to live on one of the many islands in the Shannon? Other Celtic saints found these islands so much to their taste that not one but had its group of tonsured Christian converts. The real reason for its position lies in the size of Clonfert. With its three thousand monks—as many as there were at Clonard—it was almost a town. So large a community could not afford to be entirely surrounded by water; it could only exist on the mainland.

Like most of the great saints of the Second Order St. Brendan was a presbyter. So, though he ruled supreme at Clonfert, he required the services of a resident bishop. Moenn was the name of the first bishop of Clonfert and we know that he died in 572. The date of St. Brendan's death is much less certain. It took place somewhere between 577 and 583 so that both St. Columba and St. Kenneth mourned their unique friend.

Unlike them he was not to be remembered for his missionary work nor for the size or quality of his monastery. When men wrote of St. Brendan, however inaccurately, they always felt impelled to write of the sea. In St. Cuimin's Hymn we are given the dubious information that " he spent seven years on the great whale's back: it was a distressing mode of mortification." This is an odd way to describe seven years in a small boat hunting for paradise. Yet even this hymn does point in the right direction. His fellow saints might live as close to the sea as they could—they all loved water— but St. Brendan spent his most joyful and most memorable years riding the Atlantic waves in his coracle.

Sources:

The *Voyage of St. Brendan* published by Wynkyn de Worde, 1527. Ed. by Thomas Wright, 1834.
Irish Monasticism. Ryan.
The *Historical St. Columba*. W. D. Simpson.
Mystery of St. Brendan's Voyage. James Wylkie.

Chapter VII.

ST. KENTIGERN

F the Atlantic breakers put their spell upon St. Brendan, it can certainly be said that the east wind shaped the course of St. Kentigern's life. Indeed had it not been that even in -the sixth century this keen wind prevailed in the eastern Lowlands of Scotland, he would have had no life to shape. Far out in the cold North Sea he would have been born in a drifting coracle only to die of exposure and starvation.

Joceline, a monk at the Cistercian abbey of Furness and already a well-known twelfth century hagiographer, tells the story of the saint's birth in the *Life* he was commissioned to write by that same vigorous Bishop of Glasgow who built the present Melrose Abbey. And so strange is the story that it strikes the reader as founded on fact even before it is discovered that Joceline had access not only to the standard *Life* (of which a fragment still remains) constantly read in the Glasgow Cathedral where St. Kentigern still lived vividly in the minds of the congregation, but to a much fuller and older account written in the " Scotic dialect." As Joceline says himself it is his task to " season what had been composed in a barbarous way with Roman salt." And this he proceeds lavishly to do though he frankly confesses to having found no account of the translation of the saint's relics, nor of any miracles performed after his death.

To anyone familiar with the fertile plains of East Lothian the three most outstanding landmarks of the district are the Bass Rock, North Berwick Law and Traprain Law. Urien, St. Kentigern's grandfather, knew them well. For, though it is known that he owned tracts of land all over the Lowlands to the south-west, yet in the first half of the sixth century this British chief still clung bravely to the east coast despite the fact that he was constantly harassed by the Angles who had already over-run it. Perhaps the ever increasing pressure of his enemies hardened him. At any rate when he discovered that his unmarried daughter was about to have a baby he hurried her relentlessly to the summit of Traprain Law, known in those days as Dun-pelder. On the south side of the hill there is an almost perpendicular drop of 700 feet to the plain below. He flung her over. But the girl was a Christian; and through her desperate prayers she "sustained no injury; since, as it seemed to her, like a bird bearing feathers, she came down with easy descent to the ground lest she should dash her foot against a stone." This miracle did nothing to soften her father's heart. Far from it. He had her escorted to the coast some eight miles away, and decreed "that that poor little pregnant woman, placed alone in a boat, should be exposed to the sea. In order therefore that the sentence thus determined should be carried into effect, the king's servants, embarking, took her far out to sea, and committing her to fortune alone in a very little boat of hides, made after the fashion of the Scotti, without any oar, rowed back to the shore." A glance at the map shows that she was abandoned somewhere about the middle of the wide entrance to the Firth of Forth. Maybe the tide turned, and surely the east wind sprang up. For the little coracle sped purposefully up the Forth till it grounded on the north bank at Culross in what is now the Kingdom of Fife. There, on the shore, the child was born.

Close at hand stood the buildings of the *muinntir* of the great and already aged St. Serf who died about 543; and it is through his association with him that St. Kentigern links up with Candida Casa. It seems almost certain that Dr. Scott is right when he maintains that the various dedications to St. Serf to be found in the south-west of Scotland show not only that he worked there (early Celtic churches were always called after their founders) but that this must have been his first group of foundations, planted within easy reach of his spiritual home, the great training school at Candida Casa. Later he worked among the British refugees in Strathclyde having a church at their capital, Dumbarton, and baptising their Christian king Roderick's younger brother. St. Serf also planted a group of settlements in Aberdeenshire in touch with those of the Briton St. Drostan and his three disciples, already active there at the beginning of the sixth century. Finally St. Serf made his headquarters at Culross where, in his monastery, he ran a flourishing school for small boys while planting that group of Christian settlements in Fife to be restored and strengthened later by St. Kenneth working from St. Andrews.

It was to this missionary-teacher of mixed Iro-Pictish and British descent that some kindly shepherds brought the mother and child. Joceline relates that on first seeing the baby " the blessed old man was filled with spiritual laughter." He named him Kentigern but always called him Mungo, which Pictish pet name (meaning " my dog ") so became his pupil that there is not a single one of St. Kentigern's original foundations called after his proper name. The child could not have selected a better foster-father. One of the secrets of the strength of the Celtic saints lay in their discovery of the necessary rhythmic swing between the active and the contemplative life. In the direct line from St. Ninian, St. Serf had the equivalent of the Glasserton cave in his famous Dysart to which he retired for spiritual refreshment at regular intervals. He passed on this invaluable spiritual pattern to the young Kentigern together with the fruits of his active experience and his typical love of beasts and birds.

One of the most attractive inmates of St. Serf's monastery was his pet robin—so tame that " sometimes even it perched upon his head, or face, or shoulder, or bosom ; sometimes it was with him when he read or prayed, and by the flapping of its wing, or by the sound of its inarticulate voice, or by some little gesture, it showed the love it had for him. So that sometimes the face of the man of God, shadowed forth in the motion of the bird, was clothed in joy, as he wondered at the great power of God in the little creature, to whom the dumb speak and the irrational things are known to have reason."

One day while the old saint prayed, young Mungo's school fellows, " availing themselves of the absence of the master, began to indulge in play with the aforesaid bird, and while they handled it among them, and sought to snatch it from each other, it got destroyed in their hands and its head was torn from its body. On this, play became sorrow, and they already in imagination felt the blows of the rods, which are wont to be the greatest torment of boys." But Kentigern took the bird in his hands and " putting the head upon the body he signed it with the sign of the cross, and lifting up holy hands in prayer to the Lord, he said : ' Lord Jesus Christ, in whose hands is the breath of every rational and irrational creature, give back to this bird the breath of life, that Thy blessed name may be glorified for ever.' " Miraculously the bird revived and " in its usual way it flew forth with joy to meet the holy old man as he returned from the church."

When he was fifteen, and shortly before his foster-father's death, St. Kentigern left St. Serf's preparatory school to continue his religious training under St. Fergus of Carnoch in the county of Stirling. Carnoch must have had an outstanding reputation at that time; for St. Serf would select only the best school for his favourite pupil. There St. Kentigern remained till the death of St. Fergus some ten years later when he and many of his fellow students took to the road following in the wake of two wild but willing bulls yoked by St. Kentigern to a cart containing his dead master's body. The strange procession travelled east, till on reaching the site of the present city of Glasgow the weary beasts " halted near a certain cemetery which had been long before consecrated by St. Ninian." There, significantly, they buried St. Fergus; and there St. Kentigern founded a *muinntir* so joyful that it came to be known as Glesgu or " the Happy Family."

It is easy to understand why St. Kentigern's settlement seemed to the refugee Britons of Strathclyde so miraculous an island of peace and security. They had been thrust north by the broad wedge driven between them and their kinsmen in Wales by the flood of west-moving Angles from the Humber region. And even among themselves there were fierce dissensions between the pagan and Christian elements. In consequence of these troubles so desperate was the position of King Roderick of Strathclyde that in St. Columba's opinion (his words are recorded by Adamnan) he appeared to be merely " that wretched man, who is quite unable to tell at what hour he may be killed by his enemies." This uneasy state of affairs existed in the reign of his predecessor Tudevallus and continued till about 573 when Roderick won the battle of Arderyd near Carlisle. He was assisted in the battle by Maelgon[1] the wise and generous pagan king of the southern Britons, by Urien, St. Kentigern's grandfather and by the local chief Morken; while the opposing party consisted of the pagan British from the Solway region and their curiously selected allies the Angles and the exiled Scot, prince Aedhan from Ireland.[2] Roderick's victory welded the north Britons into a nation and ensured for the Celtic Church a new era of peaceful expansion.

But when St. Kentigern first arrived in Strathclyde about 550 what the British Church needed above all was a strong young enthusiast to rebuild—to put new heart into the weary Christians and to reconvert those British who had, in their despair, reverted to their ancient gods. Large-scale missionary work was out of the question while civil war was imminent but the example of a Happy Family could and did do wonders. St. Kentigern had barely settled into his new home when the king and his friends decided that though he was only twenty-five, he was obviously the very man to be head of their church. Therefore, " having called one bishop from Ireland, after the manner of the Britons and Scots of that period, they caused him to be consecrated bishop." Joceline not only rescues this, to him, unorthodox custom, but he gives the authentic Celtic flavour to his story by adding that the bishop " dressed in the roughest hair cloth," " shook off drowsiness rather by tasting than taking sleep," and " bore a pastoral staff, not rounded and gilded and gemmed, as may be seen nowadays, but of simple wood, and merely bent." Following in the footsteps of St. Ninian and St. Serf the young bishop always spent Lent alone in his Desert. It was partly

[1]Maelgon and Roderick were both descendants of that Coroticus to whom St. Patrick wrote his famous letter.

[2]Shortly after the battle St. Columba placed Aedhan on the throne of Dalriada. He is said by Dr. Douglas Simpson to have been Roderick's ally at Arderyd: while Dr. Scott gives even more impressive evidence to show he fought on the opposite side.

the spiritual poise he gained there that " attracted the hearts of all who beheld him. His outward cheerfulness was the sign and most faithful interpretation of that inward peace . . . which the Lord bestowed on him."

A cheerful abbot ensured the happiness of the whole *muinntir*. " The man of God joined to himself a great many disciples, whom he trained in the sacred literature of the Divine law, and educated to sanctity of life by his word and example. They all with a godly jealousy imitated his life and doctrine, accustomed to fasting and sacred vigils at certain seasons, intent on psalms and prayers, and meditation on the Divine word, content with sparing diet and dress, occupied every day and hour in manual labour. For, after the fashion of the Primitive Church under the apostles and their successors, possessing nothing of their own, and living soberly, righteously, and continently, they dwelt, as did St. Kentigern himself, in single cottages from the time when they had become mature in age and doctrine." This routine and the separate huts are both in a direct line from St. Anthony, St. Martin and St. Ninian.

St. David with his aversion to cattle, must have enjoyed the following story of how St. Kentigern farmed.

" It happened once upon a time that he had no oxen whatever, and from the deficiency of these, there being no ploughing, the land lay fallow. When the man of God saw this, lifting up his eyes, he saw on the edge of a neighbouring wood a herd of deer bounding along here and there through the forest. Straightway offering up a prayer, by the mighty power of his word he called them to him, and in the name of the Lord whom all dumb unreasoning beasts and all the cattle of the plain obey, commanded them to be yoked in the place of the oxen to the plough, and to turn up the earth. They at once obeyed the command of the man of God, and like tame oxen used to the yoke, ploughed the land, to the astonishment of many. . . . Once upon a time, as the stags were going and returning like domestic animals, a hungry wolf, rushing upon one of the stags, which was wearied with his labour and was cropping some food as he lay upon the green turf, throttled him, and filled his voracious stomach with his carcase. When the saint learnt this, extending his hand towards the wood, he said: 'In the name of the Holy and Undivided Trinity, I command that the wolf, who hath wrought this injury on me who deserved it not, appear before me to make satisfaction.' Wondrous words! More wondrous deeds! Straightway at the voice of the man of God, the wolf, leaping forth from the wood, fell howling at his feet, and with such signs as he could, declared that he begged pardon and was willing to make reparation." St. Kentigern ordered him to take the place of the dead stag. "Verily the wolf obeyed the word spoken by the saint and, yoked with the other stag, ploughed up nine acres, whereupon the saint freely allowed him to depart."

After some seventeen years as abbot, bishop and chief adviser to the king, St. Kentigern fell foul of Morken, that local authority who was later to help Roderick to win the battle of Arderyd but who reckoned both St. Kentigern and his grandfather to be politically dangerous. He threatened the bishop with his life; and that St. Kentigern's action in fleeing south was only prudent is seen when we learn that Morken not only quarrelled also with the saint's grandfather, but did eventually succeed in killing the old chief.

St. Kentigern's aim was to join the Christian Britons in Wales. But he took some time to reach them for his on way he had to pass through Cumberland where he found many unhappy Britons thrust into the hills by the Northumbrian Angles. To these refugee Christians he ministered; leaving behind him no less than eight foundations. They can still be traced by the primitive equal-armed crosses on their ancient stones. But almost all their names were changed beyond recognition in Anglo-Saxon times and only Mungriesdale still speaks clearly of St. Kentigern's first, though unprepared, work in the mission field.

Joceline omits to mention more than three of the monstrous regiment of Celtic saints who strode across the sixth century, many of whom must have been St. Kentigern's friends. But what is far more disconcerting—not one of their

ST. KENTIGERN IN THE LOWLANDS

biographers deigns to mention the eminent St. Mungo. Fortunately, in Dr. Simpson's reliable opinion St. Kentigern's missions are among the best authenticated of any in the Celtic Church, otherwise one might almost be tempted to wonder whether he really did exist. But how satisfying a cross-reference would have been attained had Rhygyvarch thought fit to give an account of St. Kentigern's visit to Menevia! To be sure it would have been just another of his exalted panegyrics complete with a background of the beating of angels' wings and most probably with the deep humming of a swarm of converted bees thrown in for good measure: none the less it is a grave loss.

When St. Kentigern arrived at Menevia St. David had already been Archbishop of the British Church in Wales for some seven years. It was through his good friend the pagan British sovereign Maelgon that St. David was able to obtain for St. Kentigern the permission to build a *muinntir* of his own in North Wales first called Llanelwy but now known as St. Asaph's after that young relative of St. Kentigern's who succeeded him as abbot after the battle of Arderyd.

The exact site of St. Asaph's was apparently decided as follows. While St. Kentigern, accompanied by " a great multitude of disciples who had flocked to him, preferring to lead with him a lowly life in a foreign land to living luxuriously in their own," was debating where exactly God wished him to settle; " Behold, a single wild boar from the wood, entirely white, met them, and approaching the feet of the saint, moving his head, sometimes advancing a little, and then returning and looking backwards motioned to the saint and to his companions, with such gestures as he could, to follow him. . . . When they came to the place which the Lord had predestinated for them, the boar halted, and frequently striking the ground with his foot, and making the gesture of tearing up the soil of the little hill that was there with his long tusks, shaking his head repeatedly and grunting, he clearly showed to all that that was the place designed by God. . . . Then the saint, returning thanks, adored the Almighty Lord on bended knees; and rising from prayer he blessed that place and its surroundings in the name of the Lord. After that, in testimony and sign of salvation, and in earnest of the future religion erecting a cross, he there pitched his tents. The boar, however, seeing what was done, came near, and by his frequent grunts seemed to ask somewhat of the bishop; then the saint, scratching the head of the brute, and stroking his mouth and teeth, said: ' God Almighty, in Whose power are all the beasts of the forest, the oxen, the birds of the air, and the fishes of the sea, grant thee for thy conduct such reward as He knoweth is best for thee.' Then the boar, as if well remunerated, bowing his head to the priest of the Lord, departed, and betook himself to his well-known groves.''

As the crow flies, or—apparently more usual in the sixth century—as the monster swims—St. Asaph's, where St. Kentigern pitched his tents, is about equally distant across the water from Whithorn, St. David's and Bangor in Ulster. It will be remembered that the name Bangor meant a religious establishment where there were educational facilities. St. Comgall's enormous community (there were three thousand monks) was so far-famed that Picts, Britons, Gauls, and even a few Teutons studied there: it was everywhere known as Bangor the Great. Comparing St. Kentigern's rule (as recorded by Joceline) with that of St. Comgall it would seem obvious that the two communities were in close touch. One third of St. Kentigern's monks grew food, minded the cattle and did other such outdoor jobs; one third attended to the kitchen and the other manual labour indoors; and the lettered third '' he appointed to celebrate the Divine Service in church by day and by night.'' Though there were only one thousand monks at St. Asaph's the choir was divided as at Bangor the Great, to allow of the singing of a paeon of perpetual praise.

St. Kentigern and St. David probably corresponded regularly while the former was in Wales; but there can have been little or no communication with Candida Casa because it was most probably about the time when St. Kentigern and his followers set to work to build their monastery on the small hill selected by the importunate boar, that the invading

Angles finally reached the south-west coast of Alba. They burnt almost all the precious books and documents of Candida Casa and scattered for the time being most of her priests and lay-workers. Even before this disaster the monastery had gradually become more and more isolated. Had it not been for the help so generously given to the Pictish Church in Alba by the Irish Picts from St. Comgall's Bangor the original chain of settlements planted by St. Ninian, and already one hundred and fifty years old, must have perished for want of the spiritual sustenance annually given by visiting priests from the mother church.

And here again we meet with that fascinating interweaving of personalities that makes the story of the Celtic Church so like the joyful designs carved and drawn by her monks. For it was St. Finbar of Moville who was indirectly responsible for keeping alive the Pictish Church in Alba so that when St. Kentigern returned from Wales after the battle of Arderyd the ground, though sadly trampled, was yet prepared to receive his far-flung seed.

St. Finbar's monastery at Moville, County Down, was quite close to St. Comgall's at Bangor. The two abbots were friends and often met. And it was only natural that in his old age St. Finbar's chief topic of conversation should be of those far-off happy school days at Candida Casa; (whither, it will be remembered he sailed from the daughter house of Nendrum on an island in Strangford Lough) of his lively pupils when later he was promoted to teach there; and of his mission work among the Picts of Alba far north among the hills of Sutherland. It was his firm and oft-repeated conviction that because St. Ninian first brought Christianity to Strangford Lough the Irish Picts there still owed him an immeasurable debt. To St. Comgall he would read the pitiful letters from the monks of Candida Casa explaining how they were girt about by enemies and in sore need of help—they who had given help to so many; and so moved was that grand warrior saint that he sent from Bangor to the Picts of Alba band after band of stalwart monks to repay their debt to St. Ninian in the way he would most have appreciated.

These tidings, reaching him from Bangor, must have greatly heartened St. Kentigern when, by all accounts, the Britons and Picts of Alba lived in ever more chaotic conditions. And then, in 573, came news of Roderick's victory at Arderyd. Politically secure at last, the king at once sent messengers to Llanelwy asking the saint to return and help him in the work of reconstruction. Joceline informs us that St. Kentigern was already " preparing to nourish his grey hairs " in his Welsh monastery, happy in the company of his beloved young pupil and relative, St. Asaph. He debated sorely whether he must leave. But he heard the voice of an angel bid him " go back to Glasgow to thy church " ; encouraging him with prophesies of " innumerable people to be won unto the Lord thy God." The bishop had no choice. He wept; but like a true Celtic saint he kept repeating : " My heart is ready, O God, my heart is ready for whatsoever may please Thee." Next day he preached a sermon to his monks explaining to them why he must go. " When the sermon was over he enthroned St. Asaph in the cathedral see, and again blessing and taking leave of them all, went forth by the north door of the church, because he was going forth to combat the northern enemy. After he had gone out, that door was closed, and all who witnessed and heard of his egress and departure bewailed his absence with great lamentations. Hence a custom grew up in that church that that door should never be opened, save once a year on the day of St. Asaph . . . because when he succeeded to St. Kentigern in the government, their mourning was turned into joy."

In Joceline's place Rhygyvarch would undoubtedly have compared St. Kentigern's departure from his Welsh monastery followed by his cousin St. Nidan, by St. Fidan and by five hundred more of his monks, to the miracle of a moving swarm of bees. For just as the exalted humming of swarming bees can be heard afar off, so the chanting of the marching army of missionary monks must have stirred the hearts of all within hearing. Roderick met them at Hoddan near Annan in what is now Dumfriesshire. He was greeted by St. Kentigern with the words : " Glory to God in the highest and on earth peace

to men of good will.'' Small wonder that the king was moved
to subject himself to his inspiring bishop ; and thus to create a
precedent to be followed by a long line of future Christian
kings in Scotland.

Till Glasgow herself was made ready once more to receive
her bishop, St. Kentigern decided, after discussing what was
best with the king, to make his base at Hoddam. From there
he was soon sending forth the usual well-balanced parties of
lettered priests and manual lay-workers to form in his name
new *muinntirs* on the eastern fringes of Galloway and wherever
men had either relapsed from the faith (as had those Britons
of the Solway region who fought against Roderick) or, because
of the unsettled times, had learnt it wrong. Surviving
foundations bearing St. Kentigern's nickname are to be found
at St. Mungo, and as far afield as Lanark and Peebles.

Once reinstated at Glasgow St. Kentigern turned his
energies to organising the large-scale mission he was to lead
into what is now Aberdeenshire. The true Picts of Alba,
still unconquered by the Angles, held for the British and Iro-
Pictish missionaries a somewhat different fascination than
they had once held for the Roman soldiers. Though there is
no record that the Picts ever slew a missionary, and every
evidence to show that they took so kindly and intelligently to
the new religion as to prove the close kinship between the
British and Pictish languages, yet the great Celtic saints kept
arriving in north-eastern Alba one after another. First St.
Ninian reopened the road made by the legions ; then came his
early followers ; then St. Drostan, St. Serf, and, in 562, the
great St. Moluag of Lismore from Bangor. Now some twenty
years later St. Kentigern arrived in the same manner and by
the same well-worn route trodden by St. Ninian and his old
master St. Serf. He brought with him as his chief helpers his
two Welsh disciples St. Nidan and St. Finan. In this district,
with the Grampians to the south and the Moray Forth to the
north, Dr. Simpson has traced four of St. Finan's foundations,
one of which is Lumphanan (Llanfinan) where Macbeth was
killed. To St. Nidan and St. Kentigern he is able to ascribe
two foundations each. St. Kentigern's ancient church at

Kinnoir was close to Huntly where until quite recently people often used the phrase: "Like St. Mungo's work, never done." It is pleasant to think that the work of St. Finan and St. Nidan, though doubtless it did not stop till they died, nevertheless took them back together to Wales, where, in Anglesey, the sites of the two churches of Llanfinan and Llanidan stand companionably close together.

In the Aberdeenshire district too, sixth century Christian settlements must have stood companionably close together. They were certainly quite numerous enough to ensure a well-balanced education for all Pictish children. In the monastery schools they learnt farming and gardening as well as singing, carving, illuminating and reading and writing in Latin. In practising these arts in the spirit of charity they aimed to enrich the beautiful world for which Christ died. Life, they were taught, was simply a preparation for an eternity with God. The joy of discovering they were part of a mighty pattern is to be seen in the unique crosses of Pictland on which the Christian masons carved their symbols of infinity alongside those "sprightly and joyous animal forms" that represent their enduring delight in nature.

Doubtless some of the young monks trained in these "bangors" or "banchories" of Aberdeenshire were among those intrepid missionaries who, towards the end of the century, flocked to answer St. Kentigern's call for volunteers to carry the gospel to the islands of the far north. Joceline tells us that: "He sent forth those of his own whom he knew to be strong in faith, fervent in love, known for doctrine, lofty in religion, towards the Orchades, Noruuagia and Ysalanda, to announce to the dwellers therein the Name of the Lord and the Faith of Christ, for that in those parts the harvest indeed was great, but there were no labourers; and seeing that he was now too old and unable to go himself, he willed that this work should be accomplished by his disciples."

That his disciples did actually accomplish the work demanded of them in the Orkney Islands, Norway and Iceland, has been amply proved. To take the northernmost country first, here is the testimony of a ninth century Viking author.

" Before Iceland was colonised from Norway there were men living there whom the Northmen called *Pápas*; they were Christians, and it is thought they came over the sea from the west, for after them were found Irish books, and bells, and croziers, and other things, so that one could see that they were Westmen." For the word " Irish " substitute "Celtic" which is all it really means to the Viking, and it will be seen as Dr. Simpson remarks, " that there is no reason why the Celtic clerics whose traces were thus found in Iceland may not have included men from St. Kentigern's mission from Strathclyde." As in the Hebrides and the Orkneys and Shetlands the island homes of these early Christian explorers of Iceland still bear the now disused ecclesiastical title brought to Britain by St. Ninian. It is a solemn thought that Celtic *pápas* and their *muinntirs* were planted close to the Arctic circle and there followed the austere pattern of life laid down for them by their spiritual forbears in tropical Egypt.

Even at coastal settlements in Norway, relics of the Celtic clergy have been recovered to vindicate Joceline : though that mission apparently had no more lasting effects than the fabulous mission of St. David to the Jews of Palestine.

Fortunately it was otherwise in the Shetlands and Orkneys where the wealth of sculptured stones, iron handbells and chapel sites—all proved to have existed before the Scandinavian invasion—point to the maintenance of a flourishing Celtic church in the islands. As to the origin of this church the frequent occurrence of St. Ninian's name makes it quite possible that the first *muinntirs* were offshoots from Candida Casa and that St. Kentigern's mission was undertaken as much to strengthen as to convert. One thing seems certain ; and that is that this was a Brito-Pictish undertaking and that, contrary to popular opinion, the Scot St. Columba had nothing to do with it. Even if he had been able to speak the language, all political evidence goes to show that he would have been anything but welcome in the islands after the terrible raid on the Orkneys in 580 undertaken by his protégé, king Aedhan of Dalriada. Then, too, the names of the two islands Papa Westray in the Orkneys and Papa Stour in the Shetlands both point to the early clerics having been British or Pictish. Speaking a dialect devoid of the letter "p," the Scots found the word *pápa* so hard to pronounce that soon after St. Patrick's death they substituted the Syrian word *ab* now changed to abbot. Lastly, the type of Celtic cross found in the islands is the equal-armed and often wheeled cross— mostly found incised on slabs but sometimes to be seen placed on a separately decorated pedestal—which the Brito-Pictish masons evolved from the encircled Chi-Rho monogram brought from Gaul to Candida Casa by St. Ninian. The equally beautiful cross of glory evolved by the Scots has marked differences. The arms always project beyond the halo ; and the pedestal forms part of the whole design. It would seem, then, that Iona did not evangelise the northern islands. That honour goes possibly to Candida Casa and certainly to St. Kentigern's church at Glasgow.

Like his contemporary St. Columba, St. Kentigern was given to uncomfortable peeps into the future. He foresaw the conquest of Britain by the Angles, "and fear came upon all who heard him, and a shower of tears bedewed them." He was also able to tell his monks of the moment when he perceived the entry into heaven of that "most precious carbuncle of Prelates" St. David. Joceline relates too a number of miracles, some, as "How the Lord kept his clothes untouched by any drops of rain, or snow, or hail," greatly resembling those related in Aelred's Life of St. Ninian ; and others, like the following story, so peculiar that they must surely have had some distorted foundation in fact. "The saint," it appears, "was wont to use milk as food and drink." Once, while at Glasgow, he heard that his blacksmith was ailing. Naturally he sent him some of his favourite beverage, assuring him that it would cure him. But the milk was upset into the Clyde where it was miraculously changed into a cheese, portions of which were "kept as relics by many."

It was St. Kentigern's custom to place stone crosses wherever he had "won the people to the dominion of Christ." One of the Glasgow crosses was so immense that it needed, and obtained, angelic help to raise it into position.

" For the cross was very large and never from that time lacked great virtue, seeing that many maniacs and those vexed with unclean spirits are used to be tied of a Sunday night to that cross, and in the morning they are found restored, free, and cleansed, though oftimes they are found dead or at the point of death." Joceline obviously approves this drastic treatment of the insane. But such medieval practices would hardly have been sanctioned by St. Kentigern whose crosses usually replaced objects of pagan veneration and were often used as preaching stations.

When the bishop of Glasgow grew very old " he tied up his chin with a certain bandage and . . . prepared for his soul's departure." This event took place on 13th of January, 600, by which time he " was sighing in his soul for heaven " and had " gathered himself up into his stone bed " surrounded by his loudly lamenting monks. " At dawn the glory of the Lord shone around him, and the monks for fear became as dead men. But the holy old man, comforted by the vision . . . held close converse with the angel as with his closest and dearest friend." When an angelic visitor had come to St. Asaph's to bid St. Kentigern go fight the northern enemy, the saint had wept; but now he smiled. For this angel asked of him nothing more arduous than to await the arrival of the heavenly hosts due to fetch him home the next day; and to await them comfortably in a warm bath. The old bishop faithfully repeated the message; whereupon his monks hurried to prepare the bath " fortified by the Divine Sacraments " and cheered by a " fragrance of wonderful and unspeakable odour " left behind by the angel.

To a saint death is simply the end of a beginning in time. Let us therefore finish the story of St. Kentigern by giving an account of his meeting with St. Columba when both ecclesiastical statesmen were in their prime and Scotland was the field of their activities.

It was a fruitful meeting, otherwise it would not have ended with the exchange of *bachalls*—an act which, in the Celtic church, always signified the ratification of some important agreement. It took place when St. Columba was not far from Glasgow, having followed up one of Aedhan's belligerent thrusts to the east of Drumalban by planting there, at Drymen in Stirlingshire, almost the only one of Iona's original settlements to be found outside Dalriada and the Western Islands. These constant raids on British territory called forth protests. Roderick had already sent an embassy to St. Columba at Iona deploring Aedhan's aggressive tendencies. If there was to be peace between the immigrant Scots and the refugee Britons it was essential that their respective kings should remain within the boundaries already assigned to them by Brude the Pictish overlord; and that the two churches should behave with like discretion. Hence St. Columba's suggestion for a discussion with the leading British statesman on religious and political matters while he was on his way home and thus conveniently in the neighbourhood. Though their kings had long been enemies yet the two saints must have had many mutual friends, among them St. Comgall and St. Kenneth. So the meeting was arranged.

"And when the proper time came the holy father St. Columba went forth, and a great company of his disciples, and of others who desired to behold and look upon the face of so great a man, accompanied him. When he approached the place called Molendinar, where the saint abode at that time, he divided all his people into three bands, and sent forward a message to announce to the holy prelate his own arrival, and that of those who accompanied him. St. Kentigern likewise divided his followers into three groups, placing the juniors in front, the middle-aged next and himself among the aged at the back. As they approached their visitors they sang, ' In the ways of the Lord how great is the glory of the Lord,' while on St. Columba's side they sang with tuneful voices, ' The saints shall go from strength to strength, until unto the God of gods appeareth every one in Sion.' Meanwhile some who had come with St. Columba asked him, saying, ' Hath St. Kentigern come in the first chorus of singers ?' The saint answered, ' Neither in the first nor in the second cometh the gentle saint.' When they asked him how he knew this, he told them, ' I see a fiery pillar in fashion as of a golden crown set with sparkling gems, descending from heaven upon his head, and a light of heavenly brightness encircling him like a certain veil, and covering him, and again returning to the skies. Wherefore it is given to me to know by this sign that, like Aaron, he is the elect of God, and sanctified.' When these two godlike men met they mutually embraced and kissed each other, and having first satiated themselves with the spiritual banquet of Divine words, they after that refreshed themselves with bodily food.''

It is doubtful if the repast approached even present post-war standards; though St. Kentigern would be sure to bring plenty of milk with which, if not to gladden, at least to soften, the heart of his somewhat alarming guest. The conversation promised to be awkward—not because of language difficulties as both men spoke Latin—but because of the delicate subject they were met to discuss. With God and His saints, however, all things are possible. Lions and lambs lie down together without a qualm. Stags and wolves, yoked to the same plough, strain with a will to reach the kingdom of heaven. And so it was with St. Columba of Iona, the quickest-tempered and most attractive of doves; and St. Mungo, the dearly beloved and faithful watch-dog of the rival British church. There was no verbal flying of fur and feathers between them. Each put forward his point of view amicably and even humorously, while together they enjoyed their picnic surrounded by the birds and beasts they loved and who were their constant and admiring friends. It is a picture full of sunlight; all the more delightful because it is but a small, vivid patch in the heart of the Dark Ages.

Sources:
Life of St. Kentigern. Joceline. Ed. Bishop Forbes of Brechin.
The Pictish Nation. Archibald B. Scott.
The Celtic Church in Scotland. W. D. Simpson.
Life of St. Columban. Adamnan. Ed. Huyshe.

Chapter VIII.

ST. COLUMBA

T. NINIAN, St. Patrick, St. David and St. Kentigern were all Britons. A study of their lives reveals in some small measure the achievement of the British branch of the Celtic church in Scotland, Ireland and Wales. But there were two other fruitful branches; the Scotic branch, to which St. Brendan of Clonfert belonged, but which is best represented by St. Columba and his followers at Iona; and the Iro-Pictish branch represented here by St. Columban, that stalwart follower of St. Comgall of Bangor who died in Italy.

To St. Columba himself we owe the conversion of his fellow immigrants, the Scots of Dalriada (now Argyllshire) and of those Picts still living on the eastern outskirts of the district. Within his lifetime sailor monks from Iona had settled on almost every one of the hundreds of islands off the west coast of Scotland; and it was St. Columba's followers who later organised, with amazing results, the conversion of the Angles of Northumbria. The life of St. Cuthbert, the greatest of English saints in the Celtic tradition, would have been impossible without the tireless zeal of missionaries from Iona.

St. Columba was so powerful and influential politically as well as religiously that numerous ancient Irish documents mention facts of interest relating to his life. There are even in Ireland some revealing hymns and poems from his own pen. The English historian Bede naturally writes only of the saint's activities in Alba—and then always with Ptolemy's misleading map of the British Isles in his mind. It will be remembered that on this map Scotland juts out eastwards from the top of a more or less accurately placed England. Therefore when Bede wrote of St. Columba's conversion of the northern Picts it was really the Picts living to the west of Drumalban to whom he referred. But the saint's chief biographer is his relative Adamnan, ninth abbot of Iona during the second half of the seventh century. To show how much times had changed, the Celtic abbot Adamnan was actually foster-father to the exiled English prince Aldfrith; and one of his staunchest friends when later the prince became king of Northumbria. None the less he is still so close to his subject that he is able to gather from " faithful and experienced ancients " and often from witnesses, the glorious evidence of his founder's prophetic vision, his power over the elements, over disease, and even over death. He tells us much, too, of the " sweet and luminous " angels who visited St. Columba.

But as a biography in the modern sense of the word Adamnan's *Life* leaves much to be desired. He seldom mentions the first forty years St. Columba spent in Ireland. Indeed in the very second sentence of his story he hustles the saint, without explanation, into the ship that is to carry him to Iona. None the less, from reliable Irish sources we know that St. Columba was born on December the 7th, 521, on the site of the little village of Garten among the mountains and lakes of Donegal. On his father's side he was a direct descendant of that Niall of the Seven Hostages whose men captured the young St. Patrick on one of their raids on the British coast; while on his mother's side he was related to the royal house of Leinster. With such nobly born parents the child stood a good chance of being elected High King of Erin. But long before he grew up he had made up his mind to renounce this honour for the service of God. In those days all well-bred Irish boys were put in charge of foster-parents. Those selected for St. Columba belonged to a clan who dwelt in the nearby mountains and led a life of hunting and fishing well fitted to develop the courage and harden the muscles of a future warrior prince. But that the little boy might not grow up without proper Christian tuition he also had for foster-father a devout old priest who taught him to read and write. His primer was the Latin psalter; and so often did he rush out, book in hand, from the cell where he studied with his master, to answer the shrill calls of his play-fellows, that they nicknamed him Columkill, or Colum of the cell.

When he was nineteen he made a journey across country

to join the newly founded school of the Irish Pict St. Finbar at Moville, County Down. Here he met a man after his own heart, for St. Finbar was above all a scholar, and already St. Columba (in his own words) desired " to search all the books that might be good for any soul." St. Finbar is known to have been an excellent transcriber of manuscripts, so there must have been a good library at Moville. The only drawback was that he was so childishly jealous of those books he possessed that he would often refuse copyright even to his dearest friends. Reading under his tuition, however, was a different matter and it was not long before he and his enthusiastic new pupil were poring over his chief treasure. This manuscript was significantly known in Ireland as *St. Martin's Gospel*. It apparently contained not only the four gospels, but also the Mosaic Law and the psalter; the whole being translated by St. Jerome into the lovely Latin of the *Vulgate*. This was not yet the version generally used in Ireland. St. Finbar had made a copy of it while teaching at his old school Candida Casa to which place St. Ninian had brought it from Gaul.

While at Moville St. Columba was made a deacon; but even the boldest and most diligent of deacons quailed before the thought of asking St. Finbar's permission to copy such a book. But St. Columba coveted it passionately. For the next twenty years whenever he had a pen in his hand, at the back of his mind he would wish he were transcribing *St. Martin's Gospel*. The consequences of this eventually ungovernable desire changed the whole course of his life.

St. Columba is next to be found in Leinster. His teachers at Moville perceiving him to be a promising poet and singer, sent him for a course of literature and music to the aged bard Gemman. It was this short secular interlude that enabled him to write so vividly in the Gaelic and to appreciate the work of the best Irish bards.

His next abbot was the great St. Finnian of Clonard, Master of the Saints in Ireland, and the second of St. Columba's teachers to have been trained by British clerics. His monastery was in Meath and from all over the country there came to it young men eager to join one of the best religious training

ST. COLUMBA BLESSES THE DEPARTING CRANE

colleges in the land. St. Finnian chose a dozen of his students to be his Twelve Apostles of Ireland. Among this honoured group was St. Columba. Two others already known to us were the Irish Pict St. Kenneth of St. Andrews and Achabo, and the Scot St. Brendan of Clonfert. Three more of the apostles play a part in St. Columba's story; they are St. Brendan of Birr, St. Laisren of Devenish and St. Mobhi of Glasnevin. Their master was a bishop; but the twelve future abbots were ordained and remained presbyters.

St. Mobhi, an Irish Pict, seems to have been the first of St. Finnian's apostles to found a monastery of his own. It was at Glasnevin near Dublin; and there, after his ordination, St. Columba and St. Kenneth joined him, accompanied by St. Comgall, also a pupil of St. Finnian's and already their friend. But in 544 there was an epidemic of the Yellow Plague so virulent that it is said to have killed every third person in Europe. Because it was rife in Ireland St. Mobhi (who died of it the next year) closed his establishment, whereupon St. Columba took to the road and went north to join his people in his father's province of Tirconnel in north-west Ulster.

Here, in 546, he built his first church and monastic group of cells at Derry. Like most of his monasteries (and he founded a hundred in Ireland and Scotland) it stood within sight and sound of the sea. As he wrote, it was—

" That I might see its heaving waves
  Over the wide ocean
  When they chant music to their Father
  Upon the world's course . . .
  That I might hear the song of the wonderful birds,
  Source of happiness,
  That I might hear the thunder of the crowding waves
  Upon the rocks."

There followed one of the happiest periods of St. Columba's life. His outstanding abilities alone would have won him disciples; but because of his lineage he enjoyed a wide-spread additional prestige. It must have been during the next sixteen years that he led a party of pilgrims to the tomb of St. Martin in Tours. He also founded numerous monasteries in Ireland sending forth groups of ardent disciples from his headquarters at Derry. The two best known foundations are Durrow, on the border of King's County and West Meath; and Kells in Meath. A hundred years later the monks of these two Columban monasteries excelled even their tireless founder in illuminating and ornamenting the pages of the gospel they loved so well. There is still extant one manuscript from each monastery—*The Book of Durrow* and *The Book of Kells*. For those who cannot go to Dublin to see the original of *The Book of Kells* there is an excellent reproduction of a few of its three hundred and thirty nine pages. Gerald of Wales, writing in the twelfth century, thinks no man could have written them but only angels. Even a cursory glance humbles the modern art student. Here is a unique and glorious masterpiece; and *The Book of Kells* was but one of thousands of like books wantonly destroyed in the wholesale burning and plundering of British, Pictish and Scotic monasteries which was accomplished in the ninth century by the terrible Vikings.

In 561, at the age of forty, St. Columba went to stay with St. Finbar at Moville. There is nothing particularly remarkable about this: doubtless he had often visited his master before and enjoyed in his monastery the company of their mutual friend St. Comgall, recently established close by at Bangor. But this time St. Columba had secretly determined to make a copy of *St. Martin's Gospel*. Each night he stole to the library and there worked at it with the speed and accuracy of a master scribe till at last he reached the end of the book. He was not known as " the fox " for nothing. Yet in spite of all his precautions, St. Finbar discovered what had been taking place while he slept. His wrath was boundless. St. Columba's temper—all the shorter for the many sleepless nights—was equally roused. Nothing, he said, would make him give up his manuscript. He advised St. Finbar to take the case to the High King's Court at Tara there to be settled once and for all. But the unpredictable occurred. King Diarmait brushed aside the accused's exalted position in the land. His verdict was in favour of St. Finbar. "To every cow," he said, "belongs her call; and to every book her son-book." And with those words ringing in his ears St. Columba was imprisoned. Escaping almost at once, he made his way home to Ulster through the hills. At first he sought consolation in the composition of the moving poem, "Alone am I on the mountain." But by the time he reached his people the saint, the scholar, and the poet in him were all blotted out by the terrible thirst of a proud spirit for revenge. With his position, his looks and his marvellous tongue it was child's-play to rouse his clan. Besides the insult to himself they soon found grievances of their own they were only too keen to settle in battle. Allied clans from Connaught joined them and with St. Columba at their head they marched to Cooldrevney, near Sligo, and there fought and won a satisfyingly bloody victory against King Diarmit's forces.

But the High King appealed to the Church; and a synod was held at Teltown in Meath. The assembled abbots, bishops and priests discussed a situation without precedent, sitting inside a great circular building, the remains of which are still visible. Eventually they excommunicated St. Columba for the shedding of blood and for causing civil war throughout the land.

It was an even deeper disgrace than that which drove St. Patrick to the top of his lonely mountain. Because he was unjustly accused and dethroned, St. Patrick ended by fighting his own cause. But it was one of St. Columba's friends, his fellow apostle St. Brendan of Birr, who rescued him. St. Brendan fought on till he had succeeded in getting the sentence withdrawn. It is good to know that St. Columba never forgot the debt he owed him. When St. Brendan died in 573 he said a special Mass at Iona for the repose of his soul.

As soon as he was once more a member of the Church St. Columba—now fully aware of how nearly his hot Irish blood had cut him off from God—went at once, in all humility, to seek council of his soul-friend St. Laisren of Devenish in Lough Erne. The penance St. Laisren devised, though terrible for St. Columba, was extraordinarily apt. He bade him go into exile to "Alba of the ravens" (thus mournfully described by St. Columba himself) there to win for God as many souls as were lost in the battle. The following poem attributed to St. Columba and bearing unmistakably the hall-mark of his fascinatingly complex personality, illustrates what he must have felt on leaving Derry.

> 'Were the tribute of all Alba mine,
>   From its centre to its border,
>   I would prefer the site of one house
>   In the middle of fair Derry . . .
>   The reason why I love Derry is
>   For its quietness, for its purity,
>   Crowded full of heaven's angels
>   Is every leaf of the oaks of Derry.
>   My Derry, my little oak-grove,
>   My dwelling, and my little cell.
>   Oh, eternal God in heaven above!
>   Woe be to him who violates it."

With such anguished thoughts did St. Columba set sail for Alba in the year 563, taking with him the customary twelve disciples. They were to form the nucleus of the new missionary community among his fellow Scots of Dalriada. In his Song of Farewell he describes his departure—

> " My foot in my sweet little coracle
>   My sad heart still bleeding . . .
>   Large is the tear of my soft grey eye
>   When I look back upon Erin . . ."

Above the Bay of the Coracle, where the saint landed in Iona, there is a hill topped by a cairn called " The Cairn of the Back turned to Ireland." The completion of that cairn opened a new chapter in St. Columba's life.

It would be wrong to imagine that the Scots of Dalriada were completely pagan. After all they came from that north-east corner of Ireland first converted by St. Ninian; and by a strange coincidence they buried their early kings in a Christian cemetery in Iona founded by St. Oran who died there thirteen years before St. Columba's arrival. Even after St. Oran's death the sleeping kings were well guarded. For St. Columba is said to have found a college of seven bishops, two of whom hastened down to the shore to dissuade him from landing. It must have been they who gave Christian burial to Gabhran in 560. This Scotic king was slain when the Picts succeeded in driving the eastward-moving Scots back to the west coast of Alba. So complete was this Pictish victory that their sovereign Brude, ruling from Inverness, refused for the time being, to allow the Scotic overlord to be called king. It was therefore a stricken people to whom St. Columba came : and if they were still Christians it was for the most part in name only. It is true that St. Brendan had made a successful missionary tour of the Western Isles some twenty years before ; but on the Dalriadic mainland there are no outstanding missionaries mentioned before 563 when St. Columba of Iona and his Iro-Pictish contemporary from Bangor, St. Moluag of Lismore founded their respective island communities. The vast majority of missionaries followed the route through British and Pictish territory marked out by St. Ninian.

But in Dalriada they needed a Scot. Knowing this, and feeling their recent humiliation as though it were his own, St. Columba devoted the rest of his life to strengthening and enlarging their shrunken kingdom both spiritually and politically. And just as nineteenth century Quakers managed to combine a strong love of God with prosperous banking; so, St. Columba, combining the life of a typical Celtic saint with the functions of an astute Prime Minister to the King of his choice, contrived marvellously to excel in both spheres.

Adamnan concentrates on the spiritual sphere, dividing his book into three undiluted courses of Prophecy, Divine Miracles and Angelic Visitations. He actually apologises for the sparsity of the " feast of miracles " though a shrunken modern stomach may well quail at their number. None the less, like St. Columba's coracle, we are " borne along against the contrary winds with amazing velocity," so breathless is the pen of Adamnan and so infectious his faith. " Why say more ?" " Why linger we ?" he constantly exclaims, thinking impatiently in the Gaelic and writing in a Latin which he owns to be crude. And so he bears us away to St. Columba's world: long, low islands and mountainous islands are there; large islands and small islands; and always the sea and the white sand.

Iona has so faithfully fulfilled St. Columba's prophecy that after a period of desolation she would once more be famous among the nations, that it is superfluous to describe the island. It would also be tedious to describe the monastery he built on the east side of his island and the rule followed by his monks. It is sufficient to say that he followed in the steps of his British-trained masters. On so small an island the monks could not at first hope to lead more than a precarious existence. But we know they had cows, cattle, a horse and cart, and a kiln, mill and barn for the grain they harvested. They also fished from their little boats.

Every moment St. Columba could spare from his active life of statesman, abbot, missionary and preacher (he had a true poet's eloquence), he spent in his little cell at Iona, somewhat apart from the rest. Here with an ear to " the salt main on which the seagulls cry," and his eyes on the page before him, he copied again and again the Gospel or the Psalter, till he had produced some three hundred volumes in an age when books were rare and precious.

Nor was St. Columba merely a transcriber. He had a large correspondence and wrote from his cell at Iona to console his friend St. Colman for the loss of a devout fly. With twinkling feet and a hundred adoring eyes, the tiny creature had melted the heart of that would-be ascetic by its agreeable practice of exercising on the margin of the scriptures while he read, and of patiently marking the place in his absence. St. Colman mourned its death.

St. Columba, too, if not especially attached to insects, felt tenderly towards birds and beasts. Often he caught glimpses of the future, and one day, going about his duties among the Iona community, he suddenly knew that " a certain guest, a crane " would arrive exhausted from Ireland three days hence to return again three days later. He therefore begged the brethren to be prepared to receive it, not only with the usual hospitality shown to animals in all his monasteries

142

(and how they responded to it!) but with extra warmth as befitted a fellow Scot from Ireland. In due course down fell the crane on the shore. Gently it was picked up and taken to the hospice. After three days nursing, " raising itself on high in the presence of its ministering host, and considering for a little while its course in the air, it returned across the sea to Ireland in a straight line of flight, on a calm day."

Adamnan also tells the equally enchanting story of the saint as detective. " A greedy and very thievish " man of Colonsay set out one day for the coast of Mull. There he hid his boat under tufts of grass and himself in it, waiting till night, that he might slip across to a little island nearby where the sea-calves bred. These seals were both food and light to the brethren and were " ours by right " in Adamnan's words. The thief knew this, but he reckoned without St. Columba's all-seeing eye. Before night came, the monks of Iona had him standing before their master. After admonishment he was sent home, his boat weighed down with sheep to console him for the loss of the seals. For all this, he remained " a wretched robber " and St. Columba (perhaps thinking of his own feeling for books) strove only to keep temptation at bay by feeding him well. " Seeing " that he was about to die he took steps to have him sent a sheep and six pecks of wheat. The abbot of Tiree obeyed this order, but too slowly; so " the presents sent over were used at his funeral."

This abbot of Tiree was St. Columba's disciple, Baithene, another Scotic " leader of numberless souls to the heavenly kingdom," and destined to be the second abbot of Iona. One day he was about to set sail from Iona to return to Tiree. The saint warned him that a whale of wondrous and immense size was already half-way up from the depths of the ocean and purposed that day to raise itself like a mountain on the surface of the water between the two islands. Baithene remained calm. " I and that beast are under the power of God," he said, so the saint blessed him. Sure enough when they were half-way across, with a terrible commotion of waves, up came the mighty whale. But Baithene rose too, and with outstretched arms, and in the name of Christ, he so blessed that beast and those agitated waters that they sank instantly to rest.

There was a constant coming and going between the islands, and in their little leather-lined coracles St. Columba's monks were " wafted without an effort," or fought skilfully or prayerfully with the wind and the waves. Cormac, one of the boldest of them, vainly searched for an " ocean solitude." It seems strange that so intrepid an explorer should long for an island shared only by God, and even stranger that he never found one. Adamnan tells us that many of the monks shared his wish, which may account for his failure. Be that as it may, on his third great voyage Cormac made for the Shetland islands. Knowing that he was bound there St. Columba had begged Brude to protect his disciple from Shetlanders still aghast at Aedhan's recent raid on the Orkneys. But Cormac did not stop there. Finding the islands over full of humanity he left them only to be blown northwards for fourteen days. He reached a region " beyond the limit of human experience," and had his boat nuzzled and indeed besieged by " monsters never before seen and almost indescribable." He feared they would penetrate the frail lining and was in intolerable peril, being unable to alter his course till the south wind changed. Fortunately St. Columba was able to see the whole ghastly scene from his cell, and so harrowed the brethren with his description that by prayer they twisted that south wind into a vigorous northern blast and Cormac was swept rejoicing right back to Iona.

Small wonder that even after his death the saint was not allowed to rest from his labours with the wind. Adamnan tells of one such miracle, in which he himself played an enjoyable part. They were towing heavy timbers across the Sound to build a new church, and what with treacherous currents and devilish winds, made little progress across the summer sea. At last, losing patience, they started a " peevish grumbling " about their saint, taunting him in loud voices with being, after all, a man of no account with God. Pleasing it is to know that St. Columba refrained from smiting them from above for this gross impertinence, as he had often smitten sinners when below. (Once, being forbidden entry into a

library, he even cursed the very books into barren illegibility.)
Maybe, from where he dwelt, the monks appeared as small and
innocent and helpless as St. Colman's fly. Anyhow, we know
that it proved to be, Adamnan says gleefully, a highly profitable
grumble.

Space forbids more; but it is hoped that these few anec-
dotes will whet the appetite of the reader. Diormit, the
saint's devoted servant, is a person well worth meeting; and
Adamnan makes it seem only yesterday that St. Kenneth's
coracle was tossed across the Sound to Iona in a crashing
tempest; only yesterday that St. Brendan called in there to
tell of his latest adventures; or St. Comgall met St. Columba
at Tiree, the granary of the islands, where an important con-
ference was held. We learn how gentle St. Columba could
be to his monks—his " little children." Indeed no lover of
this man and his friends can afford to be without a good
translation of Adamnan's seventh century *Life*. He shares
with Bede—that far more eminent author produced by the
eighth century Celtic Church—the advantage of being delight-
fully easy to read.

But to get a complete portrait of St. Columba his political
influence in Scotland and Ireland must also be recorded.
The year after his arrival in Iona he set off up what is now the
Caledonian Canal to visit the Pictish overlord Brude at
Inverness. His object (in which, as always, he was successful)
was to get better conditions for his down-trodden fellow
Scots.[1] He took with him as advocates and interpreters, his
two Iro-Pictish friends, St. Comgall and St. Kenneth. Bede
declares that he converted the king. But Adamnan makes
Brude resemble Leary in that he was frightened enough of
the saint's power to give him permission to preach to his own
people; but that he remained a stubborn pagan and clung to
his druids.

A year after the battle of Arderyd—in 574 when St.
Kentigern was recalled to Glasgow—King Connall of Dalriada
died. St. Columba seized the opportunity. He ignored the

[1]The Scots began to leave Dalriada in Ireland to colonise Dalriada in Scotland at
the end of the fifth century.

claims of Conall's clan to the throne and placed on it Aedhan, whose father Gabhran had been slain by the Picts shortly before St. Columba's arrival in Iona.[1] It is recorded that at his enthronement the saint annointed him, thus creating a precedent to be followed by long lines of Christian kings. Indeed our own king is lineally descended from Aedhan who proved an efficient and vigorous ruler: for between them the king and his ecclesiastical minister ensured the eventual supremacy of the Scots in Scotland.

Dunadd, the capital of Dalriada, was a hill fortress rising from the Moss of Crinan. Here Aedhan planned the raids that gained for the Scots, even before his death, the whole of Argyllshire and north-west Scotland. In 580 he even led a fleet to the Orkneys; but his occupation of the islands was short-lived. Such, too, was the wrath it roused in Pictish breasts that, as we already know, St. Columba had to ask Brude for a safe-conduct even for his disciple Cormac when that would-be hermit announced his intention of seeking a lone island in the Shetlands. But in all his thrusts Aedhan was encouraged by St. Columba's never-failing support. Adamnan records how on one occasion the saint bade Diormit " Ring the bell " (his little square iron hand-bell) to assemble the monks. He had had a vision of Aedhan leading the Scots into battle against a Pictish clan dwelling in what we now call Clackmannanshire. He besought them to pray for the victory of their soldiers over the " barbarians." After some time he was able to announce that their prayers were answered though at the cost of three hundred and three Scotic lives.

The meeting between St. Kentigern and St. Columba, at which a working agreement was reached—at least temporarily —between the two nations and the two churches, has already been described. Partly as a result of it the numerous Kilcolumcilles, or churches of Colum of the cell, are almost all within the enlarged Scotic boundaries. Columba seems always to have been known by his nickname so it is a mistake to confuse his foundations with those of St. Drostan's disciple

[1]Aedhan's uncle on his mother's side was the Briton St. Drostan who worked in north-eastern Aberdeenshire at the beginning of the sixth century.

St. Colm whose church sites are to be found in Buchan and Caithness, and who is even known as " Colm, bishop in the Orkneys."

But if St. Columba ceased to trespass on British and Pictish territory, the Irish Pict St. Moluag wandered freely among the Scots. He planted offshoots of St. Comgall's Bangor in such western islands as Mull, Lewis and Skye, working from his base at Lismore. How greatly his rival irked St. Columba can be deduced from the delicious legend recovered for us by a native of Lismore, the Rev. D. Carmichael.

" St. Moluag was sailing towards Lismore when he beheld a boat carrying St. Columba and making for the Lismore shore at highest speed. St. Columba's craft was the faster. When St. Moluag saw that he was likely to be beaten he seized an axe, cut off his little finger, threw it on the beach, some distance away, and cried out, ' My flesh and blood have first possession of the island, and I bless it in the Name of the Lord.' St. Columba, seeing that he was outwitted, began to invoke various curses on St. Moluag's occupation.

" ' May you have the alder for your firewood,' wished St. Columba.

" ' The Lord will make the alder burn pleasantly,' replied St. Moluag.

" ' May you have the jagged ridges for your pathways,' exclaimed St. Columba.

" ' The Lord will smooth them to the feet,' answered St. Moluag." Fortunately for the immortal souls of both saints their meetings ceased when St. Moluag left the islands for the mainland where he seems to have followed St. Ninian's well-worn track, leaving a group of settlements in Aberdeen-shire, and finally dying at Rosemarkie, Ross-shire.

Towards the end of St. Columba's life St. Donnan, a Briton apparently trained at the lately rebuilt Candida Casa, was at work in the island of Eigg.[1] It is said that Columcille refused to meet him and had no qualms about prophesying his martyrdom there at the hands of the Vikings. But in defence

[1]The northernmost of his church sites on the mainland is in Sutherland. He followed St. Ninian's route.

of St. Columba let it be remembered that he was himself a kind of martyr. It took him his whole life completely to conquer the proud prince and the astute politician within him. Only a mighty saint could have won such a battle.

So much for the saint's position in sixth century Scotland. The year after Aedhan's coronation St. Columba took him over to Ireland where at Drumceatt, a hill now known as the Mullagh in County Londonderry, the High King was to hold an important council of chiefs and clergy. The unexpected guests were scarcely welcome; yet, with his matchless eloquence, St. Columba contrived to win all three of his petitions. He asked and obtained the release of a state prisoner; he asked and obtained permission for those Dalriadic clans still living in north-east Ireland to pay tribute to, and be under the control of his protégé Aedhan. Then—a poet himself—he pleaded for the bards. There were three learned orders in Ireland, the druids, the judges and the bards. The numbers and demands of the bards had gradually become so insupportable a burden on the country that the High King proposed the abolition of the order. St. Columba achieved a satisfactory compromise. He pointed out their invaluable services to the nation by the preservation of its history in their chronicles of great events; but he advised a drastic pruning of their numbers. So grateful were the bards that twelve hundred of them sang a poem in St. Columba's praise. They did it with such volume and fervour that the saint was moved to sinful pride. A friend is said to have pointed out that the sky above him was a mass of sniggering demons. On seeing the repellent sight the saint was cut to the heart and cried out that no one should be thus praised till he had run his full course. Baulked, the demons shrank from sight.

It is to be feared, though, that the demons relished St. Columba's next two visits to Ireland for on both occasions disagreements led to battles in which he was victorious. But without doubt they were finally routed by the angels of Derry when the saint revisited his first and most beloved foundation.

Some say that it was during this visit to Derry that St. Columba composed his magnificent Latin hymn. There is also a strong tradition that he wrote it as an act of contrition for all the blood he had caused to be shed in Ireland. So vast is the compass of the poem, and so Miltonic its flavour, that it might almost be called " Paradise Lost and Regained." Even a few extracts will show how the poet's mind ranged from the dread darkness of hell, to the glory of the heaven won for mankind by the sufferings of Christ.

> " Horror of night : when none can work,
> Wailing of men, and flooding tears,
> Opening the books by conscience writ,
> Riving of hearts with guilty fears . . .
>
> Kings' earthly glory fleeteth fast
> And for a moment is its stay.
> God hath all might, and at a nod
> The giants fall beneath his sway . . .
>
> Mark how the power of God supreme
> Hath hung aloft earth's giant ball
> And fixed the great encircling deep,
> His mighty hand supporting all . . .
>
> But we shall soar our Lord to meet,
> And so with Him shall ever be,
> To reap the due rewards amidst
> The glories of Eternity."[1]

" Horror of night : when none can work "—St. Columba could never bear to be idle. To this day his spirit is active in Iona. Yet Diormit found him, one wintry day, weeping because he felt his lay brothers were sorely over-worked. They were even harder pressed at harvest time. But Adamnan tells how every night while returning worn out to the monastery each labourer felt miraculously refreshed. Humbly kneeling they begged St. Baithene, who was in charge of them, for an explanation. He said : " Ye know that our senior, Columba, mindful of our toil, thinks anxiously about us and grieves that we come to him so late ; and by reason

[1] The whole of the *Altus Prosator* is translated by Canon Mitchell in Appendix II of E. C. Trenholme's *Story of Iona*.

that he comes not in body to meet us, his spirit meets our steps, and that it is which so much consoles and makes us glad." And hearing these words, still kneeling, with great joy and with hands spread out to heaven, they venerate Christ in the holy and blessed man."

Adamnan himself shall complete this sketch by telling in his own incomparable words of the saint's last day on earth.

" And so at the end of the same week, that is on the Sabbath [Saturday, the ninth of June, 597], he and his dutiful attendant, Diormit, go to bless the granary which was nearby. And on entering it, when the Saint had blessed it and two heaps of corn stored up in it, he uttered these words with giving of thanks, saying: ' Greatly do I congratulate the monks of my household that this year, also, if I should perchance have to depart from you, you will have enough for the year without stint.' And hearing this word Diormit, the attendant, began to be sorrowful, and to speak thus: ' Often dost thou make us sad, Father, at this time of the year, because thou dost make mention so often of thy passing away.' To whom the Saint made this answer: ' I have a certain little secret chat to hold with thee, and if thou wilt firmly promise me to disclose it to no one before my death, I shall be able to tell thee something more clearly as to my going hence.' And when the attendant, on bended knees, had finished making this promise according to the Saint's wish, the venerable man thereupon thus speaks: ' In the Sacred Volumes this day is called the Sabbath, which is, interpreted, Rest. And this day is truly a Sabbath day for me, because it is for me the last day of this present laborious life, on which I rest after the fatigues of my labours; and this night, at midnight, when begins the solemn day of the Lord, according to the saying of the Scriptures, I shall go the way of my fathers. For already my Lord Jesus Christ deigns to invite me, to Whom, I say, in the middle of this night, He Himself inviting me, I shall depart. For so it has been revealed to me by the Lord Himself.' Hearing these sad words, the attendant began to weep bitterly. And the Saint tried to console him as well as he could.

"After this the Saint goes out of the granary, and, returning to the monastery, sits down halfway at the place where afterwards a cross, fixed in a mill-stone, and standing to this day, is to be seen at the roadside. And while the Saint, weary with age as I have said, rested there, sitting for a little while, behold the white horse, a faithful servant, runs up to him, the one which used to carry the milk pails to and fro between the byre and the monastery. He, coming up to the Saint, wonderful to tell, lays his head against his breast—inspired as I believe by God, by whose dispensation every animal has sense to perceive things according as its Creator Himself has ordained—knowing that his master was soon about to leave him, and that he would see him no more, began to whinny and to shed copious tears into the lap of the Saint as though he had been a man, and weeping and foaming at the mouth. And the attendant, seeing this, began to drive away the weeping mourner, but the Saint forbade him, saying : ' Let him alone, let him alone, for he loves me. Let him pour out the tears of his bitter lamentation into this my bosom. Lo ! now, thou, man as thou art, and possessing a rational soul, couldst in no wise know anything about my departure hence save what I myself have just now told thee : but to this brute beast, devoid of reason, the Creator Himself has clearly in some way revealed that his master is about to go away from him.' And so saying, he blessed his servant the horse as it sadly turned to go away from him.

" And then, going on and ascending the knoll that overlooks the monastery, he stood for a little while on its top, and there standing and raising both hands he blessed his monastery, saying : ' Upon this place, small though it be, and mean, not only the kings of the Scotic people, with their peoples, but also the rulers of barbarous and foreign races, with the people subject to them, shall confer great and no common honour : by the Saints also even of other churches shall no common reverence be accorded to it.'

" After these words, coming down from the knoll and returning to the monastery, he sat in his hut transcribing the Psalter ; and coming to that verse of the thirty-third Psalm, where it is written : ' But they that seek the Lord shall not want any good thing.' ' Here,' he says, ' I must stop at the foot of this page, and what follows let Baithene write.'

" The last verse which he had written is very applicable to the dying Saint, to whom the good things of eternity shall never be lacking ; and the verse which follows is indeed very suitable to the Father who succeeded him and was the teacher of his spiritual sons, namely : ' Come, ye children, hearken unto me : I will teach you the fear of the Lord.' And he, Baithene, as his predecessor recommended, succeeded him not only as teacher, but also as a writer.

" After transcribing the verse at the end of the page, as above mentioned, the Saint enters the church for the vesper mass of the vigil of the Lord's Day, and as soon as this is over, he returns to his cell and sits up throughout the night on his bed, where he had the bare rock for pallet and a stone for pillow, which to this day stands by his grave as his monumental pillar. And so, there sitting up, he gives his last commands to the Brethren, his attendant alone hearing them, saying : " These my last words I commend to you, O my sons, that ye have mutual and unfeigned charity among yourselves, with peace : and if, according to the example of the holy Fathers, ye shall observe this, God, the Comforter of the good, will help you ; and I, abiding with Him, will intercede for you ; and not only will the necessaries of this present life be sufficiently supplied by Him, but the rewards of the good things of Eternity, prepared for those who keep His Divine commandments, shall also be bestowed."

" Thus far, told in brief narrative, are put down the last words of our venerable patron as he was passing away from this weary pilgrimage to the heavenly country.

"After which, as the happy last hour gradually approached, the Saint was silent. Then, when the bell began to toll at midnight, rising in haste he goes to the Church, and running faster than the others he enters it alone, and on bended knees falls down in prayer at the altar. At the same moment Diormit, his attendant, who followed more slowly, sees from a distance the whole church filled within with Angelic light round about the Saint. And as he drew near to the door, the same light which he had seen suddenly withdrew, and this light a few others of the Brethren who stood afar off also saw. Diormit, therefore, entering the church, moans out with mournful voice: "Where art thou, Father?" And as the lights of the Brethren had not yet been brought in, groping his way in the dark he finds the Saint lying before the altar, and raising him up a little and sitting down by him he lays the holy head on his bosom. And meanwhile the community of monks, running up with lights, began to weep at the sight of their dying Father. And as we have learned from some who were there present, the Saint, his soul not yet departing, with open eyes upturned, looked round about on either side with wonderful cheerfulness and joy of countenance on seeing the holy Angels coming to meet him. Diormit then lifts up the holy right hand of the Saint that he may bless the choir of monks. But the venerable Father himself at the same time moved his hand as much as he was able, so that what was impossible to him to do with his voice at his soul's departure he might still do by the movement of his hand, namely, give his blessing to the Brethren. And after thus signifying his holy benediction, immediately breathed forth his spirit. And it having left the tabernacle of the body, the face remained so ruddy and wonderfully gladdened by the vision of the Angels that it seemed not to be that of one dead, but of one living and sleeping."

So died the first abbot of Iona; exactly 200 years after the foundation of Candida Casa, and in the same year in which St. Augustine landed among the Saxons of Kent.

Sources

Life of St. Columba. Adamnan. Ed. Huyshe.
Ecclesiastical History of England. Bede. Ed. J. A. Giles.
The Historical Saint Columba. W. Douglas Simpson.
The Story of Iona. E. C. Trenholme.
The Pictish Nation, Its People and its Church. Archibald C. Scott.
The Celtic Church in Scotland. W. Douglas Simpson.
Irish Monasticism. John Ryan.
The Book of Kells. Described by Sir Edward Sullivan. Studio Publication.

CHAPTER IX.

ST. COLUMBAN

CONCLUDING a letter to Pope Boniface IV, St. Columban writes: "For the rest, O Holy Father and brethren, pray for me, most wretched of sinners and for my fellow pilgrims, near the holy places and ashes of the Saints, and particularly near Peter and Paul." Even now many a Celt is convinced that localities are affected for good or evil by what dramas have occurred in them or by what remains they contain. In St. Columban's day no Christian doubted it. Hence, throughout the Dark Ages, the never-ceasing flow of pilgrims to Rome. They went to pray at the tombs of the martyrs Peter and Paul whose written works they knew by heart and whose valiant lives they strove to emulate. It was largely because Rome contained these two graves, that her bishop, dwelling in so sacred a spot, was acknowledged by the Catholic Church in the West to be her supreme head, the Father of all *abs* and *pápas*.[1]

Countless were the abbots, *pápas* and bishops from the British Isles who made their pilgrimage to Rome during the fifth, sixth and seventh centuries. The monks of St. Comgall's Bangor thought nothing of the journey. It was they who first carried the gospel back to Teutonic Europe so that by the end of the sixth century they were planting small patches of Christian Ulster astoundingly far from their mother house.[2] St. Comgall himself was only deterred from exploring and settling on the continent by a wise superior who showed him that it was his destiny not to go abroad himself but to train others to be missionaries.

Why his disciple St. Columban never reached Rome remains a mystery. During the last years of his life he was,

[1]After the bishop of Rome adopted the title pope, or pápa, it was abandoned by lesser clerics in western Europe except in the remoter Pictish parts of the British Isles.

[2]Traces of them are to be found as far east as Bulgaria, Poland and even Russia. The British branch of the Celtic Church also sent missionaries to the Continent. But the Scots concentrated on the Anglo-Saxons.

comparatively speaking, quite close to the city. But he never made the necessary journey, remaining in the monastery he had founded at Bobbio in Northern Italy till his death on 23rd of November, 615.

Three years later his staunch friend and successor, abbot Athala, welcomed into the monastery school a small boy called Jonas who had arrived from the village of Susa in the mountains of Piedmont to be educated at Bobbio. He proved an apt pupil. It was not long before he had learnt to read Latin in his psalter and was eagerly mastering the contents of those precious copies of the classics to be found in the library. We get some idea of the standards of scholarship among the students of St. Comgall's Bangor (and indeed of the fifth century students at Candida Casa also) when we learn how many and what kind of books were still to be found in the distant daughter houses of St. Gall and Bobbio when the two libraries were respectively catalogued in the ninth and tenth centuries. At Bobbio there were still 700 manuscripts, many of them in Celtic script. Two books of special interest are a copy of St. Mark's Gospel with notes in Celtic by St. Columban himself.[1]; and a copy of his commentary on the psalms written in Latin but again with extra notes in Celtic.[2] St. Gall set out from Bangor with St. Columban and eventually founded a monastery in what is now Switzerland. There, in the tenth century, there were still five hundred and fifty volumes to be found, thirty of them entirely written in Celtic script. To emphasise how much we have lost let it be remembered that of those thirty only one survives to-day.[3] St. Gall possessed a copy of St. Paul's epistles in Greek: while both libraries contained texts of all the best Greek and Latin authors, including Aristotle, Demosthenes, Cicero, Virgil, Horace, Juvenal and Martial. Bobbio was indeed a scholar's paradise. The monks also fed Jonas' young mind with the *Lives* of many saints; loving above all to tell him of the strange life of their own special saint who had come here

[1]Now at Turin.
[2]Now at Milan.
[3]As we would expect all the books extant in the monasteries and which contain Celtic, are written, apparently, in the Brito-Pictish as opposed to the Scotic dialect.

from the very ends of the earth. Small wonder that he enjoyed his childhood.

When Jonas had grown up, attained the proud position of abbot's secretary, and journeyed about the continent on the monastery's business, he constantly met men and women who had known and loved St. Columban in the days when he lived in what are now France and Switzerland. So it is not surprising that twenty years after his arrival at Bobbio he should be chosen by the third abbot Bertulf to write the life of their great founder. After an arduous missionary campaign in Belgium Jonas gathered together the material he had gradually amassed and within the next four years he wrote the book.

It ought to have been an even greater masterpiece than Adamnan's *Life of St. Columba*. For St. Columban's story is equally enthralling and Jonas, being a quarter of a century nearer to his subject, had a far greater choice of living witnesses to question. Yet he fails lamentably as a biographer. Small details he paints to perfection. But he leaves unwritten those things which he ought to have written. It is hard to forgive the almost total neglect of the fifty years Columban first spent in Ireland; they explain so much. Again he never mentions the long, brave fight with the bishops of Gaul and with the very Pope himself, to be allowed to keep Easter on the date he and his Celtic Church were convinced was the right one. It may be that Jonas thought this episode did not redound to St. Columban's credit and that, for the same reason, he is silent on that marvellously characteristic letter written to Boniface IV on the subject of heresy. But there is no excuse whatever for writing nothing of the old saint's last months at Bobbio. It is easier to forgive Jonas when he writes those things which he ought not to have written and so misleads us with wrong dates and names which he could well have verified.

But if Jonas is oversparing with information the native annals of Ireland are worse, for they do not mention St. Columban at all. Two early martyrologies record his name and call him " The abbot who was in Italy." But it was the

ST. COLUMBAN IN THE VOSGES

custom, in the annals, to ignore saints who went to the continent. Moreover St. Columban was the more likely to pass unnoticed as he bore so very common a name. It is said that a contemporary abbot once asked a monk called Colman to go and fetch something out of the river. Perfect obedience was the rule, and behold, when he turned round there were twelve monks in the water! Bede, however, quotes from a letter written in 605 mentioning " the Abbot Columbanus in France."

And fortunately, in the seventeenth century, Father Patrick Fleming took upon himself the task of rescuing many Irish saints from obscurity. A friend in Paris, similarly engaged, and about to publish his finds, directed Father Fleming's attention to Jonas' *Life of Columban*, an edition of which he had incorporated in his new collection. Before Father Fleming was killed by Lutheran peasants near Prague he had grown so fond of the saint that he loved above all to devote himself to " my Columbanus," and, in his continental travels, he had managed to collect large quantities of the saint's own writings.

In Father Fleming's day Europe was almost as unsettled as it was a thousand years before when St. Columban lived. Ignorant though he was of Ireland, Jonas does note this contrast between it and the ever seething continent. " Ireland," he writes, " is situated in the extreme ocean and, according to common report, is charming being productive of various nations undisturbed by contests with other people. Here live the race of the Scots[1] who, although they lack the law of the other nations, flourish in the doctrine of Christian strength and exceed in faith all the neighbouring tribes."

Here then, in Leinster, St. Columban was born about 540. The famous young prince Columba had by then almost finished his studies and it is believed that like him St. Columban was of noble birth. If so, though brought up by foster-parents, he must have had a full and pleasant childhood. The great *duns* of the chiefs were almost self-supporting and any boys

[1]St. Comgall and St. Columban were Irish Picts. But on the Continent all inhabitants of " Scotia " were dubbed Scots.

living in them were an important part of the busy community. They herded the sheep, pigs and cattle and they helped to bring in the harvest. They learnt archery, swimming and riding, and the use of the sword and the spear; and so at home did they become in the forests, hills and rivers of their country that at an early age they could catch and cook their own food. It must have been partly this outdoor training that gave St. Columban such marvellous powers of endurance and made of him so wise a farmer and administrator.

Every three years well-bred boys were taken to the great gatherings of the chiefs and princes where they found all the delights of a fair and the excitements of athletic contests. There, too, they came in contact with the great ones of their land. Many were fit objects for youthful hero-worship. For the Brehon Laws show how high a standard was expected of an Irish king. He must be altogether " free from falsehood . . . and from unworthy conduct towards his people." The value of righteousness was further emphasised by the way those little Irish boys learnt to read. First they mastered their elements—the Latin alphabet. Then, at six, they were given the Latin psalter as their reader so that by ten years old they often had all the psalms by heart.

Some three or four years after he had reached this stage in his education St. Columban decided to dedicate himself to God. He told his poor mother he must at once leave home and friends and set out for St. Senell's school far away on an island in Lough Erne. St. Senell, like the two St. Brendans, and St. Columba and St. Kenneth, was one of St. Finnian's Twelve Apostles of Ireland. It seems probable, too, that he belonged to St. Columban's clan. These were both attractions though it may well have been the school's famous course of studies in the scriptures that drew the boy. Nothing his mother told him of the awful hardships and fasts ahead of him or of her bitter grief at losing him so soon, could change his mind. Though she sought desperately to block the doorway with her body, he stepped over her outstretched sobbing form and hurried away—a small, purposeful figure set on the long road to heaven.

St. Columban lived on St. Senell's little haven of an island for about six years, during which time the outside Irish world was disturbed by tribal wars and terrified by hideous visits of the plague. Jonas says, " his fine figure, his splendid colour and his noble manliness made him beloved by all," so no doubt he was happy in his new home. He found time, among his many monkish duties, to write a commentary on the psalms he knew so well, and several other works also well suited for monastery textbooks. But spiritually he began to outgrow the school. He envied those monks under the far sterner rule of his fellow Pict St. Comgall living on another island in the lough. When St. Comgall departed about 558 to found the monastery of Bangor, St. Columban took to the road once more and joined him there.

On good authority we have it that St. Comgall first trained with St. Fintan, severest of Irish abbots. His other two masters were St. Finnian of Clonard and St. Mobhi of Glas-nevin. To illustrate the great truths he taught his monks St. Comgall loved to take examples from the land he had worked in his youth. He was as much a farmer saint as his friend St. Brendan of Clonfert was a sailor. Naturally he shared with other Celtic saints their fascinating fellowship with birds and beasts. Bangor was not his only foundation and he often had occasion to travel. There is a story that while walking beside Lough Foyle he and his monks were entranced to hear in the distance a group of swans sadly singing their death song. " Holy father," they cried, " bid the melodious birds come near us that we may caress them." At the abbot's call the white birds drifted nearer and one, bolder than the rest, rose from the water and " flew into the bosom of St. Comgall."

He had also been a soldier as was his father before him. He therefore stressed the importance of loyalty and obedience to the great Commander in the battle against Evil. Because he was so hospitable a man, Bangor soon became a kind of Christian club frequented by all the great saints who hastened thither by sea and by land. Many are the stories attached to these visits. Some have a modern flavour: as when St.

Kenneth is welcomed and asked to preach on Sunday. Others, like the following episode, give glimpses of a forgotten world.

One day when St. Comgall knelt at the feet of yet another travel-worn saint to take off his untanned hide shoes and wash his feet, he gave an example of his saintly power of insight, for he perceived that there was something amiss with the shoe. He exhorted any demon within to come out. " How fortunate that he has met you," said the demon coming out of the shoe and referring to the saintly wearer, " for I should not have allowed him to rest two nights in the same place for the partiality that he has shewn to his own shoes above those of his congregation." The stricken visitor then confessed to St. Comgall that so comfortable did he find these unworthy shoes that he often wiped them with any grease on his hands in an effort to prolong their life.

St. Comgall's monks must have been overjoyed at the approach of a guest; for it meant contact with the outside world and some slight relaxation from the perpetual Lent they kept. It is not easy to imagine how they managed to do all the hard work attached to a self-supporting monastery with only primitive tools and with so little food and sleep.[1] They paused in their work eight times a day to celebrate the divine praises in their church. Indeed perhaps their secret lay in the fact that everything they did from writing in the cold library, where the books hung in their satchels on the walls, to making their own clothes or building the boats in which they fished or sailed to Alba, was undertaken in so ardent a spirit of prayer that they felt little fatigue, living, for the most part, in a rare state of peace and happiness. Seeing these men, outsiders called the Bangor way of living, " The Good Rule." " Verily," St. Bernard wrote of Bangor, " the place was holy and fruitful in saints, plentifully rendering a harvest to God." The number and quality of the saints it produced proves how truly the Martyrology of Donegal judges St. Comgall when it states that he " kindled in the hearts of men an unquenchable fire of the love of God."

[1] A meal consisted of bread, vegetables and water. Later St. Comgall (perhaps influenced by St. Kentigern) allowed the addition of milk.

St. Columban was so happy in his cell at Bangor that he remained there for thirty years. Tradition has it that he had charge of the teaching department of the monastery. This gave him the opportunity to attain the wide classical knowledge he later revealed in his letters. It is said that one of the future saints he taught was a small boy who found learning intolerably hard till an angel, pitying his plight, arrived in the classroom to give him special coaching. Thereafter his progress was so rapid that by the time he grew up intellect seemed the one thing worth praying for. The abbot became alarmed but the young man said staunchly : " If I have my intellect subject to the Almighty at all times, I would not sin against the Lord, nor yield to the devil."

Great multitudes of devils were to be seen at times warring against the outer monastery walls. They even succeeded in knocking parts of them down. But those in their little huts within were well drilled by their abbot in the art of spiritual warfare. They kept them at bay by a constant barrage of holy song and prayer. Unless we recapture some little of the burning love of Christ which transformed the Bangor monks they must remain in our minds as creatures not far removed from madmen. But they made of life so apparently harsh a battle to fit themselves and those who depended on them to join their Master in eternity : and that was a joyful labour. Their joy is still plain to be seen in the glorious colours and endless spiral designs created by the monks who illuminated the scriptures, and in the exquisite work on the metal covers which protected such treasures. The contents they had by heart ; living within them as vividly as the works of their own famous bards. St. Columban writes to Pope Gregory of " our masters and Irish ancients, philosophers and computists " plainly counting them the equals in their own spheres to anything the continent could produce.

It was St. Columban's stubborn loyalty to the practices and traditions of his beloved country that was to be his undoing in Gaul. At fifty, when he left Bangor, he had attained that inner strength which makes a man greatly loved or hated ; and though it is not clear why he went to Gaul, it is easy to see that one possessed of his gift of leadership and living the gospel as interpreted by St. Comgall, would not shelter for ever behind the pages of books. Some say he first went to Brittany to help twelve thousand British refugees fled from the onslaughts of the Anglo-Saxons, and that the conditions he found there were so appalling that he moved on. But he was never known to be daunted by bad conditions before or afterwards. Others maintain that he was imbued with the spirit of wandering common to his race and that he merely sought a place to live his monastic life in freedom.

Jonas has it that St. Columban and his twelve disciples "embarked and began the dangerous journey across the channel and sailed quickly with a smooth sea and favourable wind to the coast of Brittany. There they rested for a while and discussed their plans anxiously until finally they decided to enter the land of Gaul." Some Breton monks joined the expedition.

Although, unlike the Britons with the Anglo-Saxons, the Gallo-Romans had not contested the Frankish invasion (thus ensuring a far greater likeness between the new France and the old Gaul than between Britain and England) yet St. Columban's party arrived in a land reduced by these invasions and by civil war to a state of such abandoned anarchy " that the longing to root out the lusts of the flesh was to be found only in a few." Murder and torture abounded and Bishop Gregory of Tours writes in his history of the Franks that the church in Gaul suffered more in this period of warring factions than in the persecution of Diocletian. Bishops there still were; but their churches were used as much as sanctuaries for those fleeing from their tormentors as for the worship of God. Gregory's stories show the helpless anger of the Church confronted by brute force. After the murder on his roof of one Berthefred fleeing from Childebert of Austrasia, "the bishop was filled with grief not only because he had been unable to afford protection but also because he had seen polluted with human blood the place where he was wont to pray and where the relics of the saints were gathered together. King Childebert sent him gifts to distract him but he would not be comforted."

ST. GALL IN SWITZERLAND

King Childebert was one of the hateful Teutonic family of Merovingians descended from the first Frankish king, Clovis. They had divided most of Gaul between them murdering each other so successfully while doing so that by the year of 590, when St. Columban arrived on the scene, of four brothers, only one remained alive. He was Guntrum of Burgundy, uncle of Childebert, and known as " the good " though by Irish standards he was quite unfit to be a king. Because they were men of God and their presence (he hoped) might help to expiate a particularly horrid crime on his conscience, Guntrum welcomed St. Columban to his turbulent kingdom and gave leave to this strangely garbed party of foreigners to settle in the wild mountains of the Vosges.

No ordinary missionary would have chosen the Vosges as his headquarters; for past ravages of invading Bavarians and Huns had destroyed the Roman towns and roads and decimated the population. The district had sunk back into a wilderness of forest haunted by dangerous wild animals. But St. Columban strode into it, carrying the cross in front of him in one hand while with the other he rang his little bell to scare the affronted demons of the place. His holy books hung from his shoulder in their satchel and his only weapon against prowling beasts of prey was his certainty that they were there to serve him. His monks, the great St. Gall and his beloved young namesake among them, followed him chanting their psalms.

For Annegray, their first settlement, they chose the site of a ruined Roman town, and at once they started their pioneer work, felling the trees and draining, clearing and preparing the ground for seed. Until they produced their own food they were dependent on neighbours for help. These were few; but so urgent were the prayers of the starving brothers that always, just in time, someone felt impelled to go and see what was wrong in that part of the forest. Most of these people spoke Teutonic dialects and St. Gall began, in his pleasing Celtic script, to make a dictionary of useful phrases for conversation with their Latin equivalents. Soon the story of the wise men singing in the wilderness brought sick and sorrowing from all around. According to Jonas, St. Columban, over-worked, his monks often stricken with malaria ("either as a test or because of some sin ") was not at first best pleased to see them. But " when he was unable to rid himself of their importunities . . . he healed the infirmities of all who came."

To these dwellers in the Dark Ages the white-robed monks seemed to have come, not from a different country but from a different world. There was an echo of its peace in the sound of their bells; and " so great was the might of their patience, love and mildness that no one could doubt that the God of mercy dwelt among them." Broken bodies were healed, and for ailing souls there was available " the saving grace of Penitence." For this remedy St. Columban " perceived that the people were rushing in from all directions." He therefore decided on a second site eight miles from Annegray. This was Luxieul, also planted on the remains of Roman civilisation. Jonas relates that the monks found there " baths constructed with unusual skill." It became the chief monastery and the abbot divided his time between it, Annegray and a third foundation at Fontaines, built soon after to relieve still further congestion.

All these saints and sinners depended on their abbot. He had to establish the rule which they were to follow. He had to decide on the nature and severity of the treatment meted out to different grades of sinners by the Soul-Friends to whom they confessed their crimes against God and man. He followed the teaching of St. Comgall as far as he could; but he was confronted by many problems unheard of in Bangor. To solve these he needed quiet in which to hear the will of God. Seeking a refuge in the forest, he found " an immense cliff with precipitous sides and rocky paths difficult for men." At the top was a hollow in the rock. " Entering to explore its hidden recesses he found inside it the home of a bear and the bear itself. He ordered the beast to depart and not to return to that place. The animal mercifully went, nor did she dare to come back again."

As always in Celtic monasteries young students were welcome. Jonas mentions the names of several of the small boys at school at Luxieul whom he himself knew as bishops and abbots of France. One of these young noblemen, Domoal, often went alone to the cave " to tell the father when certain events happened at the monastery and to carry back his directions to the brethren." He usually stayed several days waiting on the saint, and though there was little work entailed in feeding him, the child complained bitterly that it " tired his knees " carrying water up the cliff. Pitying his frailty, St. Columban bade him " make a little hole at the back of the rock " and when it was dug water began to flow. It does so still ; and is locally said to have the power to heal like the water from the spring at Lourdes.

Another of these schoolboys, Chagnoald, afterwards bishop of Laon, remembered the father's ways with the beasts and birds of the forest. " These came immediately at his command and he stroked them with his hand." They would frolic round the saint " just as cats frisk about their mistresses," and he told Jonas he had often seen him " call the little animal which men commonly call the squirrius from the tops of high trees and take it in his hand and put it on his neck and let it go in and out from his bosom."

There are many pleasant stories of life in the forest clearings. At Fontaines St. Columban withholds a storm during the reaping of a precious field of corn ; he heals the cut finger of one of the reapers (" it hung by only a small strip of skin ") ; at Luxieul he parts tearfully from his dying fellow pilgrim and namesake from Ireland who has begged him to cease detaining him on earth by the strong drag of his prayers. The abbot often worked on the land with the brothers and it is interesting to note that he wore gloves to protect the hands that served the Mass. One day, at Luxieul, he took them off, laid them on a stone and went inside to dine. " Soon, in the quiet, a thievish raven flew up and carried off one of the gloves in its beak." After the meal the saint perceived what had occurred. In a loud voice he accused the raven of belonging, from Noah's time onward, to an unreliable race of birds. In even more ringing tones he added that, until the glove was returned, the guilty bird would seek in vain for food for its young. " While the brethren were watching, the raven flew into their midst and brought back in its beak the object it had basely stolen. Nor did it attempt to fly away, but forgetful of its wild nature, humbly and in the sight of all, it awaited its punishment." Perhaps this was a severer penance than it sounds; for the holy man merely commanded it to begone.

Jonas emphasises the many innocent joys that came to those who had painfully renounced their own will and had been born again into a life where every single act from eating, speaking, working to praying—was dedicated to the service of God and their neighbour. Even death came with sweet heavenly sounds and scents to men whose aim was to prepare for unbroken communion with God.

In 596 St. Augustine passed through France on his way to England. His mission to the Anglo-Saxons was to prove more memorable than successful. However, the bishops of France hastened to meet one who had so lately seen Pope Gregory at Rome. Prominent among the Gallic scandals they discussed with him and his fellow bishops, was the grave matter of St. Columban's heretical celebration of Easter. He and his friends, they said, persisted in calculating the date of Easter in the way they had originally learnt from the British bishops who had introduced it to Ireland on their return from the Council of Arles in 314—and this though they were perfectly aware that the Gallic Church had since twice changed its methods of calculation to conform with Rome. When they approached the foreign abbot on the subject (they told St. Augustine) he had the temerity to suggest that it was they who were wrong in following so feeble a mathematician as Victorious of Aquitaine[1]; and though they had appealed to the Pope's Legate, Candidus, it had been in vain. St. Columban still continued to celebrate his separate Easter in the Vosges.

It was the sort of problem shortly to confront St. Augustine himself, faced in England with an autonomous Celtic Church whose mind was as strong as her faith. "How are we to deal with the bishops of Britain?" is his anguished

[1]His system was made law for all Frankish kingdoms in 541 at the Council of Orleans.

cry from their midst. To which Pope Gregory replies very
properly from Rome : " We commit them to your care that
the unlearned may be taught, the weak strengthened by persuasion and the perverse corrected by authority." In spite of
the ability and tact of many of the bishops sent from Rome
there were still " perverse " sections of the Celtic Church
uncorrected when the Vikings arrived and mercilessly
annihilated them.

But if the Gallic bishops were scandalised, St. Columban
was equally indignant. He could get no assurance from
Candidus that the interference of the neighbouring bishops
would cease. He therefore wrote direct to Pope Gregory.
In " Scotia," he informs him, Victorian methods of calculation
would not be tolerated by learned computists for a moment.
They are only fit to be derided or pitied. Indeed what is
astonishing is that so learned a man as the Pope has not
remedied this patent error in the Gallic Church. He adds that
it is surely well nigh heretical to disagree with the great
scholar Jerome who, be it noted, praised the system of cal-
culations followed by the Celtic Church.

There was no answer to this fierce demand for reformation. St. Columban himself wrote darkly that two of his
letters to the Pope were prevented from reaching him by the
wiles of the devil. In 602, after twelve Celtic Easters had been
celebrated in the Vosges, the bishops of Gaul called a council
at Châlons. They demanded St. Columban's presence ; but
he prudently remained where he was, contenting himself with
writing a letter to be read to the assembled company. In it
he congratulates himself on being the cause of their meeting
together—a thing they would be well advised to do more
frequently for the good of the Church. " I trust more to the
tradition of my native country," he repeats, " than to
Victorius who writes ambiguously and decides nothing."
He then describes the life of well-doing his community leads
in the Vosges ; and pleads to be left in peace in the name of
their common Saviour. As for the bishops, they should study
both sides of the matter and then choose the right one. Very
tolerantly the council brought no charges of heresy against the

stubborn abbot. He continued to keep the Celtic Easter as long as he stayed at Luxieul.

After Guntrum of Burgundy died in 592 his nephew Childebert of Austrasia inherited both kingdoms. But three years later (probably from the effects of poison), Childebert also died. He left two small sons called Theudebert and Theuderic. The younger child, Theuderic, succeeded to Burgundy and was brought up by his grandmother, the redoubtable queen Brunhilda. It was entirely owing to her astute vigilance, after the murder of her husband, that her son, Childebert, survived as long as he did. Childebert had therefore good reason to be the devoted son he was; and such excellent reports of his upbringing reached Pope Gregory, that in his correspondence with Brunhilda he paid her many compliments. Bishop Gregory of Tours also knew the queen and greatly admired her courage. It comes, then, as a shock to find that in the opinion of Jonas this woman was no better than a second Jezebel.

He accuses her of attempting to mar the friendship of her young grandson Theuderic with St. Columban, and of encouraging in the boy those dissolute habits which the abbot certainly strove in vain to correct. According to Jonas it was the old queen's wish that Theuderic should remain a puppet king interested only in his common mistresses while Brunhilda continued to rule. But even the prejudiced Jonas is forced to reveal the intense interest this woman still had in the Merovingian succession she had spent her unhappy life defending. He relates that when she saw how changed were the moral views of the Burgundian and Frankish nobles through twenty years of St. Columban's influence, and understood that the bastards he deplored would no longer be acceptable to them as kings, she grew desperate. It was essential that her grandchildrens' position at court should be sanctioned by the man those nobles revered. She therefore arranged that when the saint came to the palace the illegitimate children of the young king should be present; and, as casually as she could, she asked the holy man to give them his blessing. He refused indignantly; and from then on Jonas' story reads like an Old Testament feud between a righteous prophet and a wicked king of Israel.

First the abbot's heretical Easter was used as a weapon against him, Childebert then began a systematic persecution of his monasteries. St. Columban retaliated by demanding justice. His opinion of the king's action was plainly shown when he refused to set foot in the palace or to eat " the offerings of the wicked." In revenge the king demanded access, not only to the guesthouse, as was customary, but to all parts of the monastery. No one but monks, penitents and students were ever given this honour; but when it was refused him Theuderic ordered that St. Columban be banished to Ireland.

With Domoal to serve him the abbot was taken to Besançon while further arrangements were made. But there, after washing their feet and preaching to them, he miraculously released all the condemned men in the town prison, accompanying them to the sanctuary of the nearby church. When they found the door shut even St. Columban was dismayed for behind them they could hear the horrified guard fast approaching. " Breathing anxiously," the saint prayed for help, and behold, " the goodness of the Creator opened the door " just long enough for the repentant sinners to enter. Thereafter St. Columban made his way out of the city and walked boldly back to Luxieul.

The struggle might have gone on indefinitely had not the saint's heart been moved to pity for the soldiers billeted on his monastery but with strict orders to escort him at once to the port of Nantes. In the words of Jonas : " These were in imminent peril, as they knew they would be cursed if they ejected him violently and killed if they did not." He soon decided to yield; and all his monks resolved to go with him. They followed " as if it were a funeral, for grief filled the hearts of all " so much had they grown to love Luxieul. St. Columban, however, turned to them and prayed: " Oh, Creator of the world prepare for us a place where thy servants may worship Thee "; then he comforted them telling them to put their trust in the Lord and to give great praise to

Almighty God, for this was an opportunity greatly to increase the number of monks. "The king's servants, however, declared that only those who were his countrymen or who had come to him from Brittany should be allowed to follow him. When the father perceived that his followers were violently torn from him his grief and that of his monks was increased. But he prayed to the Lord, the Comforter of all men, to take those into His own keeping whom the king's violence had torn from him. Among these was Eusthasius, the scholar and servant of Columban who was afterwards abbot in the convent. So, twenty years after he had come to this place, the holy man departed."

Jonas relates many miracles wrought by the saint on his mournful journey across France from Besançon to Nantes. On the road from Auxerre to Nevers he healed a youth possessed of a demon who had "run twenty miles with all his might" to catch him up. At Nevers the party proceeded down the Loire by boat to Orleans where they camped sadly on the river bank. The king had forbidden the town's people to feed them, and had even refused them the solace of entering the city churches. But a Syrian woman with a blind husband had compassion on these starving strangers and in return St. Columban gave sight to the man she loved and whom she had led and tended so gently year after year.

At Tours their one desire was to visit the tomb of St. Martin; but to their despair the guards were adamant and sailed the ship past the holy place. In his anguish St. Columban cried to heaven for help, and behold, "in a wonderful manner the boat sped from mid-stream to the harbour and entering it, accomplished the wish of the man of God." He was thus able to spend a whole night with St. Martin.

Next day the good bishop of Tours entertained St. Columban at his palace. It can hardly have been a merry party, for in fluent Latin and in no uncertain terms the saint informed the company of his plight. "That dog, Theuderic," he told them, "has driven me away from the brethren." When one of the king's followers attempted to justify his master St. Columban effectively silenced him by politely asking him to tell Theuderic that his entire family would, within three years, be exterminated by the Lord.

At Nantes, while they waited the arrival of a ship " which was returning to Ireland having brought Scottish wares," the wretched monks nearly died of hunger. What little flour remained from the supply given them by the bishop of Tours, St. Columban recklessly gave to the poor. As Jonas put it : " They had scarcely anything except the grace of faith and hope with which to refresh their exhausted limbs." They appealed in vain to the bishop ; but at last gifts of food and wine were sent them by two devout ladies of the neigh-bourhood. Thus fortified, the man of God passed the time of waiting by writing to his forsaken brethren at Luxieul. To " all his monks St. Columban the sinner sends salutation in Christ." After much good advice he bids them to " side with my true follower Athala, unless he wishes to follow me hither," in which event they are to choose another abbot. He fears they will be persecuted for upholding the Celtic Easter. " I am broken, I confess, by this cause, that while I tried to help all, they made war on me without reason." It is a long, moving letter, but before the end of it he mentions the arrival of the ship to take them back to Ireland, adding curiously, that if he willed it he knows he need not go ; but that he had decided to leave the future in the hands of God.

And this is what happened. When all his monks were aboard, St. Columban got permission to follow the ship in a small boat. He said he would join the brethren at the mouth of the river Loire. But he never boarded the ship because she had no sooner got under way than a huge wave came and drove her ashore. The astounded captain perceived that so incredible an event could only be caused by the reluctance of these men of God to leave the country. Very sensibly he disembarked them at once ; nor could he be induced to have anything more to do with them.

Such a sign could not be ignored. The people of Nantes understood as well as the monks themselves that God wished them to remain. They were therefore well cared for ; and their abbot decided to seek protection at the court of

Chlotair of Neustria. This cousin of Theuderic's is said by Jonas to have received the holy man " as a veritable gift from heaven " : the more so as he had been drawn into a quarrel about boundaries between the brothers Theuderic and Theudebert and knew not which to support. St. Columban advised neutrality. He even told Chlotair that within three years he would succeed to the whole country. But far from attaching himself to his new protector the saint could not be moved by the prospect of a land governed by a friendly king. He said he no longer desired to live in Gaul. His dauntless heart was set on the conquest of further lands. Chlotair was loath to let him go. But obligingly he obtained for the party of monks safe conduct through Theudebert's kingdom of Austrasia, the easiest approach to the Alps and Italy.

So once more St. Columban passed across France. At Paris he exorcised a particularly revolting demon. He stayed at Meaux with Chagnoald's noble parents and blessed his little sister Burgundofara, later to become one of the great abbesses of the country. The news of his approach to Theudebert's court at Metz reached his monasteries in the Vosges ; so that when he arrived there " many brethren had already come to him whom he received as if they had been snatched from the enemy." Among these were Chagnoald, Athala and Eusthasius.

The party set off up the Rhine in a boat provided by Theudebert. By the time they reached Mainz they had, as usual, run out of food. In vain the boatmen asked their friends for help. Then St. Columban puzzled his followers by saying gently : " Let me go for a short time to *my* friend." They only understood when they saw him enter the church. His prayers there brought the bishop in haste to the building. When he discovered the prostrate figure and heard that St. Columban and his monks were pilgrims he at once put all he had at their disposal.

Their first settlement was on the shore of Lake Zurich among the Teuton tribes arrived there from the north. They converted many of these worshippers of Wodan but were forced to flee before long from the wrath caused by St. Gall's

176

ruthless smashing and burning of their idols. They then went north to Lake Constance where they took refuge with a priest who told them of the pleasant surroundings of the ruined city of Bregenz at the head of the lake. Here they found a little church still standing in spite of the northern invasions. For three years they repeated their pioneer work in this new wilderness. St. Gall, a great linguist, preached eloquently to those curious enough to visit the settlement; while St. Columban found another cave and another amenable bear. It is true that this beast was merely asked to leave for the saint's use the apples on certain nearby trees. But Chagnoald, who told Jonas the story, was clearly impressed by its obedience. The demons of the place were not so easily subdued. St. Gall had affronted them by yet more smashing of idols; and when he fished at night on the lake he was troubled by their horrid wailings. They could only be banished by the ringing of St. Columban's little bell and the singing of psalms by the assembled brethren.

The saint had prophesied that within three years there would be no members of Theuderic's family left. In 612 the two brothers fought a final battle at Zulpich where Theudebert was beaten and later put to death. Next year Theuderic himself died at Metz; and Queen Brunhilda had no sooner placed his illegitimate son on the throne than Chlotair arrived to fulfil the prophesy. He killed all the children; while the poor old queen he placed naked on a camel that all might see how great was her fall. "Then," says Jonas, "she was bound to the tails of wild horses and thus perished miserably." A thousand years later her tomb was opened and he was proved correct in his dreadful account of her death.

For one year, therefore, Austrasia, in the boundaries of which kingdom St. Columban now dwelt, was in the hands of his enemy Theuderic. Fortunately the holy man had recently had an invitation from Agilulf, the Teutonic King of Lombardy, to make northern Italy his home. Old and worn though he was, he determined to cross the Alps. St. Gall was ill and begged to be allowed to remain among his converts. His abbot was bitterly disappointed and a painful parting took place between the two old saints who had left Ireland together so long ago. St. Gall slowly recovered and lived to found in the mountains to the south of Lake Constance, the great monastery that even now bears his name.[1] Athala followed his master, while Eusthasius and Chagnoald returned to Luxieul where the former was made abbot.

The Teutonic Lombards were not unknown to the Picts and Scots of Ireland. One of their Christian kings is said to have sent all his nine daughters on pilgrimage to the land of St. Patrick, though even in those days it was more for their valour than their piety that the Lombards were famous. Since their conquest of northern Italy they had become tainted with the same Arian heresy against which Athanasius fought so brilliantly in the fourth century. But Theudelinda, Agilulf's Bavarian wife, was a Catholic, and it may have been she who fired the ageing saint to cross the Alps by writing of the divided state of the Church in Italy. Jonas tells us that during his stay in Milan St. Columban started at once to attack the followers of the Arian heresy " which he wished to cut out and exterminate with the cauterising knife of the scriptures. And he composed an excellent and learned work against them." But he had scarcely had time to grasp the causes behind the dissensions he found within the Catholic Church itself before Queen Theudelinda had persuaded him to write and press Pope Boniface IV to define clearly the Roman attitude to the latest heresy. Without some slight knowledge of it and of the extraordinary complications it presented to Popes and Emperors it is impossible to judge or appreciate St. Columban's remarkable letter.

It will be remembered that the Arians denied the divinity of Christ affirmed so distinctly by the Catholic Church in 325 at the Council of Nicaea. But in the fifth century even those Christians who accepted the Nicene Creed—and by that time they were well in the majority—found much to puzzle, inflame and divide them when they discussed whether Christ had a single or a dual nature. Some thought He was

---

[1] His handbell is still there. St. Gall so loved music that in his monastery he had a room set apart for the use of a Celtic teacher of stringed instruments and the pipes.

wholly divine and some believed He was both man and God. In 451, at the Fourth Council of Chalcedon, both Pope and Emperor agreed that to be an orthodox Christian it was necessary to believe that Christ was both wholly God and wholly man. Believers in the single nature, the Council affirmed, were heretics. Broadly speaking the western Church approved the decision while the Eastern Church was inclined to favour the doctrine of the single nature still held by the Coptic Church in Egypt.

Successive Emperors, ruling from Constantinople, essayed in turn toleration or compromise in dealing with a question so explosive that it threatened to disrupt the Empire. By 543 it had split the Church, for in that year the Emperor Justinian, as head of the Eastern Church, thought fit to anathematise the still uncondemned writings of three clerics tainted with the heresy and who had themselves been severely admonished by the Fourth Council of Chalcedon. Unfortunately the western bishops took it that the Eastern Church, in its condemnation of the " Three Chapters " (as these writings were called), meant to condemn the orthodox judgment of the Council itself. Pope Vigilius therefore excommunicated the eastern Patriarch. But, at Justinian's command, he then went to Constantinople, where the Greek writings were translated for him, and perceiving them to be truly heretical he also cursed them soundly. On this apparent further betrayal of the Fourth Council by the Pope himself the Western Church rose against him so fiercely that Vigilius had to withdraw his anathema. From then on the tale is one of anathema and counter-anathema from west and east ending, at his death, with the broken Vigilius' final condemnation of the " Three Chapters " in agreement with the Emperor. This dubious victory for eastern factions shocked the Western Church out of all proportion to the relatively unimportant and apparently misunderstood cause of the battle. The Popes immediately following Vigilius were all suspected of heretical leanings; indeed many western bishops went so far as to withdraw from communion with Rome. Those bishops who supported the Pope lost communicants, as did the Metropolitan of Milan when Queen Theudelinda of Lombardy indignantly left his fold. As for her Arian husband, the poor man had grown so confused that he told St. Columban he was " willing to believe if only he knew rightly what to believe."

St. Columban's long letter to the Pope on this complicated subject starts humbly. Clearly the saint had a great reverence for the insulted Chair of Peter, for it is addressed to the " Most Beautiful Head of all the Churches in Europe." But it is soon plain that he feels pleasantly confident in his own judgment knowing how well his country has kept the faith. " As for us Irishmen, dwellers in the uttermost parts of the earth, we are all disciples of Peter and Paul, and all the disciples who, under the inspiration of the Holy Ghost, have composed the divine canon of the scriptures ; but the Catholic faith which we originally received from you, the successors of the apostles, we have held unimpaired." It is because of the tragically different conditions he finds here in Italy that he urges the Pope to call a synod. There is no time to be lost, he adds, voicing the opinion of the age, for " the world is hastening to an end." To St. Columban in his ignorance of the original facts and complications it appeared quite simple for Rome to clear herself of suspicions. " It is commonly said that in a certain synod Vigilius admitted again into the communion of the Church those ancient heretics Eutiches, Nestorius and Dioscorus." (The writers of the " Three Chapters.") Does the Pope condemn or condone this action of his predecessor Vigilius ? Let him make his position clear ; for if he condones Vigilius then those who have preserved the faith have a perfect right to judge the Pope. " It was through the twin apostles of Christ that Rome became truly great in Irish eyes. But if that honour is to be preserved the Chair of Peter must be left unstained. For he only keeps the keys of the Kingdom of Heaven who opens to the worthy and closes to the unworthy. If he does otherwise his power of opening and closing is taken from him." After proclaiming his faith in the Catholic creed and rallying the Roman Church to its defence, St. Columban ends by praying that " we may merit to adhere to Christ, to please Him, and thank Him, and with you and all the saints to praise Him, together with the Father and the Holy Ghost, for ever and ever, Amen."

In those printless days letters were precious possessions. Jonas tells of one so amusing that he kept it many years before it was lost. Indeed, if the devil were kind enough to permit of delivery, the recipient seldom failed to cherish the document whatever the tone of the contents. Pope Boniface IV undoubtedly read and re-read this startling challenge, and grew to know and perhaps to appreciate the fearless and impulsive character of the author. But he sent no answer; and the thoughts of the man of God turned from the defence of the faith by words to the creation of a final mountain refuge where he and his faithful monks might find peace.

Christians had dwelt before in the mountain valley of Bobbio where there still stood a ruined church dedicated to St. Peter. The soil " was unusually fertile, and the water full of fishes." Even so St. Columban was an old man to be leading a party of pioneers. The restoration of the little church and the building of the usual huts would never have been so easily accomplished had it not been that angels assisted the monks to move heavy logs up precipitous paths. Their timely visits rejoiced the hearts of all. St. Columban and Athala were further gladdened by a visit from Eusthasius from Luxieul with a message from Chlotair humbly begging the honour of the prophet's return to his kingdom. " But Columban declared when he heard Chlotair's request, that he could not undertake the journey again. Eusthasius he kept with himself for some time, warned him not to forget his own labours, to keep the band of brethren learned and obedient, to increase their numbers and to educate them according to his own instruction. To the king he sent a letter full of good advice and begged him to extend his royal protection and aid to the brethren at Luxieul. The king received the letter joyfully as a most pleasing gift and as a pledge of his compact with the man of God."

From the quiet retreat of his last mountain cave St. Columban could look back on six walled cities he had helped to build with his hands or his spirit for the servants and soldiers of Christ. St. Comgall is remembered as the founder of Bangor; but it was not for nothing that, at the end of thirty years, he could hardly bear to let St. Columban go. Abbot Waldebert is associated with Luxieul, the most important of the three foundations in the Vosges; but all three were created by St. Columban. St. Gall would never have reached Lake Constance without his tireless leader; nor would Bobbio have risen without its first abbot. In all these continental monasteries his stern rule was replaced so soon by the milder one of St. Benedict that only the monks at Bobbio continued to remember his wisdom and his miracles.

Others reaped where he had sown. In her scholarly *Life of St. Columban*, Mrs. Concannon points out that the greatest of these spiritual reapers was St. Francis. He is known to have visited Bobbio and he appears to have been deeply impressed and inspired by what he found there. It is surely no coincidence that his monks too were called " soldiers of Christ " and were clad exactly like St. Columban's or that his monasteries were built to the same camp-like pattern with the same great wooden crosses at their entrances. He even borrowed the Celtic name *carcair* for his cavernous retreats. Surely all this can only mean that St. Francis discovered at Bobbio a Soul-Friend after his own heart; that the man who preached to the birds found a true brother in him who called the squirrels from the trees.

If this be true then Jonas is proved profoundly right when in his last glimpse of St. Columban at Bobbio, he writes: " His remains are buried there where they have proved their virtues by the help of Christ."

Sources:

Vita S. Columbani. Jonas. Ed. D. C. Munro.

Writings of St. Columban contained in Fleming's *Collectanea Sacra*, including *Letters*, *The Rule*, *The Penitential*.

Life of St. Comgall, from *Lives of the Irish Saints*. O'Hanlon, Vol. V.

Vitae Galli. Wettino and Walafrido. Ed. Bruno Krusch.

Historia Frankorum. Gregory of Tours. Ed. O. M. Darton.

Literary History of Ireland. Douglas Hyde.

Ecclesiastical History. Bede. Ed. J. A. Giles.

Life of St. Columba. Helena Concannon.

The Celtic Church and the See of St. Peter. J. MacNaught.

Chain of Error in Scottish History. M. Hay.

The Pictish Church. A. B. Scott.

Irish Monasticism. John Ryan.

History of Europe. H. A. L. Fisher.

Early Christian Art in Ireland. Margaret Stokes.

CHAPTER X.

ST. CUTHBERT

Y the beginning of the seventh century—the century in which St. Cuthbert and his Anglo-Saxon friends played so important a part in the last act of the dramatic history of the Celtic Church—almost all of Christian Britain had vanished. Despite the valiant and often successful counter-attacks of the Britons, the Anglo-Saxons had by that time conquered all but the unimportant hill country to the west of the island and the indomitable Pictish kingdom to the far north. Speaking the rudiments of the language we speak to-day, and already with a strong love of popular government, these heathen from northern Germany lived in their villages and ploughed their communal open fields wherever there were suitable clearings among the huge forests and marshes of the country. After two hundred years of killing and plundering, the invaders were at last settling down.

Gildas, writing in the sixth century, is the first of many historians to accuse the Celtic Church of preferring to convert any distant race rather than her nearby enemies the Angles. Surely, though, the truth is that with a few exceptions (there were Teutons among the scholars at sixth century Bangor in Ulster) the invaders were not then in a fit state to receive the Christian message. After all they forced Gildas himself to die in exile; nor did they hesitate to murder his brave friend St. Cadoc when he returned from Brittany to his Welsh monastery. It is small wonder, then, that Britons surviving into the seventh century could only see the English as barbarians born of the accursed race that had plagued them ever since the desertion of their island by the Romans. The English appeared to have no culture; while to a Celt their language seemed as fantastic as their religion. But perhaps, to a Briton, the most disconcerting thing about the English was their complete lack of Latin. They had never even heard of Rome.

And yet, oddly enough, the origins of the British branch of the Celtic Church herself were quite independent of Rome. As has already been noted her first apostles were disciples of St. John, not of St. Peter—a fact which can not only be verified from early historical sources but which Abbot Colman still remembered in the seventh century when he stressed it so movingly at the Synod of Whitby. This did not prevent the Celtic Church from taking her place from the very first as part of the European Catholic Church. She became even more closely linked with the continent and with the capital of the civilised world when Constantine adopted Christianity. St. Ninian and St. Patrick, first educated by Celtic clerics in the British province of the Roman Empire, both finished their religious training in continental monasteries. The Pope was behind St. Ninian's mission to the Picts ; and when St. Patrick was unjustly deprived of his rank in Ireland he appealed successfully to the Bishop of Rome.

Even after the fall of the Western Empire the " Abbot of Rome " (as Celtic abbots so often called him thinking naturally in monastic terms) still remained the acknowledged head of the Western Church. It is true that fifth and sixth century Popes were suspected of heresy by some continental bishops ; yet St. Columban voiced the feelings of the sixth century Celtic Church when he told Pope Gregory that " through Christ's two apostles [Peter and Paul] you are almost heavenly, and Rome is the head of the Church of the whole world saving the singular prerogative of the place of the Lord's resurrection."

Not till the seventh century was there any clash between the Celtic and Roman churches. Even then had St. Augustine been a bigger man all might have been well. But though Pope Gregory more than deserved St. Columban's praise, St. Augustine—the man he chose to lead his mission to the Anglo-Saxons—proved sadly unequal to the task.

St. Augustine chose to land in Kent because King Ethelbert had a Frankish Christian wife. Between them, the Roman bishop and the queen had little difficulty in converting the king. In 625, when Ethelbert's Christian daughter travelled north to marry Edwin of Northumbria she took with her her Roman chaplain Paulinus through whom St. Augustine's successor was thus able to convert a second king. According to Bede Edwin's conversion was not quite so swift as Ethelbert's : for " being a man of extraordinary sagacity, he often sat alone by himself a long time, silent as to his tongue, but deliberating in his heart how he should proceed, and which religion he should adhere to." Before his marriage Edwin had fought and killed his brother-in-law the king of Bernicia thereby adding this northern kingdom to his own. While he tried to forge the kingdoms of Diera[1] and Bernicia into Northumbria and debated whether to accept Christianity his young nephew Oswald had taken refuge on the already famous island of Iona where he was welcomed by the third abbot of the monastery and educated and converted by the monks.

Ethelbert and Edwin really understood the Roman form of Christianity. But for the most part their peoples took to the new religion because they were expected to follow their rulers. St. Augustine's monks appear to have given them little instruction and to have baptised them more or less *en masse*. Such methods of conversion could only produce very superficial Christians. Nine years after Paulinus' arrival the Northumbrians reverted when the Britons rebelled and the pagan English King Penda of Mercia[2] marched north, killed Edwin and conquered their country.

St. Augustine and his immediate followers would have achieved very different results had they shown less interest in kings and queens and more in the people. It was lamentable, too, that they never troubled to learn the language, still requiring interpreters at the Synod of Whitby in 664. Judging by their activities among the Franks, St. Gall and his practical friends would have produced the necessary dictionaries within a year of landing in Teutonic Kent.

As for St. Augustine himself, his tactlessness and arrogance when confronted with the bishops of the ancient British Church gave them so keen a distaste for Roman ways, as interpreted by the Archbishop of Canterbury, that none of

[1]The land lying between the Tees and the Humber.
[2]Now the Midlands.

them would give him their allegiance.[1] In consequence of this unfortunate first impression Theodore of Tarsus—an archbishop of rare calibre—was still struggling vainly seventy years later to bring about the complete union of the two churches.

By that time the position had grown really serious. It was no longer merely the British and English Churches that were at variance. Monks from Iona, with two hundred and fifty years of Celtic missionary tradition behind them, had succeeded in thoroughly and permanently converting the great majority of the Anglo-Saxons. Bishop Lightfoot even goes so far as to write: " St. Augustine was the Apostle of Kent but Aidan was the Apostle of England."

Foremost among Aidan's English disciples was the great St. Cuthbert. He was born in Northumbria about 634. It was an auspicious time to enter the world though it was not long since Penda had slain Edwin, causing the queen and her daughter Eanfleda to flee back to Kent under Paulinus' protection. It was auspicious because into the ensuing chaos marched Oswald fresh from Iona and determined to wrest Northumbria from Penda's destructive heathen grasp.

He advanced, " with an army, small indeed in number, but strengthened with the faith of Christ." Before his famous victory against Penda he cried to his soldiers: " Let us all kneel, and jointly beseech the true and living God Almighty, in his mercy, to defend us from the haughty and fierce enemy; for He knows that we have undertaken a just war for the safety of our nation." It is good to hear Oswald's cry ring out through the pagan gloom of Northumbria and, because this king and his equally inspiring brother Oswy and sister Ebba, all three, wove themselves into St. Cuthbert's life, it is perhaps excusable to allow Bede a little more space in which to describe him.

" The same Oswald, as soon as he had ascended the throne [in 635] being desirous that all his nation should receive the Christian faith . . . sent to the elders of the Scots, among whom himself and his followers, when in banishment, had

[1]Till the thirteenth century the Welsh church was directly subject to Rome.

received the sacrament of baptism, desiring they would send him a bishop, by whose instruction and ministry the English nation, which he governed, might be taught the advantages, and receive the sacraments of the Christian faith. Nor were they slow in granting his request; but sent him Bishop Aidan, a man of singular meekness, piety and moderation. . . . On the arrival of the bishop, the king appointed him his episcopal See in the isle of Lindisfarne. . . . The king also humbly and willingly in all cases giving ear to his admonitions, industriously applied himself to build and extend the church of Christ in his kingdom; wherein, when the bishop, who was not skilful in the English tongue, preached the gospel, it was most delightful to see the king himself interpreting the word of God to his commanders and ministers, for he had perfectly learned the language of the Scots during his long banishment.''

Oswald's capital at Bamborough was conveniently close to Lindisfarne, which, like its mother house at Iona, soon became a magnificent training school for missionaries. The astounding results of their work prove that if Aidan found the English language difficult his Scotic monks were not long in mastering it. In a startlingly short time, and following the well-tried methods originated by St. Ninian, the faith started to spread all over the land.

While still pagan there was something sombrely grand about the Anglo-Saxons. They possessed a bleak kind of courage; though too often it was of the over-masculine variety that can only find an outlet in violence. To understand a little of what Christianity did for them is to appreciate the contrast between the rugged *Beowulf* and the beautiful *Dream of the Rood*. Only the gospel of " Jesus, whose name is not so much written as ploughed into the history of the world '' could have produced so great a transformation. No sooner had the Celtic saints sown the good seed than there sprang up so rich a crop of joy, love and tenderness among the people that seventh century Northumbria is like a gay field of flowers : while the brilliant culture of England in the Golden Age of the eighth century became the envy of Western Christendom.

ST. CUTHBERT ON FARNE ISLAND

Because the faith grew so fast St. Cuthbert was brought up a Christian. According to Bede, " he often prayed to the Lord when surrounded by difficulties and was counted worthy to be defended by angelic help." He may well have heard Aidan preach and watched him heal minds and bodies with the power of his glorious gospel. For Aidan himself, accompanied by his " twelve boys of the English nation," journeyed on foot all over wild Northumbria teaching English and British alike.

He had no need to walk: for his friend King Oswin of Diera had presented him with " an extraordinarily fine horse." This royal animal, however, bishop Aidan very soon gave to a poor beggar thus gravely hurting the feelings of the king who could not forbear to remonstrate with his apparent lack of proportion. " To whom the bishop instantly answered, ' What is it you say, O King ? Is that foal of a mare more dear to you than the Son of God ?' Upon this they went in to dinner, and the bishop sat in his place; but the king, who was come from hunting, stood warming himself, with his attendants, at the fire. Then, on a sudden, whilst he was warming himself, calling to mind what the bishop had said to him, he ungirt his sword, and gave it to his servant, and in a hasty manner fell down at the bishop's feet, beseeching him to forgive him : ' For from this time forward,' he said, ' I will never speak any more of this, nor will I judge of what, or how much of our money you shall give to the sons of God.' " It would seem that the noble Oswin could no more resist a Celtic saint than could such lesser creatures as St. Kentigern's wolf, or—later—St. Cuthbert's pair of ravens.

Like St. David St. Cuthbert grew up fair, strong, and of a ruddy countenance, and like him he started life as a well-born shepherd. As he tended his sheep in the mountains near Melrose he had leisure to meditate on the beauty of Aidan's Christlike life in a land still haunted by Beowulf's demon foes.

And then, like so many saints, when he was seventeen, he was given a sudden overwhelming sight of heaven. Bede, who finished writing his life about 721, knew many who had met and loved St. Cuthbert. He tells us that during the summer of 651 " he suddenly saw a stream of light from the sky breaking in upon the darkness of the long night. In the midst of this, the choir of the heavenly host descended to the earth and taking with them without delay, a soul of exceeding brightness, returned to their heavenly home." The boy roused his fellow shepherds to tell them. " And in the morning, hearing that Aidan, bishop of the church at Lindisfarne, a man of specially great virtue, had entered the Kingdom of Heaven at the very time when he had seen him taken from the body, Cuthbert forthwith delivered to their owner the sheep which he was tending, and decided to seek a monastery."

Though it was only sixteen years since Aidan had left Iona there was already a goodly choice. St. Cuthbert was torn between Lindisfarne and the daughter house of Melrose, but chose the latter " because of the fame of the sublime virtues of the monk and priest Boisil " who became his beloved tutor. The abbot of Melrose was Eata, one of Aidan's twelve English disciples. Later Eata was sent to Ripon, taking St. Cuthbert with him as prior: for St. Cuthbert " was affable and pleasant in his manners " so that all the guests loved him.

Some time before Abbot Eata and St. Cuthbert set out on their long journey south, the good King Oswald who had brought them together had been slain in battle against Penda. The Northumbrian throne was now divided between Oswald's brother Oswy and Oswy's son Alfrid. Oswy is chiefly remembered because it was he who, in 658, finally fought and killed Penda the last of the great pagan kings, thus ensuring the supremacy of Christian Northumbria for the next twenty-seven years.

It was not Oswy, however, but his son the young prince Alfrid who had asked Eata to go and found a monastery at Ripon. But, as Bede so wisely puts it, " because the whole state of the world is frail and unstable as the sea when a sudden tempest arises, the aforesaid Abbot Eata with St. Cuthbert and other brethren whom he had brought with him, was driven home and the site of the monastery which he had founded was given to other monks to dwell in." In other words Alfrid had fallen under the spell of his dynamic friend

Wilfrid, then newly back from a visit to Rome, and in 660, having caused him to be ordained, decided to give him Ripon to further the Roman form of Christianity.

All over Northumbria Celtic monasteries hummed with indignant talk of this cruel upheaval and the reasons for it. Alfrid's cousin Hilda, the great abbess of Whitby, strongly disapproved of the Roman road he and Wilfrid had taken. In her double monastery, run on the very best Celtic lines, she had educated Wilfrid among four other future bishops of England[1]; and knowing his character she could see fierce storms ahead. St. Cuthbert, given to seeing both sides of a question, began to long for solitude.

Back at Melrose, now nearly thirty, he was smitten by an illness that left him with the inward pains, the swellings and the ulcers that troubled him for the rest of his life. Only the strength of the prayers of the brethren, so eager for " his continued presence in the flesh " raised him to his feet again. He recovered to find that his beloved tutor Boisil was dying of an epidemic of the plague equally bad in England and in Ireland where at that time many English students are known to have died in the famous free schools. During Boisil's last seven days he and St. Cuthbert studied St. John's gospel together and " they were able to finish the reading so quickly because they dealt only with the simple things of the faith which worketh by love and not deep matters of dispute."

These two friends read together so bravely in the year 664, the year of the famous Synod of Whitby at which St. Cuthbert is certain to have been present. Wilfrid had thought it best to bring to a head certain " deep matters of dispute " between the Celtic and Roman churches. At the synod, with much eloquence from both sides, an inconclusive battle was fought.

St. Cuthbert, like King Oswy, perceived that " as they all expected the same kingdom of heaven, so they ought not to differ in the celebration of the Divine mysteries; but rather to inquire which was the truest tradition, that the

[1]Before going to Whitby Wilfrid had been to school at Lindisfarne.

193

same might be followed by all.'' It is also evident that much though he loved his church, St. Cuthbert was large-minded enough to make some sacrifice for the greater good of the whole Catholic Church. Bede, writing of the synod from the Roman point of view, is imbued with the same rare spirit of charity. So great is his admiration for the stubborn Celtic Church that often his pen carries him away writing passionate eulogies on the simplicity, the humility and the spiritual power of her monks and clergy. '' But enough has now been said on this subject,'' he usually adds abruptly, returning refreshed to his critic's task.

No Roman ever accused the Celtic Church of heresy in the real sense of the word. For she had preserved the Catholic faith in a manner almost miraculous considering the lurid pages of history through which she lived. Indeed, to any one acquainted with the stumbling blocks preventing the union of Protestant Churches to-day the differences between the Churches of St. John and St. Peter, because they were not doctrinal, seem almost negligible.

First and foremost came the different ways in which the two churches calculated the date of Easter. It was a problem which '' whilst Aidan lived, was patiently tolerated by all men '' but which nevertheless led to such curious situations that it cried out for solution. King Oswy, like his brother Oswald, had been '' instructed and baptised by the Scots [of Iona] and being very perfectly skilled in their language, thought nothing better than what they taught.'' He had married Edwin's daughter Eanfleda—the child who had fled back to Kent after Penda had slain her father. Like her mother before her, she arrived in Northumbria escorted by a Roman priest. '' Thus it is said to have happened in those times,'' Bede tells us, '' that Easter was twice kept in one year; and that when the king having ended the time of fasting, kept his Easter, the queen and her followers were still fasting and celebrating Palm Sunday.''

The forms of government in the two churches differed; the Celtic Church was the more democratic, being adapted to fit tribal customs; the Roman Church was the more orderly, having inherited the marvellous secular legal system of the Empire. The tonsures worn by Celtic and Roman monks were very different[1] : but in their liturgy, ritual and teaching the two churches were surprisingly alike.

What prevented the Celtic Church from conforming to Rome at once over the question of Easter was that the Scotic branch believed as firmly as did St. Columban's Pictish branch that if any one erred in this matter it was the Romans. Undaunted by Wilfrid's taunts about " Picts and Britons, who foolishly, in these two remote islands of the world . . . oppose all the rest of the universe," Colman, third bishop of Lindisfarne, answered : " It is strange that you will call our labours foolish, wherein we follow the example of so great an apostle, who was thought worthy to lay his head on our Lord's bosom, when all the world knows him to have lived most wisely." Later, when taxed with stupidity and ignorance in the matter he rejoined : " Did Anatolius, a holy man, and much commended in church history, act contrary to the law and the Gospel, when he wrote that Easter was to be celebrated from the fourteenth to the twentieth ? Is it to be believed that our most reverend father Columba and his successors, men beloved by God, who kept Easter after the same manner, thought or acted contrary to the Divine writings ? Whereas there were many among them, whose sanctity is testified by heavenly signs and the working of miracles, whose life, customs, and discipline I never cease to follow, not questioning their being saints in heaven."

During the debate Wilfrid let slip a few doubts as to whether Celtic saints had really reached heaven but on the whole he concentrated on explaining and describing the methods of computation followed by the rest of the Catholic Church, finally clinching his argument by comparing " that Columba of yours " with the great St. Peter. At last Bishop Colman was driven to admit that it was neither to St. John nor to St. Columba that Christ gave the keys of heaven, but

[1]The Celtic monks shaved the front of the head from ear to ear, leaving the rest of their hair hanging down their backs. The Roman monks shaved, and still shave, the crown of the head leaving a surrounding fringe of short hair. The custom may have started as a means of identification.

to St. Peter, the rock on whom rested all the might and majesty of the Roman Church.

One of the outcomes of the Synod of Whitby was momentous to St. Cuthbert for it drew him to Lindisfarne and the sea : and once there his life was slowly and inevitably twisted into the true Celtic pattern. Though Oswy and his council agreed to follow St. Peter yet without his abbot's permission Bishop Colman could not conform to the Roman computation of Easter nor to the Roman form of tonsure. He therefore returned to the mother house of Iona with his Scotic monks. But before he left he obtained from Oswy, who dearly loved him, the assurance that his own disciple Eata should succeed him at Lindisfarne. He rightly judged this Englishman able to act as a fit bridge between old Celtic traditions and new Roman customs. Again St. Cuthbert accompanied Eata on his new mission as prior, chosen this time because " he was a man remarkable for the strength of his patience." For " there were certain brethren in the monastery who preferred to conform to their older usage." Indeed so disturbed was the atmosphere in the Lindisfarne monastery, Bede tells us, that " very often during debates in the chapter of the brethren concerning the rule, when he was assailed by the bitter insults of his opponents he would rise up suddenly and with calm mind and countenance would go out, dissolving the chapter, but none the less on the following day, as if he had suffered no repulse . . . he would give the same instruction . . . until . . . he gradually converted them to the things that he desired."

St. Cuthbert was sent to the island of Lindisfarne because he was good with men. Both the contemporary lives are full of delightful accounts, not only of the way his great love for people flowered into miracles ; but also of how touchingly he was loved in return.

The following story is typical of many showing how great were his tact, kindness and spiritual power.

" There was a reeve . . . devoted to religious works together with all his household, and therefore specially beloved by the blessed Cuthbert, who when he happened to be travelling that way, frequently visited him. His wife, though given to works of charity and other fruits of virtue, was suddenly seized upon by a demon and most cruelly afflicted, so that she gnashed her teeth and uttered piteous cries, flinging her arms and limbs about in agitation, and so inspiring no little horror in all who saw or heard her. And when she lay cast out and apparently at the point of death, her husband got on his horse and came in haste to the man of God, and entreated him, saying: 'My wife is ill and seems already at the point of death; I beg you that you will send a priest to visit her before she dies and minister to her the sacrament of the body and blood of the Lord: and also that you will permit her body to be buried here in holy ground.' For he was ashamed to confess that she was insane because the man of God had always been accustomed to see her in her right mind. When St. Cuthbert had turned away from him for a short time to see what priest he should send with him, he suddenly realised in his spirit that the wife for whom the man was praying was afflicted by no ordinary infirmity but by the attack of a demon. And turning to him he said: 'I must not send another but I myself must go with you to visit her.' And when they were on the way, the man began to weep and to reveal the grief in his heart by the tears that flowed down his cheeks; for he feared that when St. Cuthbert found her possessed of a devil, he would begin to think that she had served the Lord with a feigned and not a real faith. But the man of God consoled him with gentle words. 'Do not weep,' he said, 'as though I were about to find your wife in such a condition as I should not wish. For I know myself, though you are ashamed to say it, that she is afflicted by a demon; but I also know that before we arrive, the demon will be driven away and she will come to meet us joyfully, as sound in mind as ever, and she will herself take these reins, and, bidding us enter quickly, will diligently perform her accustomed services for us; for it is not only the wicked who are subjected to such torments, but sometimes also in this world, by the inscrutable judgment of God, the innocent are taken captive by the devil, not only in body but also in mind.' ''

St. Cuthbert was right. When they approached the reeve's home " the evil spirit suddenly fled, not being able to endure the coming of the Holy Spirit which filled the man of God."

Reading such stories it becomes easy to understand why Bede so often emphasises that the saint " was of a happy disposition and very friendly " ; and why his constant arduous journeys on foot and on horseback so deeply affected the whole countryside. He proved, indeed, to be a marvellous missionary. No sinner could long resist " the light of his angelic countenance." He could heal men's bodies and read their minds, and like St. Columba he knew what the future held. It was only natural that such a man should be chosen to help in the great task of uniting the two churches. But as so often happens God had a different plan.

Nearly everyone knows the strange and lovely story of St. Cuthbert's visit to Oswy's sister St. Ebba of Coldingham while he was still prior of Melrose : of how he went to preach to her nuns—some of the many nuns who loved him—and discovered the sea. All night and every night while he stayed there he stood engulfed in the sea, singing his psalms to the sound of the waves. " When daybreak was at hand, he went up on the shore. While he was doing this, there came forth from the depths of the sea two four-footed creatures which are commonly called otters. These, prostrate before him on the sand, began to warm his feet with their breath and sought to dry him with their fur, and when they had finished their ministrations they received his blessing and slipped away into their native waters." So did the otters drag him back to the nuns : for only they knew how dangerously near he was to heaven.

While working by the sea at Lindisfarne he felt an ever more urgent need to abandon the social for the solitary life. At last, after twelve years and when he was forty-two, St. Cuthbert, who is so firmly anchored to the pages of history by the concrete names of his many famous friends, broke loose from his moorings and sailed seven miles away to the tiny island of Farne to live for the next nine years in the tradition of Celtic hermits—alone with God and the sea.

It sounds so peaceful. But the contemplative life was accounted the highest by the Church to the end of medieval times because it entailed such deep spiritual conflict. When the Lindisfarne monks visited St. Cuthbert in his little self-made house from which only the sky could be seen, he would tell them of devils such as later troubled St. Teresa of Avila and other great saints who have dared to explore the frontiers of heaven while still not far from the borders of hell. " How many times," he said, " have they cast me headlong from a high rock; how many times have they hurled stones at me as if to kill me . . . nevertheless they were unable in any way to mar my body by any injury or my mind by fear." And this went on to the very end. For he told Herefrith, then abbot of Lindisfarne, who sailed over to him in his last illness and who informed Bede : " My adversaries have never per-secuted me so frequently during all the time I have been living on this island, as during these five days." Herefrith adds : " I did not dare to ask what were the temptations of which he spoke."

Then he had often to forsake his meditations to reason with the birds who so joyfully devoured the crops he planted. So contented were they with his company and his corn that it required much persuasion to make them go elsewhere. Later he had to admonish " with a slight motion of the hand " that pair of nesting ravens who wilfully tore the thatch from the roof of the guest house he had built for the visiting brethren. Admonishment was not enough. Though they perfectly understood, the birds still continued to steal his straw till at last St. Cuthbert turned their happy squawks into a series of dismal, diminishing croaks by banishing them. " Now when three days had passed one of the pair returned and found the servant of Christ digging. With its feathers sadly ruffled and its head drooping to its feet and with humble cries it prayed for pardon, using such signs as it could." When the saint relented it was gone in a flash to tell its mate that they might return ; and together they hurried back bearing between them " a portion of hog's lard " with which to grease the shoes of the brethren they had injured.

His hermit's routine was also broken by his visitors. Christmas he would spend with a party of monks from Lindisfarne " indulging in feasting, rejoicing and story-telling." His great friend Herbert, a monk who inhabited an island in Derwentwater, also came annually to see him. They "refreshed each other with draughts of heavenly wisdom," talking far into the night with the North Sea waves roaring round them and with the ravens nearby sleeping the innocent sleep of the righteous. At first St. Cuthbert welcomed the Lindisfarne monks at the shore; but towards the end of his nine years on Farne he did no more than stretch out his hand from the windows of his dwelling to bless them. He was intent on the world beyond.

Meantime, the Northumbrian world outside Lindisfarne had changed considerably since the Synod of Whitby. It is true that except for the adoption of the Roman tonsure and the Roman Easter, all the great monasteries continued as before to practise the peculiar discipline and customs of the Celtic Church from which they had sprung. It is also true that soon after the Synod Oswy, always deeply attached to the Celtic Church, disinherited his pro-Roman son Alfrid. But in 668 there arrived from Rome Theodore of Tarsus, the new Archbishop of Canterbury. Being a Greek Theodore was well able to grasp the significance of certain Celtic customs and that part of the Celtic liturgy derived direct from Asia Minor. He proved so skilled and blessed a peacemaker that only five years later he was able to hold the first council of the English Church at Hertford having already become (as Bede puts it) " the first of the archbishops to whom the whole English Church consented to submit."

He only achieved this miracle through a rare combination of boundless energy and true tolerance. It is quite obvious, too, that he revered and loved the Celtic-trained monks he met on his ceaseless journeys through the land they had transformed; otherwise they could never have given him their trust and affection so swiftly. He was indeed the first Romanised priest to recognise the magnitude of their achievement, perceiving that without the co-operation of the great army of Celtic-trained monks and teachers, the most learned of whom still came over from Iona and Ireland, he could not hope to win all England for Christ. All he asked was that he might " confirm " the consecrations of those Celtic bishops so oddly under the authority of the abbots or abbesses of their monasteries. And as he divided up the land into proper diocesan episcopates, thus creating new sees, again and again he showed his wisdom by choosing his new bishop from the ranks of the Celtic-trained clergy already beloved, like St. Cuthbert, by the English people.

There was, however, a sprinkling of Romanised priests and bishops, the foremost of whom was the redoubtable Wilfrid. While Oswy was alive Wilfrid could do little; but after his death in 670 Oswy was succeeded by his younger son Ecgfrith who shared with his deposed brother an admiration for Roman ways surely learned at their Kentish mother's knee. It was Ecgfrith who was inspired to help Wilfrid build Churches in Northumbria surpassing anything before seen by the English. Indeed, at York, in which See Theodore placed Wilfrid, and at Ripon and Hexham, the new bishop built churches so magnificent that the Celtic clergy could only gasp. Of Hexham Wilfrid's contemporary biographer Eddius writes that there was no " building like it on this side of the Alps," whereas it is recorded that the frail Celtic churches were only too liable to take to the air in a bad gale. There was a striking contrast, too, in the grand style in which Wilfrid lived attended by many richly dressed servants. Celtic bishops, chosen for their sanctity, could not but deplore such worldli-ness. But Wilfrid undoubtedly possessed a genuine passion for architecture and for music—especially the beautiful Gregorian chants which so quickly captivated the English. He was a true patron, also, of the rest of the arts as represented by the Greek and Latin classics he brought back to England from Rome; by the glass, gold, silver and colourful paintings with which he enriched the spacious interiors of his churches; and by the truly gorgeous embroidery on his vestments. Hilda's educa-tion had not really been given in vain : though it is easy to see why Wilfrid was so disliked by followers of the simple Celtic tradition his innovations were a necessary, wholesome and colourful development in the history of the Catholic Church in England.

But that church needed also the very different personality of St. Cuthbert. In 684—the ninth year of his retirement—Theodore held a synod at Twyford, Northumberland, presided over by king Ecgfrith. There he was " by the unanimous consent of all, chosen bishop of the church of Lindisfarne. And when he could by no means be dragged from his place by the many messengers and letters that were sent to him, at length this same king himself . . . as well as many other religious and powerful men, sailed to the island; they all knelt down and adjured him in the name of the Lord, with tears and prayers, until at last they drew him, also shedding many tears, from his sweet retirement and led him to the synod. When he had come, in spite of his reluctance he was overcome by the unanimous will of them all and compelled to submit his neck to the yoke of the bishopric."

Boisil had told him he should rise to the rank of bishop, an honour he had always dreaded; though knowing well, as he said, that he could " not escape anywhere from the decree of the Ruler of Heaven." By the time Theodore consecrated him St. Cuthbert was far from strong. It is therefore amazing to read of all he accomplished in his wide diocese in the one year before he was allowed a last winter on Farne. When invited he gladly dedicated churches far outside his own territory, a habit of Celtic bishops most displeasing to the orderly Roman church though Theodore himself wisely ignored it. He crossed the country to Carlisle (where Herbert hastened to meet him) and the citizens proudly showed him their Roman walls and wonderful Roman fountain. But while he gazed at these remains of the past he thought sadly of Ecgfrith's recent cruel expedition into friendly Ireland (where, in mistaken zeal for the Roman cause his soldiers had " miserably afflicted and burnt God's churches "), and his mind leapt suddenly into the future so that he beheld King Ecgfrith's death in battle against the Picts.

It happened just as he had foreseen. Aghast at the invasion of Ireland the Picts rose in defence of their Church and liberties before they too should be attacked. In 685 " greatly against the advice of his friends, and particularly of Cuthbert " King Ecgfrith marched north crossing the Forth and the Tay till he met the Pictish army at Nectansmere in Forfarshire. In that terrible battle he and almost all his army lost their lives. That fateful year saw too a large scale revolt of Britons from the south. Between the two blows Northumbria staggered ; and though she went bravely on under her new pro-Celtic King Alfrid, foster-son of Adamnan of Iona and bastard brother of Ecgfrith, till then " in exile among the islands of the Scots, for the study of letters," yet she never regained the political supremacy she had enjoyed throughout St. Cuthbert's whole lifetime.

For St. Cuthbert had little longer to live. It was, indeed, only because he was dying that he was permitted to return to his island. The story of his last months is beautifully told by Bede. He had it from abbot Herefrith who, despite St. Cuthbert's longing to die alone, insisted on coming over to be with him. Every detail rings true. No one could read unmoved this vivid piece of biography. At last, on the 20th of March, 687, the end came " and stretching out his hands aloft he sent forth his spirit, in the very act of praising God, to the joy of the heavenly kingdom."

Even on his way to heaven the would-be hermit was not alone, for when they met at Carlisle Herbert had begged that they might " journey together to the skies." This favour St. Cuthbert obtained and " they departed from the body at the same moment of time . . . and together they were borne to the heavenly kingdom by the ministry of angels."

The author of a new and rational book on why great saints are not great, writes as follows : " It is difficult to escape the conviction that daily life in the company of such types would have been a burdensome experience." Burdensome ! St. Cuthbert's many friends would have laughed aloud. Living, he drew them to him so that they clamoured for his presence. He was like a magnet they could never hope to reach. When he lay dead in his stone coffin, dressed in his episcopal robes and "wearing his shoes in readiness to meet Christ" they could not bear to abandon him even at the coming of the terrible Vikings. Rather than be separated when at last they had him always with them, the monks carried the coffin containing his incorruptible body all the way from Lindisfarne to Durham.

Far from being burdensome to others, and a thing of gloom, St. Cuthbert's English life makes as lovely and buoyant a picture as does the life of his Scotic master St. Columba.

The founder of Iona stands surrounded by the hundred sea-girt churches he founded and by a border of all the beautiful books he wrote—each one as exquisitely designed and coloured as the Book of Kells. Above him, but quite close, is heaven, alive with a white rush of angels' wings.

For the outer border of St. Cuthbert's portrait there are otters and ravens and waves and wind. They all served him gladly. In the centre he kneels alone on his little island, his face turned up to heaven; but edging the distant shore and approaching in small boats from every side are peasants and nobles, nuns and abbesses, monks and abbots, stretching out their hands. He is a saint as completely surrounded by the love of his Celtic and English friends as his island is by the sea.

Sources :
Two Lives of St. Cuthbert. Ed. Bertram Colgrave.
Only Bede's prose *Life* is here used, based as it is on the shorter anonymous
Ecclesiastical History of England. Bede. Ed. J. A. Giles.   [*Life.*
Anglo-Saxon Chronicle. Ed. J. A. Giles.
The Celtic Church after the Synod of Whitby. J. L. G. Meissner.
A History of Europe. H. A. L. Fisher.
The Historical St. Columba. W. D. Simpson.

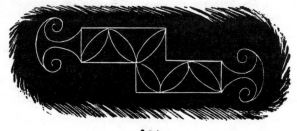

CHAPTER XI.

ST. BRIGID AND HER SISTER SAINTS

"GOOD heavens, what women these Christians have !" By the fourth century Libanius' exclamation of admiration mingled with dismay was being echoed by men in all the Latin and Greek-speaking countries surrounding the Mediterranean. Pagan races varied greatly in their treatment of women ; some suppressed them : while Jews and Teutons held them in high regard. But Christians, whether they wished to or not, were no longer able to suppress them, since Christ had given women the freedom of their homes by his prohibition of divorce ; and an alternative to marriage in the celibate life devoted to prayer and charity—a life sometimes lived quite apart from the family.

It is to the eternal credit of St. Paul that despite the dangers he risked in allowing his women converts to leave their sheltered homes and roam freely on their errands of mercy, over pagan lands where the standard of sexual morality was deplorably low, he yet led what was to become a veritable revolution. He only insisted (and it is this insistence alone that is generally noticed) that in the full practice of their religion his sisters in Christ should be shielded as much as possible from temptations very real to those brought up solely to please or to serve men. Again and again he admonishes them to cultivate a quiet, reserved manner and to dress always in the soberest of clothes. It was only common sense : and largely because of St. Paul's combined courage and common sense, Christian women won their freedom.

As the centuries rolled on men—even Christian men—were inclined, quite understandably, to resent this new breed of women. The following remarks by Sulpicius Severus, the fourth century author of St. Martin's life, are typical. "The woman should remain in safety behind the walls of the city. Her chief virtue, her crowning glory is ever to remain invisible." It is to be hoped that Sulpicius Severus never

205

heard the laughter of his female readers as they shook their heads over his absurdly masculine ideal. When he can find fault with one of his frailer Christian sisters Sulpicius Severus does so with gusto. Writing of a widow he had occasion to rebuke, he says, " She was indeed a capricious and coquettish spendthrift of a woman, and she was leading a life of flagrant folly."

St. Jerome, however, found Paula's excellent business head so invaluable that he persuaded her and her daughter to leave Rome and help him found his monastery near Bethlehem. It is not he but she who complains of the difficulties of looking after so irritable a genius. It is doubtful whether they could have remained such good friends had not Paula been followed to Bethlehem by so many women that she founded her own monastery for them, only visiting St. Jerome in her spare time. Monnica, too, was greatly troubled by her son, later to become St. Augustine of Hippo. But he, amazed at her contribution to a learned discussion, writes that " we fairly forgot her sex."

When in the fifth century St. Patrick arrived in Ireland, he found that the Celts had long respected their women. In pre-Christian times, when Hannibal made a league with their race they made the following stipulation ". . . but if the Carthaginians have anything to lay to the charge of the Celts it shall be brought before the Celtic women." The men of Ireland had even gone so far (in legend) as to imagine their beloved country to be a woman ruling over the men of Erin.

But though the women St. Patrick met already played an important part in the life of the community, even attending public assemblies and enjoying a surprising amount of power and independence, there was as yet no alternative to family life. However, as a fifth century home did not buy, but actually made almost everything possessed by the family, much of the women's work was interesting and creative. Indeed the only members of their sex who deserve our pity were the female slaves who were treated simply as bits of property. St. Patrick writes of those of them converted to Christianity that " they constantly endure even unto terrors and threats. But the Lord gave grace to many of His hand-maidens, for, although they are forbidden, they earnestly follow the example set them." He, and St. Brigid after him, worked hard to free them.

"See," wrote St. Patrick, "how in Ireland there has lately been formed a people of the Lord. . . . Sons and daughters of Irish chieftains are seen to become monks and nuns . . . and their number increases more and more." It was partly because women played so important a part in his church from the first that St. Brigid was able to attain, within her lifetime, to such a unique position in her country. But only partly; for St. Brigid herself is unique.

She was born about 453—twenty years after St. Patrick's landing and eight years before his death. In her were represented both the proudest and most down-trodden sections of the Irish community, for her father was Dubthach one of the pagan Scotic chiefs of Leinster and her mother was a Pictish Christian slave. Shortly before St. Brigid's birth the poor woman was resold to a druid owning land in the west. There the child was born, remaining till she was old enough to serve her legal owner, her father. Her mother taught her all she knew of the Christian faith and even took her, while still almost a baby, to hear the great St. Patrick preach. Here was an opportunity to be grasped by even the youngest saint. But St. Brigid not only fell asleep long before the end of the sermon; but when she woke up she ignored the old bishop and discoursed to the congregation at shocking length on the exciting dream she had just enjoyed. If the story be true then St. Patrick, who loved children, must have been the most appreciative member of her audience. Later St. Brigid was given to speaking with impressive brevity; though all her life she retained the same irrepressible gaiety. Her high spirits were partly due, no doubt, to the possession of a perfectly strong and healthy body, but even more because she so soon grew to see the world through God's eyes.

Back in Leinster she dismayed her father and scandalised his wife by her incorrigible generosity. Having nothing of her own to give away it was her father's possessions that continually disappeared. If she encountered a starved dog she flung it all the food she could find; if a beggar came to the door for bread and she thought he needed more, she ran straight out and fetched him one of her father's sheep. When reprimanded she only answered that Christ dwelt in every living creature and that from Him, to Whom all mankind owed so immeasurable a debt, nothing should be withheld.

Later, even St. Brigid's devoted nuns were to protest against the reckless measure of her giving. Small wonder then that her pagan father found her impossible. At last he drove her in his chariot to the *dun* of the King of Leinster purposing to sell her as profitably as he could. After a searching look at that lovely stubborn young face he left his daughter in charge of the horses (no beast or bird but adored St. Brigid) while he tried to explain the situation to the king, making as light as he could of the girl's unfortunate habit and extolling her strength and her exceptionally good looks.

Meanwhile a begging leper had crept up behind the chariot in which St. Brigid sat awaiting her fate. She turned round and gazed through the terrible remains of his face right into his lonely soul. Beside her lay her father's skilfully wrought sword, beautiful in itself, and, to him—a proud chief of "Leinster of the Battles"—his most treasured possession. None the less lifting it up she smiled at the leper. Then she passed it to him humbly, as though to a king.

But she did not look at all humble when she stood before the king of Leinster that he might examine her. Dubthach could not concentrate on the deal so "mightily enraged" was he to discover what had happened to his sword. He refused to listen though St. Brigid kept explaining calmly that through the leper she had given the sword to God, choosing it just because of its great value. But the King of Leinster was a Christian; and suddenly, as her father was about to strike her, he intervened commanding Dubthach to let her alone "for her merit before God is greater than ours."

As he drove her home again, Dubthach decided that there was nothing for it but to give his problem daughter her freedom. No sooner given, than, like a wild bird released

ST. BRIGID IN THE CURRAGH

from a cage, St. Brigid flew rapturously across the country to make a present of her freedom to her mother. The work of most bondswomen was extremely monotonous. They ground corn by the hour, they stood, holding lights, while their masters supped; they formed indeed a substitute for the scientific inventions we employ to ease our drudgery. But St. Brigid found her mother (who must surely have been a remarkable woman) in charge of a dairy. The management of twelve cows may be arduous but it is not unpleasant. The only thing that St. Brigid found intolerable was that her mother had no choice but to do what she was told or starve. Relegating the tired, ageing woman to the kitchen she herself set about reorganising the dairy. She was on her feet from morning till night; yet because she did the work of her own free will her energy was boundless and she sang daily to her enchanted cows. Needless to say she found time to give away to those less happy than herself quantities of her master's butter and even some of his best cows. It seemed to make no difference. Under her care the dairy so flourished that at last the grateful druid who owned it granted his dynamic dairymaid what she desired above all—her mother's freedom.

For the second time St. Brigid left the west to go to her father. But this time it was she who chose to return to "Leinster of the Battles" and she who decided that it was best that her mother, now safely ensconced in her own cottage, should remain in peace in the west.

When she returned to her father's *dun* she found that he had taken the trouble to arrange a marriage for her. The husband selected for her by Dubthach shows how greatly St. Brigid had risen in his estimation. He was an eligible young poet; and in fifth century Ireland bards, because of their great learning, ranked next to kings. But St. Brigid told her father that she was already dedicated to God as were many other "virgins in Christ" already striving to follow their vocation in their homes. "They did it," writes St. Patrick, "not with the consent of their fathers; but they endure persecution and lying reproaches from their kindred." It is possible that Dubthach was hurt enough by his daughter's refusal to accept the poet to behave as did those other fathers. But it seems more probable that by this time he had grown to appreciate her and that he supported her next move.

First she went to Bishop Mel, a disciple of St. Patrick's, and after due preparation, he received her final vows. Then she gathered about her seven more nuns and, dressed in white with a white veil over her long hair, she hastened to the rescue of all those persecuted Christian women whose invaluable lives were being wasted simply through lack of a leader.

Alice Curtayne has remarked on the paradox that for St. Brigid, entering a convent meant " becoming one of the most indefatigable travellers in the land." This was because she had no sooner filled her first foundation with nuns and found a sister competent to run the place in her absence, than she was off in her chariot, accompanied by a few chosen helpers, to plant a similar one elsewhere.

When St. Brigid started her great work the First Order of Saints, the bishops, still ruled supreme in the Celtic Church in Ireland. At once they recognised the crying need for her innovation and not only did they protect her communities of women but so invaluable did they consider her Christian settlements as havens for the poor, the sick and the tired traveller, and as schools for prospective converts and Christian children, that they all besought her to come and found convents in their own special districts. It is because St. Brigid never failed to respond that her name is written across the length and breadth of Ireland.[1] Among the hundreds of bishops who consulted and appealed to her were St. Finnian, Master of the Saints of Ireland, Bishop Fiacc the poet (who played so dramatic a part in the life of St. Patrick) and Bishop Erc whom we have also met as the man who selected St. Brendan's first school. All St. Brigid's travels in Munster were organised by Bishop Erc.

But however influential the bishop in whose cause she travelled, he could not make smooth roads for her through the huge forests and bogs and lonely mountains of fifth century Ireland. Nor could he control the incessant discord among the

[1] There are innumerable Kilbrides and Kilbreedies (meaning the cells or churches of St. Brigid). Glens and rivers too were named after her by her contemporaries.

chiefs about which St. Patrick complained and which is a feature also of the period in which St. Brigid lived. So, often, she was thrown out of her chariot when it overturned in a hidden ditch; and often she was held up by would-be robbers and murderers. Once her two horses bolted. But she always arrived at her destination ready to make a good story for bishop friends out of her misadventures. For St. Brigid could enjoy her mishaps; but it is to be feared that the sisters who travelled with her did not so much enjoy as endure the shocks and bruises they sustained through bravely following their intrepid leader.

When any bishops visited her at Kildare—and once seven arrived on the same day—she treated them as fellow saints. One, indeed, who dared to murmur, as he descended from his chariot, that he felt hungry after his long journey, she sharply reprimanded. " So are we hungry—for instruction," she told the wilting man. " Go into the church and speak first and then we shall eat."

This story probably belongs to the later part of St. Brigid's life when, towards the end of the fifth century, she had established Kildare on the site given her on the Liffey plain by her friend the King of Leinster. Because she not only designed and supervised its structure (as she did with all her foundations) but remained its abbess, using it as the base from which she worked, Kildare quickly became the largest and most famous of her monasteries. It grew so fast that she soon felt the need of a resident bishop to ordain priests, consecrate nuns and supervise her many male workers. She appointed Conlaeth—a monk already famous for his exquisite metal work—and he was duly consecrated by one of the numerous bishops she knew. Close to St. Brigid's convent he founded a school where he taught his art so successfully that thousands of handbells, staffs, chalices, patens[1], book-rests and book-covers were produced by the monks of Kildare and sent off to become the treasures of little churches all over the land.

It is possible to visualise the plan of Kildare because all the early Celtic mission stations were adaptations of the *duns*

[1]Gold or silver salvers used for the consecrated bread at the Eucharist.

of the chieftains, as was that very early Ninianic settlement of Nendrum on Mahee Island, Strangford Lough, the remains of which have fortunately been scientifically examined.[1] They reveal an impressive picture of how wisely these Celtic Christians arranged the pattern of their lives.

There is no trace left of the original Kildare, but like Nendrum and the contemporary *duns*, three thick walls probably separated the community within from the outer world. The walls were far enough apart to allow of two sheltered walks much favoured by nuns in cold windy weather. A strong wide gate across the entrance through the outermost wall could be closed at night but generally stood hospitably open so passionate was St. Brigid's championship of the poor. An avenue bordered on each side with the little wooden workshops, producing all the requirements of the community, led straight from the gateway to the centre of the enclosure at which focal point stood the church. Cogitosus, a Kildare monk who wrote St. Brigid's *Life* in the seventh century, tells us that the church St. Brigid built for her large community was "elevated to a menacing height." The word Kildare, however, means the oak church; and its roof was most likely thatched, so that Cogitosus's statement cannot mean more than that the building exceeded the size of most modest Celtic churches. But inside, either by the light of the "many windows" or when the torches were lit, the place must have been truly beautiful so great was the Celtic love of colour. As is customary in the Greek Orthodox Church, a rood screen concealed the altar, and this screen was covered with the celebrated tapestry and paintings so wickedly destroyed by the Vikings. The walls of the church, too, were decorated with hangings and pictures, the latter no doubt the work of those monks who made Kildare famous above all for the brilliance of its illuminated books; while the former were spun, woven and designed by the happy sisters. Gold and silver work were also introduced to the glory of God; but perhaps the most interesting feature of the interior was

[1] Among these remains has been found a sundial. Such clocks were probably in use in most Celtic monasteries to tell at what time the bell should be rung for the different services. Celts were always keen astronomers.

the partition running up the centre aisle. St. Brigid wished her monks and the local Christians to sing and pray with her nuns; but that the sisters might not be distracted she used this sensible means of separating the sexes. "Thus," says Cogitosus, " in one very great temple a multitude of people of different order and rank and sex and situation . . . but with one mind worship Almighty God."

Behind the church St. Brigid and her nuns dwelt in the innermost part of the enclosure. A whole village of little huts stood there in which the sisters prayed, meditated, and slept. The huts probably contained no furniture at all but their floors had a warm lining of rushes.

To the right and left of the front of the church there was space enough for the pigs and poultry; though the enclosure was small and almost all the cultivated land owned by the monastery naturally lay outside its walls.

St. Brigid loved her farm. She helped with the harvest; and we read in an ancient life that " she came from her sheep to welcome Brendan." The chronology of the story is a little dubious as St. Brendan could have been no more than twenty when St. Brigid died; and yet we know that he never invoked her aid in vain when wrestling in his coracle with intractable sea-monsters. He surely called out to her in heaven because he had actually seen her walking in her earthly meadows surrounded by her beasts and birds. Perhaps she had shown him the once wild boar which had astonished the workers in the little huts by dashing past them up the avenue to take refuge in the church from a host of pursuing huntsmen. Naturally, St. Brigid refused to give up the terrified animal and stayed to soothe it after they had gone. As for the boar, it decided to abandon the joys of the forest and remained for the rest of its life a biddable and respected member of her herd.

The rhythmic disciplined freedom of the wild duck which visited her marshes so regularly, entranced the mystic in the practical St. Brigid. One day, while they were feeding, she called them to come to her where she stood watching them in the field. They gathered round her obediently while she stooped to caress them marvelling at the beauty of their bodies. But after she had given them her final blessing they could not be induced to leave her. Dimly they felt that she had discovered an even more joyful freedom than theirs.

One day, while St. Brigid was returning from a visit to one of her convents a baby fox sprang into her chariot and thrust its red head confidingly into the folds of her habit. Doubtless it had lost its mother and suddenly knew instinctively that here was the perfect substitute. St. Brigid found it irresistible; nor did she have the slightest trouble over its education as its sole desire was to please her. But the more accomplished the little fox grew the more she felt what a perfect present it would make for her friend the King of Leinster. At last she drove it with her to his *dun*, showed him how exceedingly clever it was, and left him playing delightedly with his new pet. But the little fox felt exactly as did that poor lady whose gift of choice apples St. Brigid there and then distributed among the lepers at her gate. "I did not bring the apples for those lepers," she cried. "I brought them for *you*." The lady got short shrift; but the little fox, who had learnt its tricks solely to please its fascinating mistress, fared much better. As soon as possible it escaped from the king's *dun* and "went safely back through the wood, the hosts of Leinster behind, both foot and horse and hound." It knew well that St. Brigid could never refuse sanctuary.

If the dogs of twentieth century Highland shepherds accompany them regularly to church we may be perfectly sure that their ancestors did exactly the same in the Dark Ages. Everyone would take the congregation of dogs at Kildare as a matter of course; but prominent among the dogs was a glorious splash of red-gold, and few there were who could resist a glance at the fox which always lay at the back of the church silently worshipping St. Brigid.

Perhaps no woman has ever had so many legends woven round her life. Long before she died on the 1st February, 523, they were everywhere in the making, so greatly did her country rejoice in her existence. When taken literally many of them seem incredible; though it is well to remember that legend, like poetry, often contains a higher degree of truth than do the bare bones of history. Out of the wealth of miracles there emerges, somewhat surprisingly, the picture of one of the most downright, practical and human of all the Celtic saints. St. Brigid never fought for her causes; somehow they were always won as soon as she championed them. Neither did she feel the need for long retreats from social life so boundless was the energy she drew from her love of the Creator. She always saw Him through the fallen world of nature, animals and human beings He had redeemed. What she did for Him was to give ceaselessly of everything she possessed. It is said that she preached; but for the most part it was through continual practical giving that she taught her country the lesson of charity it so badly needed.

Sometimes it was quite literally herself that she placed before sinners. The chiefs of Ireland filled the land with bloodshed because they were too proud to forgive an injury. But St. Brigid knew nothing of pride. When the two sons of the High King of Tara determined to have a battle over a boundary, St. Brigid and her nuns fell in humbly behind the army of one of the brothers and persisted, despite their entreaties, in following them over the hills to the battlefield. There the women stood in a row and watched while the opponents approached each other. But somehow that regiment of calm white nuns brought the brothers to their senses and instead of fighting, the whole party gathered together to enjoy a merry picnic.

St. Brigid's idea of heaven was just such a joyful banquet; but with enough food to last her guests for eternity. Great was her wrath, one day during Lent, when two sanctimonious nuns refused the chance of a good meal despite the fact that a famine had brought the convent to the verge of starvation. She always loved good cheer; and when, as often, the food at her earthly banquets ran out, she turned for refreshment to music, drawing forth, even from those who had never played the harp before, melodies so infectiously lively that soon she had the whole company singing. Often the peasant girls and slave girls who loved her blended their voices with the visiting bishops and kings. For to St. Brigid, who could see Christ clearly in everyone, class meant nothing. And it is amusing to read that she so delighted in cleanliness that bishops and slaves alike had often to wait patiently to consult her till she had finished enjoying her daily bath.

She revelled in water; though unlike most Celtic saints it was the rivers of Ireland she loved, having little to do with the sea. But the green pastures of Leinster are the proper setting for St. Brigid. " One day walking in the Curragh and admiring the beautiful fields rich in clover blossoms, she said that if these fields were hers she would offer them all to the Lord of the Elements." The tale is told in one of the ancient *Lives* and the author adds that St. Columba (who wrote a poem to St. Brigid) was so impressed when he first heard it that he cried: " God is as pleased as if she did in fact own the fields and make this offering to him."

But St. Brigid's offering to God was her whole being. Cogitosus realised this. When he wrote her *Life* in the seventh century the Celtic Church considered, as it always did, that frequent and regular Holy Communion was essential to the well-being of the soul. St. Brigid, he said " was a consecrated casket for keeping Christ's Body and His Blood." The casket was not ornate; it was simply and beautifully shaped by God out of the clover and the corn and the wind and the rain of Ireland.

St. Brigid may be said to have invented the double monastery. To her it seemed only commonsense to have a neighbouring community of monks under her rule; then they could concentrate on the heavier outdoor work while the sisters, so to speak, ran the house. In this way the monks and nuns between them were able to achieve her goal of a self-supporting monastery that yet had leisure to devote to the outside world.

The biographers of St. Ninian, St. David and St. Kentigern make little or no mention of women; and in sixth century Ireland almost all the saints belonged to that Second Order of presbyters who, unlike St. Patrick and his immediate followers (" they feared not the blast of temptation "), seem

to have made little use of women as active members of the
Celtic Church.

But the human heart, male or female, was an open book
to all the great Celtic saints of the Dark Ages. Again and
again they were called upon to take the place of the modern
judge or psychiatrist. Adamnan tells us how St. Columba
hastened to the help of a couple reported to be living miserably
together on one of the western islands of Scotland. First he
saw the husband, an ill-shapen, heart-broken man whose wife
refused to sleep with him. Then he saw the wife. She was
desperate. That one thing excepted she would, she said, do
anything he bade her. "I do not refuse to do all the house-
work, or, if thou do so bid me, even to cross the sea and
remain in some monastery of maidens." Had she lived in the
next century and consulted Wilfrid he would doubtless have
added her to the list of unhappy wives he placed in convents.
But the Celtic Church held different views on marriage.
St. Columba's one idea was to make it possible for these two
to remain together. So he said: "Let us three, namely I,
and the husband with the wife, pray to the Lord fasting."
They agreed to try. To make quite sure St. Columba prayed
all that day and right through the night. Next day he called
them before him and asked the woman if she still pined for a
monastery. "Now I know," she said, "that thy prayer to
God for me is heard. For him whom I hated yesterday I love
today, for my heart this night past—how I know not—has
been changed in me from hate to love." Fortunate pair!
"From that day to the day of her death the soul of that wife
was indissolubly cemented in love to her husband."

That a sixth century woman living on a remote island
should know of the existence of "monasteries of maidens"
on the mainland proves that these, though rarely mentioned,
were still numerous. Most of these monasteries seem to have
followed the sensible pattern of Kildare; and almost invariably
the abbess ruled supreme, the resident bishop being under her
authority just as he would have been had he worked with an
abbot. If this had not been so in the sixth century double
monasteries (in which the churches were partitioned as at

Kildare) could never have been so marked a feature of the Celtic Church among the English in the seventh and eighth centuries. Only the Italian clergy protested at the enormity of a woman in full control of both sexes. The whole principle of the double monastery scandalised them. But Tacitus had remarked with surprise that Teutons "neither scorn to consult [their women] nor slight their answers." The Northumbrian kings, therefore, though somewhat dismayed that their wives and daughters should prefer God's company to theirs, soon learnt to benefit by the Celtic recognition of the equality of the sexes. Indeed Hilda, the great abbess of Whitby, and her successors, were often sorely pressed by the queues of kings, princes and bishops who sought their advice. Of Hilda Bede writes that "she was a woman devoted to God" and that "all who knew her called her Mother." Though closely related to the thoughtful King Edwin and therefore to the rest of the Christian kings of Northumbria, she was brought up a pagan and it was not till after her conversion, when she was already thirty, that she decided (there being as yet only one convent in Northumbria) to go to Chelles, a monastery near Paris much frequented by English girls.[1]

Fortunately for England bishop Aidan of Lindisfarne heard of her plans during one of his missionary journeys through Northumbria. They met; and the Celtic bishop, whom no one could resist, succeeded in changing Hilda's mind. He was one of the many to profit by her life at Hartlepool[2] and later at Whitby for he "knew and loved her and diligently instructed her because of her innate wisdom and inclination to the service of God." She was not only an efficient organiser but became one of the most brilliant teachers of her age. She educated no less than five outstanding bishops at a time when there were only fourteen throughout the land.

[1] Seventh century English girls were also educated at Faremoutiers where Burgundofara, the little girl once blessed by St. Columban, was abbess of one of the most famous monasteries in France, founded for her in 617 by St. Columban's disciple Eusthasius.

[2] The names of St. Hilda's nuns at Hartlepool can still be read cut in their stone pillows, each pillow incised with a cross.

Such was her position in the Church that it was in her monastery that the Synod of Whitby was held in 664 though her pupil Wilfrid well knew her to be one of the staunchest upholders of the Celtic traditions brought to England from Iona. Indeed so strong was St. Hilda's party that the Romans could do little to alter Celtic peculiarities; and there was never any question of abolishing the many obnoxious double monasteries, so greatly were they valued by the English people they served. Secure in their love St. Hilda made no changes at Whitby after the Synod.

In her monastery there was a stable hand called Caedmon so shy and tongue-tied that when at an entertainment (and like St. Brigid St. Hilda loved a party) '' it was agreed for the sake of mirth that all present should sing in their turns '' this man always slunk away from the fireside and went back to his horses before it should be too late. St. Hilda must often have smiled at his ways. One night, after he had slipped away as usual and was drifting off to sleep in the stables, a voice commanded him : '' Sing the beginning of created things.'' Whereupon he presently began to sing praises of God which he had never heard.'' In the morning he still remembered them, and the steward, amazed, conducted him to St. Hilda. She listened to him carefully and when she had made her decision she called together her learned clergy to hear him recite his poetry and to decide '' whence came his verses.'' They agreed unanimously that these were from God. After they had further tested Caedmon with passages of holy writ which they expounded to him and which he duly returned to them the next morning transformed into the sweetest verse, St. Hilda instructed him to leave his horses and become a monk. She herself supervised his education to be quite sure that he was taught '' the whole series of sacred history.'' So was St. Hilda responsible for the first flowering of our English sacred poetry that was to culminate gloriously in Milton's ''Paradise Lost.'' The great abbess died on the 18th November, 680, after six years of continual fever, active to the last. That night, thirteen miles away from Whitby, in the daughter house of Hackness, one of the nuns woke up and was greatly alarmed to see through the roof St. Hilda's soul departing, "attended and conducted to heaven by angels."

The next abbess of Whitby was Elfleda, St. Hilda's young cousin, and one of King Oswy's four remarkable children. Her brothers we have already met; they were Wilfrid's pro-Roman friend Alfrid; Oswy's successor King Ecgfrith; and (after Ecgfrith's death in battle against the Picts) Ecgfrith's successor King Alfrith who, it will be remembered, remained until 685 "in exile among the islands of the Scots for the study of letters." Alfrith shared with Elfeda a passionate love of the Celtic form of Christianity in contrast to Alfrid and Ecgfrith who both met disaster through their zeal for the Roman cause.

St. Elfleda was brought up at Whitby by her cousin Hilda, herself a disciple of Aidan. So her views are not to be wondered at. Nor is it very surprising that St. Hilda should have chosen as her successor the child Oswy had dedicated to God as a thank-offering for his final victory over Penda though the two women had very different personalities. More dependent than her cousin, St. Elfleda owned that in her responsible position she found in her bishop (who was, of course, under her authority as abbess) "extraordinary assistance in governing and comfort to herself." She was also given to leaning on St. Cuthbert and "always had a great affection for the man of God." He loved her dearly; though at times her curiosity must have tried his patience. Just before St. Cuthbert left his tiny island of Farne to become bishop of Lindisfarne a message was brought to him by one of St. Elfleda's monks. "She humbly asked the hermit of God in the name of the Lord to cross the sea and meet her at Cocquet Island." Obediently he sailed down the coast. St. Elfleda had prepared a list of questions which she felt that only St. Cuthbert could answer. Among them she demanded "by the nine orders of angels" to be told how long her brother king Ecgfrith would live. St. Cuthbert had the gift of prophecy and though he tried for her sake to prevaricate, it was quite useless. She insisted on hearing the truth. When he told her that Ecgfrith would die within the year, the foolish creature burst into tears and had to be comforted. No sooner was she recovered, however, than she pressed him afresh—this time to find out who would succeed to the Northumbrian throne. But St. Cuthbert was devoted to the incorrigible woman and during his year as bishop of Lindisfarne he always accepted her invitations to cross the boundaries of the diocese within which Theodore had so earnestly begged him to remain. For Roman customs, however orderly and logical, were not to be compared with the importance of serving a friend. If St. Elfleda wished him to dedicate her new churches—however far away—he responded joyfully at the first possible opportunity.

St. Elfleda confided to Herefrith (a friend both of St. Cuthbert and Bede) that at one time in her life she was so ill that she almost died. The doctors could do nothing for what seems to have been a rheumatic complaint. By divine grace alone her condition did improve slightly but unfortunately " she could neither stand upright nor move about except on all fours." She found it next to impossible to run a large monastery from this position and at last, in desperation, she cried out: " Would that I had something belonging to my Cuthbert." No sooner were her words reported to him than St. Cuthbert sent her his girdle. " She girded herself with it, and in the morning she could stand. In three days she was cured." She could neither return nor treasure the miraculous girdle, because, after curing one of her nuns of " an intolerable pain in the head " it mysteriously and, she decided, discreetly, vanished.

The last glimpse we have of St. Elfleda is the more impressive because it is not preserved by Bede, but by Eddius who wrote the *Life* of his pro-Roman master Wilfrid. Though educated by St. Hilda, bishop Wilfrid was wont, as we already know, to send what Bede pleasantly calls " a veritable breeze of trial " through any Celtic monastery he attempted to remould. Indeed his outspoken Roman views and his shockingly loud, rich style of living soon grew so unpopular that the kings, ministers and bishops of Northumbria, ignoring Wilfrid's champion the Pope, continually met together with

223

the sole purpose of banishing or even imprisoning him. This had to be done at frequent intervals, because, when banished, Wilfrid made straight for Rome always reappearing with fresh documents demanding his reinstatement. In 705 the indefatigable man appeared yet again and at once a synod was held by the river Nidd to consider his claims. St. Elfleda was present, "always the comforter and the best adviser of the whole province." Though she must have disliked the tactless, tempestuous man as much as anyone she felt it her duty to rise and tell the assembly that when, a short time before, she and her friend Oedilburga had attended the death bed of her brother, King Aldfrith—that loyal patron of all that was Celtic —he had told her that when he had recovered from what proved to be a fatal illness he had decided to reinstate Wilfrid and do his best to live at peace with Rome. On hearing this the assembled bishops proved themselves to be truly English. Their consciences were even stronger than their inborn love of independence and, after further discussion, they agreed with St. Elfleda that the late king's wishes must be granted. But they were also English in that they compromised; and Wilfrid found himself shorn of much of his former power.

St. Elfleda's friend, Oedilburga, was abbess of Hackness. Her monastery still stands; and in the church, even now, there are visible signs of how greatly she was loved by her nuns. Carved in stone are the words ' Mater amantissima '— dearest of mothers.

Another Northumbrian princess who spent her life governing and founding double monasteries was St. Ebba, sister of King Oswald and King Oswy. She usually chose to build her large settlements on the sites of Roman forts, thus intelligently saving her masons the trouble of laying foundations. Like her niece St. Elfleda she was devoted to St. Cuthbert whom she knew first when he was the young prior of Melrose. She asked him to stay with her at Coldingham; and we have already heard the story (first told by one of her monks) of how the saint spent his nights in the sea. St. Abb's Head still recalls Ebba's active life in the district; but there is little left of the original Coldingham. And this is scarcely surprising. The last entry for the year 679 in the Anglo-Saxon Chronicle reads as follows: "And Coldingham was burned by fire from heaven." Bede goes further and says, "it was consumed by fire for its great wickedness." It is apparently an unspeakable kind of wickedness for though he also mentions the event elsewhere in his *History* Bede's pen becomes so distraught that the reader is merely confused. Coldingham was a double monastery and in that fact (though this is the only hint of scandal to be found) the explanation would seem to lie.

Until this tragedy the reputation of St. Ebba's monastery stood so high that, though the presence of monks there was entirely against his principles, Wilfrid yet chose Coldingham as a retreat for Queen Etheldreda when he had at last succeeded in wresting her from her unhappy husband. It must be confessed that though for nine years his influence over the queen nearly drove King Ecgfrith mad, Wilfrid did discover a potential saint in Etheldreda. Her nature was ill-suited to marriage with a king; but in the convent she was perfectly happy. "It is reported of her that from the time of her entering into the monastery, she never wore any linen but only woollen garments, and would rarely wash in a hot bath unless just before any of the great festivals . . . besides, she seldom did eat above once a day, unless some considerable distemper obliged her." After a year at Coldingham she went south to be abbess of Ely where, after seven years, she died of the plague. Though St. Etheldreda may seem to us the least attractive of the Anglo-Saxon abbesses, yet after her death she became a famous saint through the many miracles she worked. So widespread was the homage paid to her that gradually her frothing mouthful of a name (it should really be spelt Ethelthrytha) shrank to the simpler form of Audrey.

She was succeeded at Ely by her sister Sexburga who had likewise forsaken her husband the king of Kent[1]. After sixteen years, during which time St. Etheldreda's fame grew continually, Sexburga decided that a wooden coffin was not good enough for so powerful a saint. Her monks therefore sailed

[1]She and her husband sent their small daughter to Faremoutiers. By no means all the pupils in these monasteries took the veil. They were excellent boarding schools, as are many convents to-day.

across the Ely marshes to an abandoned Roman town where, providentially, they found a fine marble coffin. Both St. Etheldreda's doctor and Wilfrid were present when Sexburga prised open the lid of the old wooden coffin and cried: " Glory be to the name of the Lord!" For the body was incorruptible. The doctor who had, in her last illness, lanced a great swelling in her neck, testified that the wound he had then made was now reduced to " an extraordinarily slender scar." As for the new coffin, it was " as if it had been made purposely for her, and the place for the head particularly cut, exactly fit for her head, and shaped to a nicety."

Coldingham, Hartlepool, Whitby, Ely—they are four out of many missing links in a chain of double monasteries stretching from the north to the south of England, and all deriving from Iona. The monastery of Wimborne is in what is now Dorset—away to the south-west of Ely—and there, in the eighth century, lived Leoba. Later she went to Germany as a missionary where she fortunately rescued from oblivion some few of the escapades of her attractively frivolous companions, by relating them to her biographer, Fulda. On one occasion the young nuns decided they needed extra sleep. They argued that if they could steal the keys of the church, of which the sister in charge had a bristling bunch, they would surely escape the early service. Accordingly with great cunning, it was done. But to their disgust Tetta (as they nick-named their abbess) had them roused as usual. They merely prayed elsewhere. Afterwards, as they passed the closed church they were all (or nearly all) astonished to see lying on the doorstep, a small, dead fox holding the lost keys in its mouth. Tetta did not hesitate. Seizing the keys and briskly removing the fox, she unlocked the door and led her five hundred nuns into the building. There they held a long, full service of thanksgiving for the miracle.

It is shocking to relate that these same young women so disliked a particularly severe sister that when she died they danced on her grave till the newly made mound became a hollow. Again their joy was short-lived, for Tetta ordered a three days' fast for all, with constant prayers for the departed.

Tetta's vivacious brood was probably dressed much as are young novices to-day and their rule, though more Romanised, still owed much to the Celtic Church. But girls in the earlier monasteries under the Pictish rule of Columban wore white habits over what seem to have been brightly coloured tartan petticoats—a charming sight when they, too, danced on the green grass.

St. Leoba herself, though she became a very great abbess, often erred endearingly in her youth. She was determined to captivate her famous cousin Boniface, later to become known as the Apostle of Germany: and so thoroughly did she succeed (though perhaps not quite in the way she had first intended) that the bishop ended by desiring her bones to be buried with his that they might rise together. Here she is, then, at Wimborne, writing to him for the first time and intent on impressing him with her learning. As they are cousins she sends a little present " to remind you of my littleness." She begs that " the shield of your prayer defend me against the poisoned darts of the hidden foe." Then comes the master-piece that is to take his breath away. " These verses under-written I have tried to compose in accordance with the rules of poetic tradition, not audaciously but in the desire to exercise the rudiments of a slender and feeble intellect and needing thy assistance. This art I learned under the teaching of Eadburga." In writing the four lines of Latin verse that then follow she was, alas, assisted by no other than ' the hidden foe,' for as Bishop Browne has pointed out, and as Boniface no doubt observed delightedly, they are copied whole-sale from the contemporary treatise on Latin composition by Aldhelm of Malmesbury.

By the time St. Aldhelm and St. Boniface lived, Canter-bury, through political changes in the country, had almost lost contact with York. The Archbishop of York dealt direct with Rome; and his Northumbrian Church, though gradually conforming more and more to the church of St. Peter, was yet strongly imbued with the spirit and learning of the Celtic Church of St. John, to which both Bede and Alcuin[1] owed so

[1] In 785, while he was Archbishop of York, Alcuin sent special help to Candida Casa " because of the holy men who had laboured there."

much. In Northumbria women like St. Ebba and St. Elfleda took part in all important synods till the coming of the Vikings.

In the south-west of England where St. Aldhelm worked, and on the continent where St. Boniface strove to convert the Germans, an ever-widening breach separated the two churches. Both men considered the Celtic clergy as little better than heretics. And they were everywhere. St. Bernard compares the widespread continental activities of Celtic missionaries from the British Isles during the fifth, sixth and seventh centuries to a great flood so many of them poured across the channel. Though in the eighth century Celtic missionaries still refused to conform to Rome except in the matter of Easter, Pope Gregory III thought so highly of their work in Germany that Boniface had to use many dubious tactics before he succeeded in getting them expelled as heretics—and then it was only for such reasons as that his Celtic rival Firgil, Bishop of Salzburg, was mad enough to declare that the earth was a globe on the under side of which people probably dwelt just as they did on the upper.

St. Aldhelm of Malmesbury frequently came in contact with British bishops from the west; but the contacts rather resembled collisions from which both parties withdrew hurt but unchanged. It was even in vain that he wrote them the letter that starts so persuasively: " We entreat you on our knees, in view of our future and common country in heaven, and of the angels our future fellow countrymen, do not persevere in your arrogant contempt of the decrees of St. Peter and the traditions of the Roman church, by a proud and tyrannical attachment to the decrees of your fathers[1]." The appeal was in vain because Celts have even longer memories than those Indian elephants they so correctly described in seventh century Ireland to their astounded students of geography. They could not trust Aldhelm of Malmsbury remembering as they did the arrogance of St. Augustine who had failed to rise and greet their predecessors a mere hundred

[1]Aldhelm wrote the best Latin among English scholars of his day because he learnt it from a Celtic teacher, Maeldubh.

years before. St. Aldhelm was an able and ardent exponent of the Roman cause and it is regrettable that he had to suffer for the sins of his fathers.

St. Boniface is equally touching when, about 746, he writes to his cousin Leoba (as St. Cuthbert might have written to Elfleda) asking for her prayers that his work in Germany might not prove fruitless. St. Leoba had long since put away such childish things as the deceitful copying of verses. She perceived at once that he was in sore need of help discouraged as he was by the multitudes of heathens and heretics that swarmed about his exile home. No doubt she prayed for him —and prayed as well as any Celtic saint. Indeed it seems almost certain she prayed to St. Brigid for advice : for the miracle she achieved was exactly what St. Brigid would have wished. At Kildare men and women worked side by side to promote the kingdom of heaven on earth. There were apparently no monks at the more Romanised Wimborne. But less than a year after St. Boniface appealed to his cousin there set out for Mainz a party of twelve monks from Malmsbury and twelve nuns from Wimborne. St. Leoba led the nuns ; and from the time of the arrival of the sisters St. Boniface's mission began to flourish. Indeed it is not too much to say that without St. Leoba and the practical St. Brigid behind and above her, St. Boniface could never have gained the proud title of " The Apostle of Germany."

To love people—even when they are saints—it is necessary first to know them. In making their acquaintance you may, of course, grow to dislike them. No materialist or completely rational scientist could be expected to relish the kind of human beings produced by the Celtic Church. But, given the chance to meet them the average Christian responds to them warmly. When, in 1928, the members of the Provincial Synod of the Episcopal Church in Scotland met in Edinburgh to revise the Scottish Book of Common Prayer, they compiled a Kalendar of one hundred and twenty saints to be commemorated throughout the year. No less than a third of these saints are men and women mentioned in this book. It is a fascinating list ; though the preponderance of men's names used to dishearten me even when I knew no more about the Celtic saints than that their names in the Kalendar made stout armour against a dull sermon. But now I am convinced that had the women of the Dark Ages not been so occupied in organising their monasteries and teaching future bishops (work which the men naturally took for granted) many more of their names would have been added to the Kalendar. As it was they had no leisure to write each other's *Lives*.

But thanks to Cogitosus, Bede and Eddius four of the saints we have met in this chapter have achieved excellent places among the heavenly ranks of the Kalendar. St. Hilda is there. She is flanked on each side by an eminently suitable Englishman, the one a king, the other a bishop. St. Ebba is there. She makes a ready listener for her mighty companion St. Augustine of Hippo. St. Etheldreda has an enviable position next the Beloved Physician, St. Luke. But to St. Brigid falls the greatest honour: for the date of her birth into eternity enables her to take part in the lovely feast of Candlemas, placing her as it does next to Mary, Mother of God.

Sources:
Enjoying the New Testament. Margaret T. Monro.
St. Ambrose, His Life and Times. Homes Dudden.
Irish Monasticism. John Ryan.
Lives of the Irish Saints, Vol. II. Ed. O'Hanlon
Lives of the Saints from the Book of Lismore. Ed. Whitley Stokes.
Acta Sanctorum Hiberniae. Ed. John Colgan, 1647, containing Cogitosus' *Life of St. Brigid,* and five other *Lives.*
Vitae Sanctorum Hiberniae. Ed. Plummer.
St. Brigid of Ireland. Alice Curtayne.
Ecclesiastical History of England. Bede. Ed. J. A. Giles.
Anglo-Saxon Chronicle. Ed. J. A. Giles.
Importance of Women in Anglo-Saxon Times. G. F. Browne.
Scottish Prayer Book, 1929.

CONCLUSION

HEN throughout the ninth century, Viking invaders disrupted life in the British Isles, spreading havoc and terror wherever they appeared, the people turned for help to the Celtic saints.

St. Kiaran of Clonmacnoise, like his friend St. Columba, had prophesied a passing earthly disaster in no uncertain terms. He even begged those who should pray to him after his death to " hasten to other places and leave my remains just like the dry bones of the stag on the mountain; for it is better that you should be with my spirit in heaven than to be alongside my bones on earth with scandal." They were wise words. None the less tremendous efforts were made by ninth century clerics to preserve the bodies of their beloved saints from pollution. St. Cuthbert was moved from Lindisfarne to Durham. St. Brigid was lifted from beneath her beautiful altar at Kildare where she and her bishop lay side by side, their resting places marked from above by gold and silver crowns. Her monks carried her to Downpatrick where St. Patrick still lay at peace. Iona was from the first so exposed to Viking raids that by 831 the monks there felt bound to part with the body of their beloved founder. Diarmat therefore escorted St. Columba's coffin across the Irish Channel: and he too selected Downpatrick as the most promising refuge.

But though their original tombs were empty the spirits of the saints remained to strengthen those confronted with the most prolonged and appalling carnage these islands have ever known. All over the country men fought the ruthless Vikings : in Northumbria with the help of St. Cuthbert; in Wales under the banner of " God and St. David." St. Patrick, St. Brigid and a host of later saints were constantly called to the help of

231

Ireland. While in Scotland the Annals for 909 inform us that : " Valiantly also in this battle did the men of Alba fight because Columcille was assisting them, for they had fervently invoked his help, seeing that he had been *their* apostle, and that through him they had received the Faith." Just how unquenchable was that Faith is shown by Iona's splendid Cross of St. Martin carved by tenth century Scotic masons after the island had been repeatedly sacked. In the Celtic Church of St. John the accent, as always in his gospel, is on the glory and tenderness born from earthly suffering : this, then, is no Crucifix abounding as it does with lively animals and joyful serpentine spirals. The central plaque shows Mary and the Child attended by adoring angels and surrounded by the ring of glory. Combined with the symbol of the cross itself we have here a perfect picture of eternal Love and Peace incarnate even at the heart of a fallen world at war.

For in the ninth century the Vikings still remained unconquerable, even by Alfred the Great. Yet, with God's help, Alfred achieved something far more constructive than their expulsion from the British Isles : he changed the course of history by converting them to Christianity. As with their Anglo-Saxon cousins the conversion of the Vikings meant the transformation of daring pirates (unhampered in their lust for robbery and slaughter by any sense of sin) into disciplined and creative human beings. It is often said of Canute that so deeply did he fall in love with the religion and customs of his adopted country that he became more Roman than the Pope, more English than the nation he ruled for God.

So did the Catholic Church triumph once more : though in the long struggle the Celtic branch, which had weathered seven hundred stormy years, was almost entirely destroyed. During the raiding stage of their invasion the Vikings persistently plundered and fired so many churches and monasteries in the land that had it not been for King Alfred's timely victories and his wise division of the land with the newly-converted settlers (to say nothing of his zest for history[1]) we might never have discovered the existence of the Celtic

[1] Alfred compiled the Anglo-Saxon Chronicle and translated Bede's *History* into English.

232

Church. Indeed there would have been no-one left to tell the tale had the Vikings overwhelmed Western Christendom. The fact that they were miraculously incorporated into the Christian culture they so nearly wrecked by the frequency and deadly efficiency of their widespread raids, should cheer those who dread the power of physical force in the hands of the ungodly. It can maim; but if there is sufficient spiritual power to oppose it, it cannot kill.

Substitute for the Viking invasion the coming to the British Isles of a second Theodore, and it is easy to believe that his wisdom and tact (combined with the tenacious independence of the Celt) would have ensured the preservation to the present day of all that was best in the Celtic Church— if not in England at least in those Celtic strongholds of Ireland, Wales and Scotland. For in reality the Churches of St. John and St. Peter were one and the same; only differing in minor details because they originated respectively from western Rome and eastern Ephesus. And after all no Catholic thinks any the worse of the Uniate Church because, like the Celtic Church, she invented a liturgy, ritual and tradition of her own through her geographical remoteness from Rome. It is sufficient that she teaches the Catholic doctrine and acknowledges the supremacy of the Chair of Peter.

If, then, the descendants of the Celtic monasteries still stood where (as St. Columba wrote) they could hear " the roar by the side of the church of the surrounding sea ": and if even now they produced contemplatives like the Culdees, and active evangelists of the calibre of St. Ninian, St. Brigid and St. Columban, those men and women and their settlements would very closely resemble the saints and monasteries produced right down the centuries to the present day by the Roman Catholic Church.

For the Celtic Church taught the whole doctrine of Latin Christendom,[1] since pruned and deformed by most Reformed Churches to an extent that would have horrified her. Her monks had so few illusions about human nature that only their firm belief in the power of the Holy Spirit saved

[1] At a council in Rome in 680 attended by 120 bishops even the hostile Wilfrid testified to the orthodoxy of the Celtic Church.

them from the sin of despair at the darkness of their age. By the quality of their lives they proved the tonic social value of the discipline of asceticism: of chastity; of poverty; of obedience; of penitence; of the " white martyrdom " which meant entire lives offered joyfully to the service of God. That the people outside their islands of prayer and worship could scarcely be expected to attain the standards achieved by the monks and nuns within the monasteries was of little consequence. Their beloved directors stood to them as living examples of practical, creative sanctity, ever pointing to the wisdom of humility we have so nearly lost to-day. Education has become compulsory because we have learnt the value of knowledge. Celtic teachers too stressed learning and crafts-manship; but far more they emphasised the peril—the drifting helplessness—of a soul undeveloped and undisciplined by the sacraments and regular worship ordained for its fuller life and liberty by God Himself.

The Latin services in the monastic Celtic Church tended to be very long. The Roman Church always knew better how to temper the wind to the weaker lambs which form so large a part of any congregation. But in both churches the sacrifice of the Mass formed the central act of worship: while regular and frequent communion taken fasting (and taken at least once a week) was considered by the Celtic Church to be vital to the well-being of the soul. Though not compulsory, weekly confession, either to a chosen Soul Friend, or in public before the priest and the people, was also strongly advised. Unlike the Roman Church, the Celtic Church did not give absolution for sins confessed till after the completion of the prescribed penance; but the services were fully choral and we read so often of the use of the sign of the cross by Celtic monks that they must have employed it to consecrate every significant act.

Lastly, the Celtic Church undoubtedly held the present Roman doctrine that saints in heaven hear and answer the prayers of those still on earth; having the power (which they delight to use) to intercede with God for sinners in distress. It is only reasonable to believe that anyone spiritually advanced enough to work miracles while still on earth will continue to do so for those who invoke them after they have passed into heaven: and so it was with the Celtic saints, acclaimed holy by the Catholic Church through the strength of popular devotion alone. Later the Roman Church devised the Congregation of Sacred Rites since when no one may be given the title of "saint" unless it can be proved that, in addition to the miracles worked while alive in this world, the person beatified has miraculously answered the prayers of those who invoked his spirit; for this is looked on as a final proof that the saint has passed through purgatory into heaven and is therefore worthy of canonisation.

Without the inspiration of St. Anthony there could have been no monastic Celtic Church. On his precepts, as interpreted by the more active St. Martin, her founders based the firm structures of their missionary bases. His *Life* by Athanasius was greatly treasured by Celtic saints, all of whom knew well his final counsels.

"Be you wary, and undo not your long service to God, but be earnest to keep your strong purpose as though you were but now beginning. . . . Let Christ be as the breath you breathe; in Him put your trust. Live as dying daily, heeding yourselves and remembering the counsels you have had from me. . . . So do you be earnest always to be in union first with the Lord and then with the Saints; that after death they may receive you in everlasting tabernacles as known friends."

Dorbbene, the seventh century scribe who copied Adamnan's *Life of St. Columba*, shared with other industrious transcribers of the period the excellent custom—since abandoned—of ending each *Life* he copied by asking a service of all his readers in return for his humble, because purely derivative, labours. Parts of what such patient monks preserved for us so long ago, I have copied as faithfully as I can; making a like use also of a long line of scholars, historians and archaeologists, some of whom are still working creatively to-day.

I may be said with some truth, then, to have joined the ranks of the scribes; and can but hasten to add my belated request to theirs. To them, as they vigorously forged a way through the Dark Ages (and I believe to us, too, wrestling as we are with a no less alarming world), only one thing really mattered: that through their labours here they might be assisted towards their true goal. I therefore plead, in the form used by Dorbbene and his friends, that

WHOSOEVER READS THESE LIVES OF THE SAINTS, LET HIM PRAY GOD FOR ME, DIANA, THAT AFTER DEATH I MAY POSSESS ETERNAL LIFE.

EDINBURGH, *Feast of St. Martin*, 1947.